DISCOVERING THE ENGLISH LOWLANDS

42 Historical Walks

DISCOVERING
the ENGLISH
LOWLANDS

42 HISTORICAL WALKS

Martin Andrew & John Cleare

The Crowood Press

First published in 1991 by
The Crowood Press Ltd
Ramsbury, Marlborough
Wiltshire SN8 2HR

British Library Cataloguing in Publication Data

Andrew, Martin
Discovering the English lowlands : 42 historical walks.
1. England. Walking recreations
I. Title II. Cleare, John
914.2204859

ISBN 1 85223 448 2

Photographs

Page 13 *Ridge and furrow at Kirby Gate, Kirby Bellars, Leicestershire.*
Page 43 *Poulton (Gloucestershire): vicarage cottage.*
Page 55 *Hamdon Hill (Ham Hill), Somerset.*
Page 79 *The River Nadder at Ugford, Wiltshire.*
Page 95 *Glynde (Sussex): Georgian parish church.*
Page 107 *Shackleford (Surrey): Lydling farmhouse.*
Page 115 *View across the Thames on Richmond Bridge.*
Page 125 *Whitehorse Hill, The Ridgeway, Oxon.*
Page 145 *Kentwell Hall, Long Melford, Suffolk.*
Page 161 *Olney (Buckinghamshire): view over the Great Ouse River.*

Dedication
To Jill, Charlotte, Rebecca and Harriet with love

Typeset by
Footnote Graphics
Warminster, Wiltshire

Printed and bound by
Times Publishing Group, Singapore

Contents

6 · **CONTENTS**

Acknowledgements

There are many people to thank and mention, not least my walking friends from the now defunct Greater London Council Historic Buildings Division which has been absorbed into English Heritage. Of most significance is Mike Kilburn who first invited me to join their monthly walks and introduced me to a love of landscape history to add to that of historic buildings and walking. Several of the routes owe much to these good companions, particularly David Atwell (the cinema historian), Peter Smith, Paul Calvocoressi, Mike Stock, Geoff Bosher, Jeff George, Brian Rayment, Bob Rigg, Philip Wilson, Charles Beeden and Des Lowry. I should also like to mention Michael Ashton and Philip Murray who did some of these walks with me.

Although within the tight format of the routes described in this book one might get the impression of a people-less England, I would like to pay tribute to all the friendly vicars and other people I chatted to in villages, in pubs and shops, and while leaning on farm gates.

The photographs in this book reflect the skills of John Cleare, who was a splendid companion and a fund of mountaineering anecdotes on the walks we did together.

Finally, I would like to thank my wife, Jill, and my daughters for all their help and encouragement. My eldest daughter, Charlotte, aged fourteen, did many of the walks with me, and if they passed her scrutiny as a young participator then I can be confident in their appeal! It is not easy doing a full-time job and turning out to walk and then writing up each walk on a regular basis and I think without my wife's encouragement the book would have taken years.

View over Westbury valley above Little Norton, Somerset.

INTRODUCTION

*Know most of the rooms of thy native country
before thou goest over the threshold thereof*
Thomas Fuller

I first met John Cleare in 1989 when I was the Conservation Officer for the part of Wiltshire in which he lives. We knew of each other through our writings and the idea for this collaboration emerged sitting with a drink in hand in his sun-soaked garden. John, of course, is best known for mountain photography while I have written on lowland walking, so it was a different venture for him. He arranged a meeting with his publishers and this book is the outcome. I should say that the photographs make the book and they are wholly John Cleare's: he decided on all the views to be photographed, while I merely assisted at a late stage in the selection process. My contribution is the walks themselves, the choice of routes and the maps. Any defects in these are thus entirely my own.

We chose a cut-off point south-east of the Fosse Way. This convenient limit follows the course of the great Roman road driven by Roman military engineers across middle England around AD 47 from Axminster in Devon to Lincoln. It formed the frontier briefly before the legions moved on to conquer the unruly British tribes beyond and the highland zones of England and Wales. This obviously divides lowland England in two but the chief advantage is that it allows coverage of at least one walk in every county in the south-east. Also of course it opens the way for Volume II . . .

This book is aimed at the walker who is prepared to spend the whole day afoot. There are many books for the motoring walker with short circuits and very detailed route descriptions, but this book is aimed at the discerning walker interested in the historical evolution of the countryside and the buildings in it. It aims to place you within the countryside for a whole day to get the feel of an area and its history.

For those people who think lowland walking a soft option I can only say: try it and see. It is as demanding as fell-walking with constant stopping and starting and with even more testing routes than in the hills. You will need to make an early start to complete some of these routes in one day! Another benefit of lowland walking is that you have the countryside to yourself. With thousands of miles of footpath all over England it is astonishing how few walkers you meet: they are all queueing to get on to the Pennine Way or in line ahead along Striding Edge.

The walks in this book follow a style evolved in the 1970s when I was in the Greater London Council Historic Buildings Division. A group of friends, all specialists in historic architecture, thought it a good idea to combine a love of old buildings with a love of walking. From this the concept of the 'historic buildings walk' evolved, later expanded to include historic landscapes: walking through history.

This may not sound wildly different from other walking concepts but in fact it introduces a remarkable flexibility whereby emphasis can be laid on one of the three elements involved: scenery, landscape history or buildings. This means that superb buildings could compensate for less exciting scenery, such as the Fenland churches of west Norfolk where marvellous churches are in flat uninspiring landscape. Alternatively, splendid scenery or ridge walking can compensate for less interesting buildings. Landscape features such as deserted village earthworks can also play their part: the permutations are limitless.

Walking is now one of the most popular pastimes but it seemed to us that there was a gap between the fell-walking and long-distance path guides and the motorized walker books giving short walks all over the country. This book aims to fill that gap by providing full day walks all over southern England, all within approximately two hours' drive of London and south-east of the Fosse Way. For those who live in the south-east it is hoped these walks will offer an alternative to the middle of the night start for the dash up the M1 and M6 to spend a day walking in the Lake District or down the M4 to the Brecon Beacons.

Also, the book is intended as an antidote to the lowland motorways of the walking fraternity, the Countryside Commission Long-Distance Paths, which have also spawned siblings in every county, such as the Viking Way, the Greensand Way, the Grafton Way, the Weald Way, the Sussex Border Path and the North Bucks Way. On the whole the only walkers you will meet will be where the routes in this book impinge on the official long-distance footpaths such as the Ridgeway, the South Downs Way, the North Downs Way or the Dorset Coast Path. Even on the lesser waymarked long-distance paths like the Greensand Way you will hardly ever meet any walkers, apart from those exercising dogs. On ordinary footpaths it will be astonishing if you meet anybody at all.

These walks therefore offer more solitude than you can find on Kinder Scout. You have only to do the Three Peaks Walk in Yorkshire, the Lykes Wake Walk or the start of the Pennine Way to see what intolerable pressure is put on the hills, their surfaces eroding at an alarming rate. I hope this book will help to increase awareness of lowland virtues.

For those who, bedecked in complex equipment, set off to the fells and sneer at the lowlands, we can assure you that it is just as challenging. In the early days of our walks when I was at the Greater London Council, over-equipped people joined us, veterans of the Munros and the Welsh 3000s, but their initial contempt soon gave way to exhaustion. They had not allowed for the constant stopping and starting, climbing stiles, opening (and shutting) gates, searching in nettled field margins for any sign of a foot-bridge marked on the Ordnance Survey map, for pushing through chest-high barley or rape, or for muddy ploughed fields that quadruple the weight of your boots. Lowland walking is a constant battle between the green line on the map and the reality on the ground.

In fact, the problems of plough-land deserve a paragraph all to themselves. From the increase in weight of boots in muddy conditions and damp-growing crops snagging feet and saturating clothes, often eliminating any sign of the path at all, to the failure of many farmers to honour their obligations to remake the path after ploughing or ploughing right up to the hedge. If you plunge in to re-establish the right of way it may prove to be as exhausting crossing a large field of wheat as scaling Cader Idris. I may exaggerate a little – but many sections of the routes in this book were amended to follow lanes rather than direct the reader out along statutory footpaths shown on the map but to be seen nowhere on the ground.

That said, it is hoped that you will enjoy following the routes in this book. On the whole there are few navigational problems. The walk routes are deliberately not described in detail, as in our view there is nothing more tedious to read than a com-

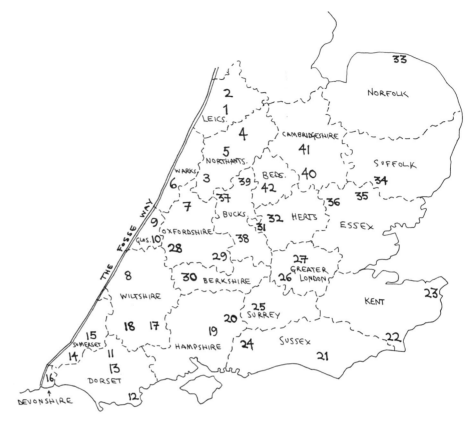

KEY MAP ONE: THE WALKS BY COUNTIES

plete route guide. I have therefore tried to integrate the route with the text, so that each chapter can be read for pleasure whether the walk is undertaken or not. The maps are provided to supplement the text. These walks are aimed at the intelligent reader who has much common sense and is well used to the Ordnance Survey 1:25,000 Pathfinder maps. These are the 'bible' of the walker and the second edition which now covers most of the country is a work of art and aesthetic pleasure in itself. The maps each cover 20 by 10km and show the footpaths and bridleways in green. I recommend that you buy them.

There is no need to give exhaustive safety advice: you will rarely be far from human aid and do not need to take supplies and emergency blankets with you. There are usually shops in villages and certainly pubs and inns. However, it should be remembered that pubs often have limited lunch-time sessions. There is nothing

more disappointing than arriving hot and hungry to find the kitchens have closed and the cook disappeared by 1.30 p.m., or no catering is done on that specific day. An increasing trend is the existence of a locum landlord who just keeps the place open for drinks while a major revamp or new licensee is organized. Many are the variations on these themes and sometimes the glee with which the barman will impart the information does little for morale.

Besides the maps little else is needed, though I would recommend that you always have the relevant volume of Nikolaus Pevsner's magisterial *Buildings of England* series (Penguin) in your pocket. Now entering second editions, these books are without parallel for anyone interested in the buildings of England. Professor W. G. Hoskins' *The Making of the English Landscape* is also most useful. There is a brief booklist at the end of the book if you would like to read further.

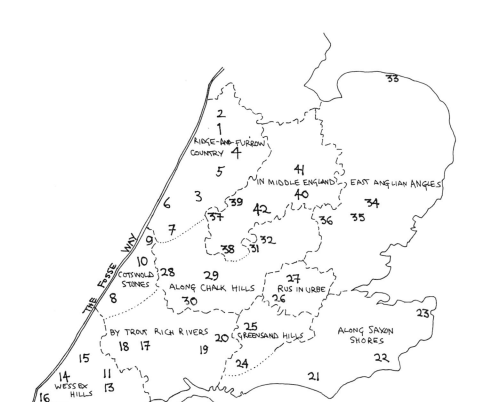

KEY MAP TWO: THE TEN GROUPS OF WALKS

Lowland walking offers unrivalled variety of scenery from bare chalk downs and oak-wooded greensand hills to wide water-meadowed valleys; from historic townscapes and villages to rolling hawthorn-hedged midland pastures corrugated by ridge and furrow; from Iron Age hill-forts to deserted village earthworks, from riverside paths to salt-marshes; from high hedge-banked small-field Devon to barley-land Suffolk; from vast skies above the Fens to intimate valleys in the Somerset limestone hills. I could go on for ever. There is something for everyone.

There is an equally formidable range of buildings and building materials to be seen. These range from all types of stone such as flint, pebbles, limestone, greensand, chalk and sandstone, to earth wall or cob and witchert, to brick, tiles, thatch, slate, render and timber-framing. Most important of all, virtually all these building materials were quarried, processed or grown locally in the areas in which they are used, thus giving each area its particular character. This is evident everywhere on the walks.

But a word of caution: generally speaking, buildings erected after the mid-nineteenth century will not follow this dictum, for cheap transport by railway meant building materials could be mass-produced and transported more cheaply than they could be produced locally. The result was initially the spread of Welsh slate all over England, followed by other materials until in our own day standardization means that a housing estate of the 1960s could be in Bootle or Bournemouth. To get the feel for an area's historic character look therefore at the buildings; you will soon see a pattern emerge. For example, in Suffolk and Essex there is little building stone so older houses are almost always timber-framed and usually plastered or pargetted and later houses are brick, although plastering remained popular. In Gloucestershire or Somerset the walks pass through good building stone country so the villages and towns are almost all built of local stone. In the Weald sandstones are used as well as oaks for timber-framing.

Parish churches are often the focus of the walks, as they are usually the oldest buildings in a community and can also be entered. They preserve in stone the history of that community and are invariably fascinating. A donation in the fabric fund box is always appreciated, as these buildings are expensive to maintain. They are an invaluable link with the past and also the focus of the living community.

For those interested in landscape history, I think you will find the Midland walks most interesting with their acres of ridge and furrow. In the south along the Avon, Nadder and Itchen the remains of complex water-meadow systems and deserted village sites, old parkland, woods and field systems will appeal to others. England has a wealth of landscape history, even in the most populated areas, and each walk will offer some insight into the evolution of the existing farms, villages and towns.

Each walk is circular for maximum flexibility. This means you do not have to worry about using public transport to get back to the start or about needing two cars. You can do a walk on the spur of the moment if, say, it is a fine day. The snag of course is that on some walks there are no short cuts or loops to serve as escape routes. However, others can be cut up into sections like the Salisbury walk and the London ones can be subdivided using public transport.

The distances vary from 7 to 17 miles. While this may not sound much to the hill walker who might cover twice as far on an uninterrupted day in the mountains, it is certainly sufficient for walkers frequently stopping and starting to visit places every mile or so. I have grouped the walks into themes, but this does not mean doing them in that way: it is purely for convenience.

And one last proviso: at the start of each walk is the month and year that the walk was done. I walked all these routes between July 1989 and September 1990 and the text and maps relate to this. Any subsequent changes to footpaths may make sections difficult to follow but this is inevitable in any walking book. I can only apologize but as you know *all is flux*.

I conclude, with the following quote from Shakespeare's *A Midsummer Night's Dream:*

> *Over hill, over dale,*
> *Thorough bush, thorough brier,*
> *Over park, over pale,*
> *Thorough flood, thorough fire,*
> *I do wander everywhere.*

We hope that you will enjoy these walks, marvellously photographed by John Cleare, and will learn to appreciate, if you do not already, the quieter virtues of the English lowlands.

KEY TO TEXT MAPS

○	Start of walk
⊕	Start of walk at a parish church
=	Roads
--	Public footpaths and bridle ways
▦	Towns and villages
⁘	Earthworks or sites of deserted medieval villages
≋	Other earthworks
◩	Ridge and furrow
ENCLOSED 1631	Date when a village's open fields were enclosed
⬡⬡	Lakes and other water
♠♠♠♠	Woods
♠ ♠ ♠	Parkland

Ridge and Furrow Country

LEICESTERSHIRE, NORTHAMPTONSHIRE, WARWICKSHIRE AND OXFORDSHIRE

Sheep have eaten up our meadowes and our downes
Our corn, our wood, whole villages and townes,
Till now I thought the proverb did but jest
Which said a black sheep was a biting beast.
Thomas Bastard

Walk 1

AND SHEEP DO NOW DEVOUR MEN

Ingarsby and Billesdon, Leicestershire. 13 Miles. June 1990.
OS Pathfinder Sheet SK60/70.

In the uplands east of Leicester the celebrated Quorn Hunt rides over classic rolling Midland hawthorn-hedge country dotted with small woods. These heavy Triassic claylands are ideal for pastoral farming which in turn is ideal for fox-hunting. Many of the present woods date from the late eighteenth century when they were planted for foxes to live and breed in. The most notable is Botany Bay Fox Covert near Billesdon, its name dating from the 1790s after the Australian penal colony was founded.

This walk is a homage to Professor W. G. Hoskins who has contributed so much to Leicestershire history and was one of the founders of the discipline of landscape history, that is, the history of villages and the countryside rather than of country-house landscapes. He opened the eyes of people to the antiquity of man's influence on its shaping: many readers will recall his fascinating television series. His influence on this book is all-pervasive and this walk takes in four of his *Seven Deserted Village Sites in Leicestershire*, published as long ago as 1956. This countryside retains vast acreages of ridge and furrow and Hoskins was influential in proving that this was of medieval origin and not modern, or Napoleonic at best. I walked this route with Mike Kilburn, a devout follower of Professor Hoskins from Leicester, who first introduced me to this paradise for the 'humps and bumps' (or earthworks) enthusiast.

We started the walk in Hungarton where a number of the houses have date-stones going back to the 1760s such as

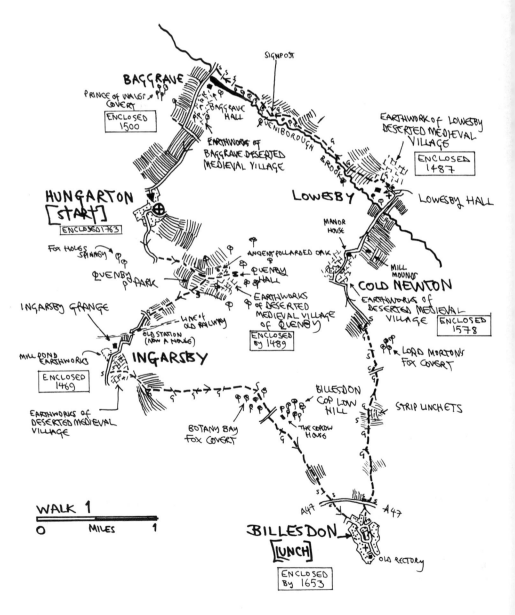

BAGGRAVE
PRINCE OF WALES COVERT
ENCLOSED 1500
BAGGRAVE HALL
QUENIBOROUGH BROOK
SIGNPOST
EARTHWORK OF BAGGRAVE DESERTED MEDIEVAL VILLAGE
EARTHWORK OF LOWESBY DESERTED MEDIEVAL VILLAGE
ENCLOSED 1487
HUNGARTON [START]
ENCLOSED 1763
LOWESBY
LOWESBY HALL
MANOR HOUSE
FOX HOLES SPINNEY
QUENBY PARK
ANCIENT POLLARDED OAK
QUENBY HALL
MILL MOUNDS
COLD NEWTON
EARTHWORKS OF DESERTED MEDIEVAL VILLAGE
ENCLOSED 1578
INGARSBY GRANGE
LINE OF OLD RAILWAY
EARTHWORKS OF DESERTED MEDIEVAL VILLAGE OF QUENBY
ENCLOSED BY 1489
OLD STATION (NOW A HOUSE)
MILL POND EARTHWORKS
INGARSBY
ENCLOSED 1469
EARTHWORKS OF DESERTED MEDIEVAL VILLAGE
LORD MORTONS FOX COVERT
STRIP LINCHETS
BILLESDON COP LOW HILL
BOTANY BAY FOX COVERT
THE COPLOW HOUSE
A47
A47
BILLESDON [LUNCH]
OLD RECTORY
ENCLOSED BY 1653

WALK 1
0 MILES 1

Sycamore Farm, Hungarton, dated 1766. Part of Squire Shukbrugh Ashby's rebuilding of the village after the 1763 enclosure of its open fields.

Hope Farm (1772), Sycamore Farm (1766) and the Manor House (1767). These tall flat-fronted brick houses in typical Midland red brick represent a surge of building that followed the Enclosure Act of 1763. Unusually, this rebuilding took place in the village rather than out in the newly enclosed fields. The church in rusty ironstone with banding of Clipsham limestone has a recessed spire crusted with crockets and inside on squire Shukbrugh Ashby's 1792 monument is the information that he rebuilt a large part of the village. This explains why the farmhouses remained within the village.

South of the village along the road we crossed a stream and saw on the left very clear ridge and furrow where four or five selions or individual ridges were separated into blocks by wider ridges. A common phenomenon but not often evident from the ground, it must have helped identify strips in the former common fields. Where the road turned right we continued straight on, following the signpost 'Quenby Hall Bridleway only', along the drive to Quenby, one of Hoskins' 'seven deserted villages'. Immediately past the modern lodge we entered parkland overlying very obvious ridge and furrow. These were the open fields of Quenby, enclosed for sheep in the 1480s. By 1563 the Ashby family had eliminated the village whose earthworks are west of the Jacobean E-plan mansion they built in the 1620s. With its straight parapets entirely concealing the roofs it is an austere brick house of three storeys, but set amid delightful oak-tree-lined parkland. Retracing our steps

Quenby Hall from the site of the village the Ashbys cleared away for sheep. By the 1620s they were wealthy enough to build a palace.

we noticed probably the oldest oak in the park, a gnarled pollarded tree, possibly a survivor from the village hedgerows. Beyond an old bridge spanning nothing in particular we turned left and, through a gate, descended south-west out of the park.

At the road we turned right and left (signposted Ingarsby Station and Houghton) to ascend past the old Great Central

Railway station and the station-master's house (1882). Both are now private houses and the railway line is dismantled. Beyond the old bridge the road curves right to skirt some of the finest deserted village earthworks in England at Old Ingarsby. This village desertion has different origins to Quenby: Leicester Abbey, which had been granted the manor in 1352, spent the next hundred years

acquiring the rest of the lordship to such good effect that they were able to enclose the manor in 1469. Most was converted to sheep and cattle pasture and the very large village destroyed. The Abbey built a grange or estate farmhouse and this survives in much extended form as Ingarsby Old Hall, although it looks more 1540s-like with its Tudor-arched windows. These may be alterations by Brian Cave who bought the abbey estate after the Dissolution. The road winds past a 1977 Silver Jubilee Plaque relating the history of the village and earthworks west of the village with the flat expanse of the long dry millpond on the right. At the bridleway sign we turned left and climbed a holloway, the main east-west street of the village. To the right and especially to the left are superb earthworks of village streets, houses, gardens and crofts. The roads are of remarkable depth and are used for grazing by the villagers' supplanters: ubiquitous sheep.

At the top we went through a gate and headed south-east and then east through pastures. Reaching arable we bore right into the Botany Bay Fox Covert woods to the road, then right and left between the eagle-topped gate piers to pass the Coplow, an eighteenth-century house enlarged in the nineteenth century into a hunting box much visited by Edward VII and 'friends'. This stuccoed mansion nestles in the lee of Billesdon Coplow whose wooded peak is a landmark for miles around. The footpath on the map looks easy but reaching Billesdon is a real challenge and the faint-hearted would be well advised to deviate east to the parallel road. Eventually, perspiring, we reached the new bypass which overlays ridge and furrow, crossed it and struggled through barley to Billesdon.

Billesdon is an interesting village, apparently built round an open green which has subsequently been built over. There is a choice of pubs for lunch but, as in other areas of Leicestershire, there is a reluctance to prepare food after about 1.30 p.m. There is an interesting maze of back lanes, some mud or cob-walled barns and a lot of attractive cottages, many with

Quenby Park's oldest tree: a magnificent pollarded oak that probably survives from the hedgerows of the village that disappeared in Tudor times.

Ingarsby: the earthworks of one of England's most spectacular deserted medieval villages, destroyed by Leicester Abbey in the fifteenth century for sheep pasture.

their front doors opening directly on to alleys or lanes. The eighteenth century added many brick houses, some dated, to a village whose open fields were enclosed by 1653. The church is at the south end, somewhat over-restored, while south of it The Old Vicarage is seventeenth-century stone with an enormous bay window added to the south in 1770 and a cob garden wall. The nearby stone Old School (1650) has arched mullioned windows and was in use until 1876. We completed the circle before turning right up Long Lane and over the bypass, right up a metalled track and left over another stile. From here we headed generally north through fields, passing through a valley with strip-lynchetted sides and eventually reaching Tilton Lane, a ridgeway since Neolithic times. Across this we skirted left of a hut and continued to join the road north of

Sludge Hall Farm. Following the road we turned right into Cold Newton, technically a shrunken village with half a dozen houses but with fine deserted earthworks following enclosure for sheep by 1586. The road skirts the mellow ironstone seventeenth-century Manor House and bends north into ridge and furrow with two windmill mounds on the right besides the one within the village earthworks.

At Lowesby, whose church has interesting Perpendicular tracery windows and a mainly Georgian tower, we turned left and just past gates sharp right onto the path that runs parallel to the drive to Lowesby Hall. On the right are the earthworks of the village cleared by the Ashbys by 1487, again for sheep. The north front of Lowesby Hall is Queen Anne brick and very fine with projecting wings, a pedimented centre and long, relatively narrow

sashes. We continued through ridge and furrow parkland north-west, crossing a road and walking alongside the Queniborough Brook through pasture, passing at one point an old signpost looking most odd in the middle of nowhere which marks a footpath crossing. Just before we reached the next road we had glimpses of the service ranges of Baggrave Hall. Turning left onto the road we passed the mid-eighteenth-century stone west front which has the three centre bays of seven set forward and pedimented. This front conceals a sixteenth-century core built by Francis Cave. He acquired the estate from Leicester Abbey who had enclosed the parish in 1500 and cleared the village whose earthworks lie south of the house and east of the road. We followed the road south past much good ridge and furrow back to Hungarton.

Walk 2

IN RIDGE AND FURROW COUNTRY

Gaddesby and the River Wreake, Leicestershire. 15 Miles. 14 June 1990. OS Pathfinder Sheet SK61/71.

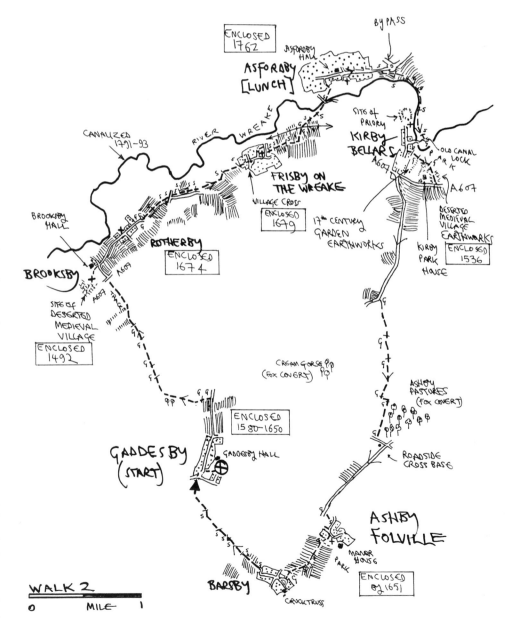

Leicestershire is one of my favourite counties: the people you meet when walking are invariably friendly and many of the rural villages are still working villages. The rolling landscape is most attractive with hawthorn-hedged fields and small woods, many planted as fox coverts for the renowned Leicestershire hunts. On the negative side, many people say to walkers, 'I bet you had fun trying to follow the footpaths!' To some extent true where the plough rules rather than the hoof. Where sheep and cattle are dominant the pastures overlie old plough-land ridge and furrow and the stretch between Brooksby and Kirby Bellars south of the River Wreake is truly spectacular. It resulted from enclosure, mainly for sheep, but at wide intervals: Brooksby in 1492, Kirby Bellars in 1536, Rotherby and Frisby in the 1670s and Asfordby as late as 1762 (the last date when the plough worked their common fields).

There is ridge and furrow elsewhere on the walk but the other 'humps and bumps' highlight is at Kirby Bellars. North of the church are prominent earthworks reputedly of an Augustinian priory which disappeared at the sixteenth-century Dissolution. Almost immediately in 1536 the parish was enclosed and Kirby Park formed. Early in the seventeenth century Sir Erasmus de la Fontaine demolished several cottages and enlarged his park eastwards. The east and south park walls remain beyond the earthworks of the cleared village. His house has gone but the earthworks of its gardens remain and

A corrugated landscape: superb ridge and furrow seen from the walk route at Kirby Gate near Kirby Bellars.

the service buildings became a hunting box for Sir Francis Burdett who died in 1844 and combined two main interests which sound a curious combination to modern ears: social reform and fox-hunting. The garden earthworks are a surprisingly little known example of late sixteenth-century formal gardens. A prospect mound remains by the road and a long rectangular close runs northwards to the site of the mansion. Beyond it was the main formal court with a raised promenade terrace on the left and a square moated area at the end. To the immediate left of the moat is another high prospect mound which gave views over this part of the gardens and over the west parts bordered by the remains of ornamental fish-ponds. Obviously, the formal parterre beds, gravelled walks and hedges have gone but the remaining earthworks are remarkably evocative and in places stone walling breaks through the sheepcropped turf.

I started at Gaddesby church whose churchyard is a forest of Swithland slate headstones, quarried in the Charnwood forest north-west of Leicester. The aisles

The prospect mound from Kirby Park's remarkable Tudor garden remains, vast and carpeted by ancient sheep-cropped turf.

are a lavishly decorated work of the 1320s when chantries were established. The south aisle looks like a separate church with a west door below a spherical triangular window. Above, the wall is encrusted with niches and gablets and has a richly carved parapet, all with that writhing tactile quality of Decorated sculpture at its best. The north aisle is simpler but with exciting flowing tracery, while inside is just as rewarding with simple fourteenth-century pews. There are two fine monuments in the north aisle. Overwhelming the chancel is the monument to Colonel Cheney by Joseph Gott (about 1848), a bizarre sight: the colonel is depicted, life-size, on a dying horse at the battle of Waterloo. This monstrous piece was transferred from Gaddesby Hall so the poor taste is of a later age.

From Gaddesby church I walked west along a path which gave glimpses of the Hall, largely restored after dereliction in 1950, and turned right to walk uphill along Main Street – a typical Leicestershire

village street with a mix of brick and rendered houses, some thatch and pantile and a lot of slate, much of it from Collyweston in Northamptonshire. At the end I continued straight on, and just beyond Carlton Lodge Farm climbed a gate to a green lane, the left-hand hedge decayed and with barkless dead elm trees. There is ridge and furrow pasture initially but then the path runs through arable, curving north to Spinney Farm where it picks up a lane.

I reached the road and crossed over to Brooksby Agricultural College, based on Brooksby Hall where the Stuart favourite George Villiers, Duke of Buckingham, was born. Some is seventeenth century and battlemented, but it received stone-architraved sashes in the early eighteenth century when Sir Nathan Wright inherited from Sir Nathan Villiers whose excellent memorial dominates the isolated church beyond the car-park. He and his wife stand, life-size, striking poses side by side in front of pilasters and arches. Back to

the road I crossed a cattle-grid on to the unfenced road to Rotherby through superb ridge and furrow. This and its continuation east was the main route to Melton Mowbray before the turnpike road, now the A607. I walked through Rotherby village with its stumpy church and left the road by a cattle pen and headed east through more outstanding ridge and furrow with the old hay meadows along the River Wreake to the left, both now grazed by sheep and cattle.

At Frisby on the Wreake the path emerges by the village cross, somewhat decayed on a base and three-step plinth. Past the Bell Inn in painted brick, dated 1759, I walked up Main Street, noting a number of timber-framed houses, and turned left into Church Lane. Just before a thatched and timber-framed cottage I turned right past the school of 1854 into the churchyard. The church has a good fourteenth-century south transept and delightful rustic corbels to the chancel north chapel arch. Out of the church I walked east to Mill Lane then right and left into the fields and more ridge and furrow before turning north to cross the railway line, water meadows and the Wreake into Asfordby.

This industrial village expanded with coal mining but there are several older buildings, including the Jacobean brick Old Hall with three gables and eighteenth-century sashes, now at last being repaired after years of dereliction and the old Rectory with its four by four bays in brick of about 1808 south of the church. The church has a graceful crocketted recessed spire and a churchyard full of Swithland slate headstones. Inside, the tower has an octopartite rib vault and the nave roof has carved musicians to the wall posts. The chancel screen is medieval with a modern rood-loft above and in the south aisle are fragments of an Anglo-Saxon cross shaft.

There are three pubs to choose from for lunch.

I walked east from the village and before the bypass turned right into the fields to follow the east bank of the Wreake to Kirby Bellars. Before recrossing the river

A thatcher at work in Gaddesby village on a timber-framed cottage.

There's always a spire in sight in Leicestershire. Kirby Bellars church spire reflected in the River Wreake.

I saw the ruins of a canal lock which dates from the canalization of the Wreake in the 1790s, part of a cut across a meander. Over the river I visited the church which has good Decorated tracery and a blocked north arcade where the aisle was demolished. Back south across the railway I turned left on to a path which skirts Kirby Park's seventeenth-century garden earthworks and crosses the village earthworks within the park, noting the park wall to the east and south. I climbed out of the park by the footpath sign and walked west along the road past Burdett's remodelling of the service buildings with five coped gables and an elaborate porch in Jacobean almshouse style.

By Kirby Hall, an enormous yellow brick house, I turned left where signposted Gaddesby, and continued south for a mile with excellent ridge and furrow to the left, and then left at a bridleway sign to battle south to the road beyond Ashby Pastures wood, a fine fox covert planted by the Quorn Hunt. Here I turned left then right, noting the 'cross' on the OS map as a stone stump in a field. I turned right and continued south, eventually turning right through a gate across ridge and furrow to Ashby Folville, partly an estate village with the mansion largely rebuilt in the 1890s for the Carington family. The church is another excellent building, although the key is held in South Croxton! I continued south-west down a footpath and then through ridge and furrow to Barsby, an unspoilt village. Here Springwell House shows off an exposed cruck truss in the gable and there are a number of timberframed houses, rare in Leicestershire. I crossed the junction to Main Street, with good brick houses of 1701 and 1707 on either side and continued past the King William pub into fields and back to Gaddesby.

Walk 3

DISPLACED BY SHEEP

Fawsley, Northamptonshire. 15½ Miles. September 1989.
OS Pathfinder Sheets SP44/54, SP45/55, SP65/75.

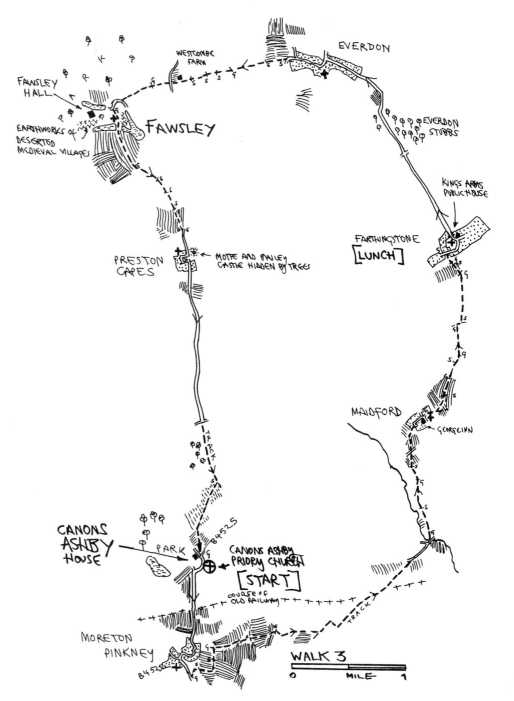

To me there are two distinct types of landscape walk. The first is hill-walking where the landscape is spread out below the hilltops with the patterns clear; the broad perspective is closer to an aerial photograph. The second is lowland walking with patterns which are not necessarily clear beyond the next hedge but which need to be unravelled along the route. Only small glimpses and insights are therefore possible as one walks. The attraction of hill-walking is precisely that it provides a broad sweep of history, while that of lowland walking is the intimate; things gradually revealed.

The Midlands offers the latter sort of walking and because of the nature of medieval and later farming retains much physical evidence of old landscapes. Villages are surrounded by evidence of their former open-field agriculture in the form of the characteristic corrugations of ridge and furrow, the selions that made up individual strips which in turn made up parcels of strips or furlongs. Much of the Midlands was converted to pasture from the fifteenth century onwards, preserving this older field pattern. It is remarkably persistent and makes walking in the Midlands a joy.

Much of this walk passes through or beside considerable acreages of ridge and furrow, much still under sheep pasture and one can 'read' the landscape more clearly than elsewhere. An added sense of history comes from noting later hedgerows cutting across the ridge and furrow. Generally speaking, the straighter the hedges the later the enclosure, as new field hedges followed furlong edges until about 1700 and are therefore often curv-

Canons Ashby. The Drydens' Tudor tower rises from Queen Anne-sashed flanks, all lovingly restored by the National Trust.

stored, was the home of the Dryden family from 1551 (National Trust: open March to October, Wednesdays to Sundays). The house dates substantially from then with a stone-dressed brick road front, an ironstone south-east elevation and a rendered north-west front which looks out on to a serene enclosed garden with Jacobean obelisk finial gate piers. In 1976 when I last walked here the house and church were in poor repair.

Walking south with ridge and furrow to the right and, beyond, the lake glinting, I crossed the bridge over the former railway line. Amid the undergrowth Midland Railway diagonal-paling fencing and the platforms partially survive. Beyond I was in Moreton Pinkney, a parish of the seventeenth-century and earlier enclosure rich in ridge and furrow with hedges following the furlong edges. The village is attractive and winding with some sub-arts and crafts roughcast council cottages as well as ironstone houses. Some houses are attractively banded in brown ironstone alternating with whiter Weldon limestone, for example Pear Tree Cottage (1701). In the centre a wide archway and lodge with conical-roofed turret of 1860 leads to the Victorian Manor House. The church has plain ironstone arcades, a distinguished Early English chancel and sheep grazing the churchyard.

Back past the Manor Lodge up the sycamore-tunnelled lane, under a footbridge I glimpsed the Manor House through gate piers, then turned left through

Banded limestones (the darker one is an ironstone) produce a rich effect on a thatched cottage in Moreton Pinkney.

ing, whereas parliamentary enclosure surveyors ignored the earlier pattern.

I started the walk in Canons Ashby, a deserted village site where the Augustinian priory, founded about 1150, evicted the villagers in the 1490s to convert their manor into sheep runs. Ironically, the

prior and his canons were in their turn evicted in 1536 by Henry VIII. The west end of the priory church survives and has been very well renovated by the National Trust: an imposing Early English west front but only two and a half bays of nave remain. Canons Ashby, beautifully rea kissing-gate on to footpaths through sheep-cropped ridge and furrow. After a mile and a half the path joined Banbury Lane, a splendid old drove-road which headed north-east, becoming a road past Adstone Lodge, a nineteenth-century stone cottage with reset 1697 datestones. I turned left at Fulling Mill (the sign says 'Glebe Gallops') and headed north beside a stream to Maidford where the George Inn is most welcoming. Across the road Manor Farm has a blocked medieval gable window and, facing the churchyard, a stone range with sixteenth-century doorways and blocked stone-mullioned windows. The church has a saddlebacked tower and is usually locked.

Beyond Maidford church I headed north into the fields to follow footpaths to Farthingstone, ridge and furrow giving way to arable. I crossed a valley with a stream, heading right of a stableyard up to the village. I walked downhill, noting on the right just before the sombre former school a terrace of cottages called Pension Row, a curious building with giant brick arches

and faced with broken crockery. Round the bend the very picturesque King's Arms has a front of three-gabled projecting bays and cast-iron lattice windows, a resolutely early nineteenth-century Tudor composition. All in all, an attractive venue for lunch. The church is relatively plain. I walked north-west along the road, passing Farthingstone House, a polychrome brick-banded house of about 1860 with a slated hipped roof; not lovable but of its time. I walked steadily north before dropping down through Everdon Stubbs, a coppice wood mixed with oak, ash and sweet chestnut and oddly in a salient of Farthingstone parish.

Everdon village is very fine, built mostly of ironstone. The seventeenth-century bridge over the stream, a feeder of the River Nene, is narrow. It has two arches with cutwaters and a refuge to the south facing the flow, and stepped buttresses to the north. Many of the houses, though, have ill-proportioned standard windows, and cheap concrete roof-tiles marring an otherwise most attractive village. The

Church Farm Farthingstone, reflected in the waters of the pond.

church is excellent: a very spacious lofty nave with tall, elegant columns and a medieval roof. The fifteenth-century chancel screen has a polythene sheet above it filling the chancel arch. At the end of High Street I took the left fork, and where the road bends left, climbed steps to a stile into the fields to walk west, soon through stubble, with the tower of Fawsley church appearing on the horizon before dropping downhill to Westcombe Farm.

Across the road I climbed uphill and at the summit the parkland of Fawsley Hall spread below me. Downhill to the road and I was in the park and on The Knightley Way, a Northamptonshire County Council waymarked path. Fawsley Hall and its park were created by the Knightley family. This picturesque scene conceals fifteenth-century misery: the ejection of the inhabitants of two villages to create a great sheep-rearing estate, one village around the church, the other near the Hall. Richard Knightley bought the manor in 1415 and systematically destroyed the villages for wool production. South of the

Pension Row Cottages in Farthingstone with giant brick arches and walls bizarrely surfaced with broken crockery of all shapes and colours.

The Knightleys at rest in Fawsley Church. Two villages were cleared to make way for for their sheep as the family rose from graziers to the knightly classes.

lakes is a huge 'launde' or sheep run still unsubdivided and covered in ridge and furrow formed before about 1420.

The Hall is part medieval but mostly Anthony Salvin of the 1860s, a suitably baronial pile. The church out in the greensward, surrounded by sheep and encircled by a ha-ha, is beautifully situated. Entered by a curiously narrow north door it is full of superb monuments to the Knightley family, a remarkable collection from the sixteenth to the nineteenth century. Out of the church I crossed the causeway between the lakes to head east of south, ignoring the obvious path to obey the Knightley Way waymarks. I was now in the great sheep field, acre after acre of ridge and furrow, still sheep-cropped. The Way then crosses arable fields, descends into spectacular ridge and furrow before reaching the road into Preston Capes, all well waymarked with white discs on posts.

Up the hill into Preston Capes on the left is a tree clad motte-and-bailey castle. In the village the church has its chancel painted a rich tomato colour and in the east window there is etched glass by Annabel Rathbone; all right on a goblet but dreadfully ineffective in large windows. It is a pleasant village with ironstone cottages and some wealthy expansion. Out of the village ridge and furrow soon gives way to arable lands, with many hedges removed compared with the 1970s map. At the junction I continued straight on down Oxford Lane, past another drove, Ashby Gorse, and a wood full of small lakes. Beyond an arable field I turned right over a half-hidden stile to head south-west across fainter ridge and furrow, then a last field of superb corrugations, back to the road in Canons Ashby.

Walk 4

THE TRESHAMS BEAR WITNESS

Rothwell and Kettering, Northamptonshire. 11 Miles. 24 March 1990. OS Pathfinder Sheets SP87/97, SP88/98.

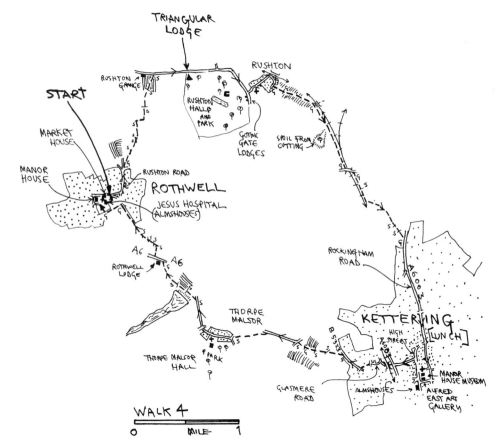

WALK 4

0   MILE   1

The Triangular Lodge at Rushton gives an extraordinary insight into the sixteenth-century mind barely comprehensible to-day. It is a stone testament of faith by a recusant Roman Catholic who refused to worship in the Anglican church of Eliza-beth I. Its builder, Sir Thomas Tresham, converted from Protestantism to Catholic-ism in 1580, spent years in prison with the zeal of a convert for his refusal to con-form. He also built several small buildings, two of which are included on this walk. Lyveden New Bield, which is not included, lies beyond Brigstock and is full of sym-bolism relating to Christ's Passion. Sir Thomas died in 1605 with Lyveden incom-plete and his Market Hall for Rothwell roofless: it was finally completed by Gotch, a local architect, in 1895!

The Triangular Lodge, built between 1594–97, demands close study in its sym-bolism. At a superficial level everything is in threes, partly punning on the Tresham name but mostly gloriously celebrating the Mass and the Trinity. The plan and pro-portions are based on the equilateral triangle; it has three sides; there are three storeys, each with three windows per side, and it is crowned by three gables and a triangular stack. It is covered in mystic numbers and inscriptions and is a fine example of that peculiarly Elizabethan phenomenon of a 'conceit', an architec-tural display of convoluted intellectual games stating the faith for which Tresham was prepared to suffer persecution.

This is the 'boot and shoe' country of Northamptonshire running in a crescent from Northampton past Kettering to Rothwell on the northern fringes. Roth-well has a core of buildings of great quality but much of the town is quintessentially Midland with hard red-brick houses. Immediately west of the church the Manor House, today offices but formerly the Urban District Council headquarters, is a quite exceptional mid-eighteenth-century house of five bays and two storeys in ironstone with white limestone dressings.

These include Gibbs surrounds to the ground-floor windows, a Venetian central window with Ionic pilasters to the first floor and a fluted Doric pilastered door-case.

However, Market Hill is where the walk starts with the parish church on the west side. This is a large stone church which was even larger for it has lost chapels and transepts over the years.

Tresham's Triangular Lodge at Rushton: an eerie and defiant witness to one man's faith.

Rothwell Manor House with Gibbs surround ground-floor windows and Venetian first-floor ones. Beyond is the church whose spire was lost to lightning in 1660.

Inside, the nave arcades are very tall with stiffleaf foliaged capitals and medieval choir stalls with carved misericords in the chancel. To the south Jesus Hospital, founded in 1585 for twenty-four poor men, was enlarged in the eighteenth century and again in 1833, and today it has been well converted into flats where the occupants live rent-free. The Hospital consists of three ranges and its best elevation is seen from the south towards the end of the walk. On the north side Sir Thomas Tresham's Market House has had a chequered history. It was designed in 1577 by a William Grumbold who was paid £62, but work was abandoned. Gotch completed it in 1895 using drawings found at Rushton Hall. The rest of the town centre has a few good buildings, some with eighteenth-century datestones. Rothwell House Hotel, formerly the Vicarage, in

Jesus Hospital almshouses, founded in 1591, present a mellow limestone south front to the occupants' vegetable plots.

Bridge Street is an elegant late eighteenth-century brick house.

I walked east then bore left on to Rushton Road until just beyond the junction with Shotwell Mill Lane. I crossed mainly pasture fields north to the Desborough Road where I turned right. Soon I reached the Triangular Lodge built in thin bands of ironstone and whiter limestone at the north-west corner of Rushton Hall's park. It is more extraordinary in reality than photographs can convey. Beyond one gets glimpses of the gables and chimneys of Rushton Hall which is now a school for the blind and is basically Tudor and 1620s style. I skirted the park wall of limestone with a brick coping. Rushton Hall Farmhouse is a big H-plan eighteenth-century house in stone with a fashionable brick east front of five bays but the whole house sashed. To the south of the junction is the main drive to Rushton Hall beyond a gate

screen with charming Gothick lodges dating back to the early nineteenth century. I got the key to Rushton church from the North Lodge and walked to the church which has two fine tombs, one of about 1300 with a cross-legged effigy of a knight, the other of Sir Thomas Tresham who died in 1559. He was the father of the builder of the Triangular Lodge and the alabaster effigy was moved here in the eighteenth-century when the church near the Hall was demolished.

Rushton has several good buildings including the old, late Georgian Rectory opposite, and the Manor House and Rushton Manor, both seventeenth-century buildings with mullioned windows. I turned right down Chapel Lane, then left into High Street with a number of ironstone cottages; and right into Manor Road. At the bridleway sign to Kettering I turned left and headed south-east towards

the railway. Ignoring the bridge, I continued along the west side, passing spoil heaps from the railway cutting looking remarkably like ancient tree-clad earthworks. At the road I turned left to cross the railway and then immediately right to follow the waymarked route across country to the Rockingham Road which leads into Kettering.

Kettering starts a long way out with modern estates, then Satra House, the footwear technology centre, and soon late nineteenth- and early twentieth-century expansion with houses dated between 1880 and 1914. The centre of town has been much rebuilt but Gold Street and High Street are pedestrianized and pleasant, if architecturally undistinguished. South of Market Place is the very fine parish church with three tiers of lucarnes to its crocketted spire, and then the seventeenth-century Manor House with a Georgian west front, now an interesting local museum. On Sheep Street is the library of 1904 in red brick with stone dressings in Domestic Revival style and beyond the Alfred East Art Gallery of 1913 by Gotch. East was a local artist of some note and the top-lit gallery gave Gotch the chance to design monumentally in the Tuscan Order with paired columns, blank walls and heavy cornices. There are other attractions in Kettering including Horse Market, a pleasant space, and Staples Factory in Green Lane nearby, a warehouse (1875 to 1891) with arched windowed lower storeys and deep bracket eaves to the slated hipped roof.

I lunched and then turned off High Street west down Meadow Road. Beside Macdonalds hamburger restaurant, I crossed the main road, under a railway bridge and then through a housing estate to the B5323 where I turned right. At the end of houses I continued past gates to a stile in the hedge to cross fields, some with ridge and furrow, then a road. I left the road to cross arable fields aiming for Thorpe Malsor church spire. From the churchyard there is a good view of Thorpe Malsor Hall, a Jacobean E-plan house re-sashed in the eighteenth-century. In the village are several estate cottages (1910–11) and other older ones, including Bonnette Cottage and May Lodge, both thatched. The church has a good Victorian south porch and vestry with turret, the porch vaulted and the squire's way in. This dates from about 1877 but the rest of the church is mainly thirteenth century.

Out of the village and over the cross-roads I left the road to skirt a reservoir in a copse, then across ridge and furrow and arable to Rothwell Lodge. Briefly along the A6 before dropping right to a footpath that crossed narrow closes running down to Slade Brook. I crossed the brook and walked through a park. At the Rothwell Community Centre I turned left through a chunky kissing-gate on to a path that gives marvellous views of the symmetrical 1585–93 south front of Jesus Hospital. Soon I went through a gate on the right into the park that leads to the superb south front of Rothwell Manor House and back to Market Hill.

Walk 5

PROUD HATTON'S GARDEN

Holdenby and Althorp, Northamptonshire. 13 Miles. April 1990.
OS Pathfinder Sheet SP66/76.

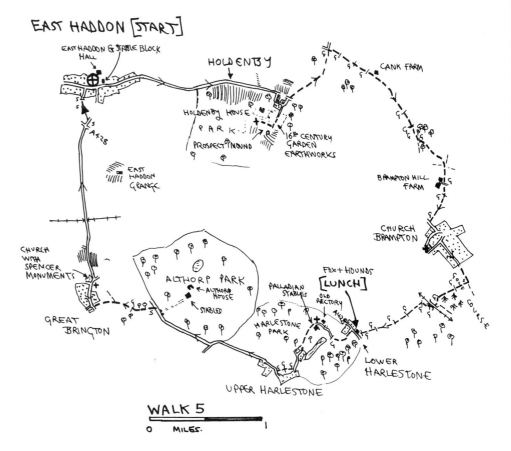

The story of Holdenby House is a remarkable one of brash Elizabethan showmanship for this enormous mansion 350 by 225ft, arranged round two courtyards, was just one of the houses of a rich bachelor. He was Sir Christopher Hatton who became Lord Chancellor in 1587 after working his way up as a courtier and civil servant to Queen Elizabeth in positions that allowed him to accumulate great wealth and influence. Hatton also built Kirby Hall east of Corby: another 'Prodigy House' as these gigantic palaces such as Burghley House and Hardwick Hall are called. Kirby survives, albeit partially ruined, but Holdenby has almost disappeared. They were not primarily intended for ordinary living but for the courtly life and many were built in the hope that the Queen and her entourage would visit. Holdenby was virtually the same size as Hampton Court and saddled Hatton with enormous debts. He died in 1591 and a nephew struggled on until he sold it to King James I. The house was largely demolished in 1651 by Captain Adam Baynes who bought it during the Commonwealth. The remnants were incorporated into a Victorian house about one-eighth the size of Hatton's monster but in the same style, with mullioned and transomed windows, pedimented eaves dormers and elaborate stone chimneys.

Even after these vicissitudes the great formal gardens laid out under Hatton remain as earthworks, ponds and terraces and are perhaps the best preserved Elizabethan formal gardens in England. Immediately south of the house a huge platform 260 by 330ft was formed to give views over the countryside and this was the heart of the gardens. To the east was a base court which led to the great east gatehouse and from the north and south walls of this court two grand archways survive. South of the platform the hillside was terraced and ornamental ponds and small lakes dug while at the south-east corner there is a prospect mound. At the south-west the parish church is all that remains of the medieval village Hatton swept away for his pleasure gardens and 'Prodigy House'. It is poignant to contemplate these fragments of past splendours and all the labour and finance that was expended on a house that enjoyed such brief glory.

I parked in East Haddon, a busy stone village with a long low church and the

Sic transit gloria mundi: *the base court archways of 1583 are almost all that remain above ground of Sir Christopher Hatton's prodigiously vast double-courtyard palace.*

home of 'Haddonstone', a reconstituted stone whose urns and balusters are displayed in their Show Garden. North of the church the Hall (1780) is a Palladian mansion with a rusticated ground floor, sashes and a pediment. The house is in grey Barnack freestone while its 1663 stable-block by the road, now a house, is in rust-brown ironstone or Marlstone. Both limestones occur everywhere in this area but the Barnack tended to be used for better quality work and dressings. I walked east along the road between arable and vulgar yellow rape fields and passed Haddon Spinney which marks the north-west corner of Holdenby Park. Glimpses through the shelter-belt reveal vast areas

of ridge and furrow under the sheep-cropped turf of the Park, the common-field strips of vanished Holdenby village not ploughed since the 1570s.

Soon I reached the north drive to Holdenby House with an elaborate Elizabethan style gateway arch (1920). From here I saw the north front of the house, mostly 1873 and 1887. The gardens are open some afternoons from Easter to the end of September. Beyond a Tudor-style Lodge (1890), I turned right to the village centre, a mixture of ironstone and tilehung estate cottages round a square green with limes, oaks and blossoming cherries. I turned right to walk down towards the church with glimpses of the base-court

archways through the trees on the right. At the end I turned right before the prospect mound and walked up to the church with ponds and other garden earthworks on the left and the tree-clad rampart of the main garden platform on the right. Inside the church are Jacobean black-letter painted texts on the walls and a series of wall tablets to the Whites who took part in the infamous 1895 Jameson Raid into the Transvaal. The late seventeenth-century chancel screen in dark-stained oak with fluted Doric columns and pilasters appears to have been brought in from elsewhere.

Retracing my steps through the village I crossed the main road on to a path across arable and then uphill through rape. Then I

Northamptonshire limestone cottages: a typical pair in Harlestone.

I descended through a conifer wood, crossed a stream, walked under the railway, and up a farm track into Harlestone and lunched at the Fox and Hounds (no food on Sundays).

Harlestone is a delightful ironstone village scattered over rolling small-scale hills with thatched seventeenth- and eighteenth-century cottages. I walked north briefly up the A428 and turned left by number 34, soon leaving the lane through a gate on to a path through pastures that skirts the walls of Harlestone Park. I then bore right to descend past a good stone farmhouse with stables and barn into a valley, then climbing out to the church past Devey's School, and the rectory, now Harlestone House, a three-bay Palladian house with a recessed centre and rusticated ground storey. At the top on the left are the magnificent but dilapidated Palladian stables of Harlestone House, demolished in 1940. They form a quadrangle with hipped-roof corner pavilions and a col-

turned right to follow a bridleway south-east between fields of rape and barley, passing through Cank Farm and its eighteenth-century stone farmhouse and eventually Brampton Hill Farm, a huge early nineteenth-century model farm with double yards in ironstone with brick inner elevations. The path then descended to the road into Church Brampton, a village with Tudor-style estate cottages of 1848 built for the Spencers of Althorp. East of the church opposite former almshouses of 1858 I turned right down a pleasant suburban lane, past the entry to the golf club and down a green lane, soon turning right over a stile to cross the fairways.

Gothic and Palladian side by side in Harlestone: the Decorated Gothic church beside the monumental decaying stable block to long demolished Harlestone House.

umned and pedimented centre, are all in ironstone, and have a stark grandeur. The church is decorated with reticulated tracery windows. Most of it dates to 1320 but the tower goes back to 1294. Inside is good woodwork, and a west gallery.

I walked west past the north elevation of the stables through the Park with its ancient sweet chestnuts and oaks. The park is being converted to a golf course and a large clubhouse occupies the site of Harlestone House, looking out over the lake in the valley. The tarmacked footpath enters Upper Harlestone, a more scattered hamlet with thatched stone houses and estate cottages. I walked through the village and headed north-west along the road which skirts the south-west edge of Althorp Park, the home of the Spencer family, first as tenants and then as owners from 1508. Their wealth came from sheep and wool and in 1512 the present 300-acre park was created, now surrounded by a high stone wall. At the foot of the hill are a pair of lodges to the west drive. Beyond

Harlestone House stables looking through the giant columned and pedimented yard entrance into noble rot.

the wall becomes railings and I could see the west front of the house and to the left the ancient parkland with pollarded oaks, cedars, limes and beeches. A glimpse of the ironstone Palladian stables with Tuscan portico and hipped-roof corner pavilions can be seen, undoubtedly a better building than the somewhat anaemic-looking house with its white gault bricks.

Beyond the view of Althorp I turned left into a copse and then fields to Great Brington, another good ironstone village whose excellent church contains a marvel-lous collection of monuments to the Spencer family in the north-east Spencer chapel. The series starts with Sir John who bought the estate and includes the peculiar one of 1655 in which Sir Edward appears to be climbing out of his urn! Opposite the church Blore's Old Rectory (1822) has a Scottish-looking octagonal tower with spirelet. From the church I walked north towards East Haddon, bearing left across the A428 junction through ridge and furrow pasture into the village.

Walk 6

HILLS OF RUSSET HORNTON STONE

Tysoe and Edgehill, Warwickshire. 13 Miles. November 1989.
OS Pathfinder Sheets SP24/34.

On this walk the villages are almost wholly built of Hornton stone, the local name for the rich, golden toffee-coloured Jurassic limestone still quarried on Edgehill. This marlstone was extensively used even beyond Banbury, giving a homogeneity to the villages that unites disparate building styles. Used as ashlars and rubble-stones its high iron content produces a rich rusty colour. It forms the basis of the Edgehill escarpment and plateau that looks out over the Warwickshire plain. The level top is cut into by deep valleys, such as that of the Sor Brook, which make for attractive walking. The views north-west from the escarpment are striking, for below the field patterns are made clear and Enclosure Act hedges can be seen zigzagging their way into the hazy far distance.

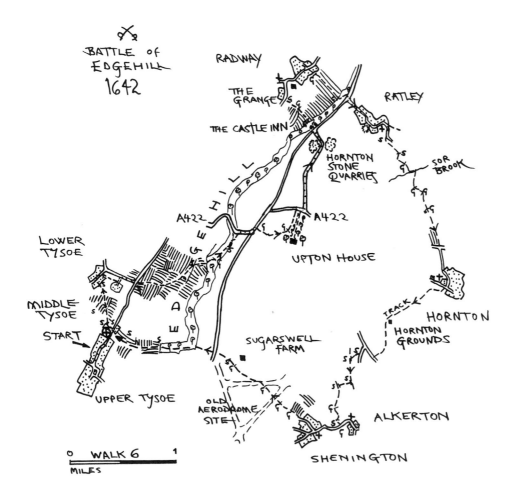

Edgehill is of course associated with the English Civil War battle fought inconclusively in October 1642. While the battlefield is inaccessible on Ministry of Defence land, the Castle Inn at Edgehill is on the route. The Inn is on the site where the Royal Standard was raised during the battle. Below in the valley Radway Grange was the house of Sanderson Miller, an architect who was influential in the Gothick Revival of the mid-eighteenth century. It is said that the ogee-arched windows of Ratley church inspired him and his stamp is to be seen in the area, including a cottage, the Castle Inn at Edgehill and alterations to his own house. Miller was insane when he died but his work survives widely and includes the Shire Hall in Warwick and the sham castle at Wimpole Hall, Cambridgeshire.

Parking in Middle Tysoe I walked to the church, admiring the quality of the Hornton stone houses including Home Farm with its windows and unusual central doorway of Venetian type. The church is attractive and large with a Norman south door that has a paschal lamb plaque above. Inside, although 'scraped' and pointed in dark mortar, there is also much of interest including Jacobean pews at the west end, some medieval pews, traces of Norman windows and a rustic Jacobean effigy on the north side of the chancel.

All this is a preliminary to Midland landscape at its best, for north-west of the refined 1856 Gothic school by Sir George Gilbert Scott, one is in ridge and furrow, overlaid by eighteenth-century enclosure hedges. I walked through spectacular examples to Lower Tysoe and then beyond Hopkins Farm with its selions gathered into interlocking furlongs that carefully

A distant view of battle: the site of the Civil War battle of Edgehill seen distantly from the limestone scarp at Spring Hill.

followed every variation in slope to assist drainage. From amidst it on the Lower Lias clay plain I climbed the escarpment and its layout became clearer, like in an aerial photograph, all etched crisply in the low autumn sunshine.

Once over the ridge I walked past Upton House (National Trust), a nine-bay smaller country house of 1695. However, its broken segmental pediment, which looks like Yorkshire seventeenth-century artisan mannerism, dates only from 1927 when alterations were made by Morley Horder. The view down the double pine avenue from the north gates is rather disappointing yet unforgettable. Towards Edgehill, quarries are still producing Hornton stone, but the chief treasure of this village is the Castle Inn consisting of two unequal sized battlemented towers, the larger inhabited and octagonal with machicolations, the smaller square and now, humiliatingly, the toilets for the inn. These towers date from 1746–47 and are by Sanderson Miller in the then novel Gothick style. They occupy the site of Charles I's headquarters for the 1642 battle on the plain below.

Down the escarpment across more ridge and furrow with the Grange on the right, I was in Radway, a very picturesque village whose Victorian church has a convincing broach spire and plain memorial tablet to Sanderson Miller of 1780. In the field north-east of the church are good earthworks that show that Radway was formerly a larger village. The Grange is basically a square Elizabethan house with gables, but Miller added the south-west bay windows and largely rebuilt the south-east front. In the park to the south is an obelisk of 1854 embossed by beeches and limes. Through more ridge and furrow and back up the ridge I walked into Ratley whose church is delightfully situated at the head of a valley with houses on three sides, including the Rose and Crown Inn. The church has ogee-headed north nave windows with reticulated tracery and, inside, nave and chancel arches of continuous moulded type with no capitals.

Walking down the valley to the southeast I looked back at the spectacular earth-works of the motte-and-bailey castle before continuing south, crossing the Sor Brook into Oxfordshire. I reached Hornton and walked south along its winding main street which opens up into three small greens at various points. It is a delightful village with many fine cottages and farmhouses, ranging from small mullioned windowed cottages to more formal sash-windowed houses. Opposite the Methodist Chapel, an overblown Gothic-style structure of 1884, is a particularly fine thatched stone house of four bays with a cross passage between the right-hand bays and fireplaces backing on to this, as well as many moulded mullioned windows. In the churchyard the hillside to the south gives a satisfying feeling of enclosure. Inside, the church has scalloped capitals to the north arcade and wall paintings, including a fourteenth-century Last Judgement or Doom over the chancel arch. Note the corpses rising from their coffins and, behind the pulpit, St George.

I lunched at the Dun Cow and joined the Oxfordshire Circular Walk just before a good seventeenth-century house on the

The Castle Inn at Edgehill on the site where the Royal Standard was raised in 1642: a mid-eighteenth-century sham castle by Sanderson Miller.

The Dun Cow in Hornton: a thatched village inn for lunch.

south side of The Green which has, behind the creeper, a doorway hood-mould with diamond stops. I saw several of these on the walk – they must be a local feature. I followed the Circular Walk, leaving it to walk up the hill to Alkerton whose church-yard gives a superb view of Shenington church. The church, approached by stone steps, has a tall narrow nave of *c* 1200 and a Decorated clerestory with a corbel frieze of great variety carved with animals, an organ player, musicians and grotesques. Inside, the central tower has an elaborate west arch with annulet rings to the shafts and a Jacobean pulpit. South of the church the Old Rectory of 1625 is of lobby-entry plan type with the irregularly placed single-light staircase windows above the door with its diamond label stops, and behind this the large stone stack has three diago-

A Hornton stone plaque in Shenington records a fire in 1721.

nal ashlar flues. It is a very fine house with mullioned windows, coped gables and stone roof slates.

Shenington village is another show-stopper with a green surrounded by fine houses and cottages, though one, Glasfryn, has a corrugated asbestos roof. The church has a tower of about 1504, but the remainder is fourteenth century. It was heavily restored by Pearson who, inexplicably, relocated the Norman chancel arch with its chevron and a cable hoodmould into the chancel north wall. Pearson's chancel arch apes the distinguished south arcade foliage capitals in white limestone.

I walked past the Bell Inn of 1700 and out into the countryside with very fine ridge and furrow on the right in the valley. Soon I crossed the old wartime airfield, now much quarried, descended through woods down the Edgehill escarpment, and back through ridge and furrow of very high quality into Tysoe.

Walk 7

KING'S MEN AND WHISPERING KNIGHTS

The Rollright Stones and Chastleton, Oxfordshire. 15 Miles. July 1989. OS Pathfinder Sheets SP22/32, SP23/33.

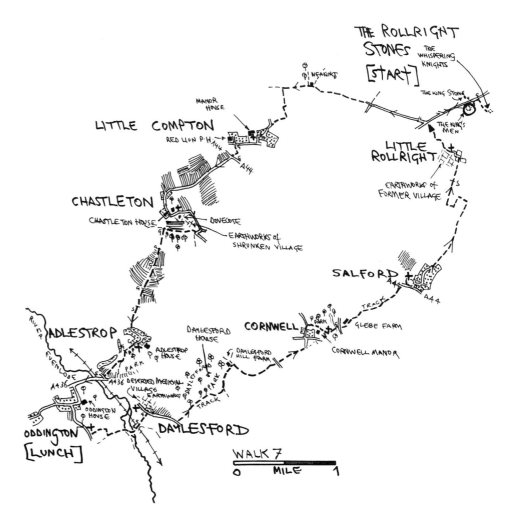

Along the ridge where three counties meet runs an ancient neolithic trackway, now known as the Jurassic Way. It ran along the Jurassic limestone ridges from Lincolnshire to Salisbury Plain and was subsequently used as a drove road for sheep and cattle and for pack-horse trading well into the last century. The route passes through much arable land but in places, particularly in Chastleton and Adlestrop parishes, pastureland preserves the earlier open field ridge and furrow.

Much of the field enclosure in this area is eighteenth century when elms, the 'Warwickshire Weed', were planted as standards in hawthorn hedges around the new fields. Dutch elm disease has killed the elms leaving a few ashes as standards. There are also a number of landscaped parks along the route, but arable is the commonest land use in this expansive Wold country. The villages and farms are almost entirely built in mellow Cotswold oolitic limestone. This is also extensively used for roofing, usually graduated in size from large at the eaves to small at the ridge. Stone field boundaries are rare and in fact hedging is the norm in this part of the Cotswolds. It is a beautiful area to walk and there are few navigational difficulties.

I parked in one of the two lay-bys at the Rollright Stones, a Bronze Age stone circle, originally of eleven stones but now broken up to edge a circle 100ft across. These are in Oxfordshire as is the Whispering Knights to the east, a stone chamber tomb without its soil mound, while the King Stone on the north side of the road is in Warwickshire. From here I had splendid views north across the Warwickshire Plain, the Bronze Age remains remote and unrelated to the hedges and fields they sit in, their religious purposes long forgotten.

I followed the ridgeway west before taking the second turning right. I headed straight on past quarries on to footpaths and tracks into Little Compton, a delightful Warwickshire stone village where the Manor House occupied by Reed College

The Whispering Knights confer: a Bronze Age chamber tomb bereft of its soil mound sits eerily in an eighteenth-century landscape.

wraps round the saddlebacked church. The Manor is best seen through the south gate where Altantean piers with giant ball finials pierce the high dry-stone boundary wall. The house is seventeenth-century stone of half-H plan with gables and stone-mullioned windows. At the west end of the village the Red Lion Inn, if open, is welcoming.

I crossed the A44 and followed the road to Chastleton with much ridge and furrow on either side, some enclosed early out of the open field strips into narrow, long rectangular closes, other areas cut across by later hedges. Climbing up to Chastleton is visually exciting, seeing first the parkland to its south surrounding the eighteenth-century dovecote, a square building on arches with a cupola above gables. Turning my back on this, Chastleton House is set beyond its arched and pedimented gateway, a complex and serene small-scale country house of about 1603–10 built for a Witney wool merchant, Walter Jones. It is remarkably unaltered inside and the composition of advancing and receding bays is highly accomplished (Open Easter to September; Fridays, Saturdays and Sundays, 2.00–5.00 p.m.). Next to it the church is similarly unspoilt with whitewashed walls and some good wall-paintings.

Following the road round, note the ridge and furrow to the left and the earth-works on the right around the dovecote. At the top of the hill on the Z-bend follow bridleway signs into the insect-rich

woods. Coming out of the woods views of Chastleton confront one. Turning left at the lime avenue to drop down towards Adlestrop through sheep-cropped pastures there are spectacular interlocking blocks of ridge and furrow on either side. Emerging at the road a shelter with a Great Western Railway sign from the defunct Adlestrop station has a plaque with the famous poem by Edward Thomas, who was killed in the First World War and which begins 'Yes I remember Adlestrop'.

Chastleton House: Jacobean symmetry at its best, framed by its pedimented forecourt gateway.

Through the pretty stone village I visited the church and from the graveyard glimpsed Sanderson Miller's Gothick south-west front of 1756–62, a marvellous crenellated and bay-windowed mansion looking out over Repton's gardens and park. Past the cricket pitch the parkland contains ridge and furrow and a long narrow lake. Along the A436, across the railway and the diminutive River Evenlode (heard rather than seen) and into Oddington, a long polyfocal stone village with two pubs, both serving good food: the Horse and Groom in Upper and the Fox in Lower Oddington.

The church is isolated south of the village and indicates where the village centre was before migrating to the east–west road. It is a superb church in a walled graveyard and has a wall painting of about 1400 depicting the Last Judgement, and a provincial but colourful Royal Arms of 1835 above the chancel arch. Across the fields and over the Evenlode again to Daylesford, another deserted village with a moated site opposite the church. The church is a splendidly Victorian one by Pearson, the architect of Truro Cathedral: cruciform with a central tower capped by a pyramidal spire. Inside are tablets to Warren Hastings and his wife, the resoundingly named Anna Maria Apollonia. East of the church is a beautifully restored Coade stone memorial urn to Warren Hastings dated 1818 and chastely Greek. Hastings was Governor of Bengal for the East India Company until 1783, but his career ended in controversy and impeachment. Daylesford House which he built remains unseen in its heavily wooded park on this walk. Daylesford 'village' is at the park gates, a superb collection of nineteenth-century vernacular stone cottages, betrayed only by their too-regular layout.

Adlestrop Park where a towering cedar sets off Sanderson Miller's airy, superbly composed 1750s Gothic windows and pinnacles.

The route skirts Daylesford Park and eventually reaches Cornwell, a curious village largely reworked or rebuilt by Clough Williams Ellis (the architect of Portmeirion) before the war, in a highly self-conscious manner. But most of this is round a private village green and I had to walk past and on to the footpath east to the church which gives good views of the Manor House with its mid-eighteenth-century south front concealing earlier work. The church is out in the parkland linked to the house by a narrow lime avenue.

Climbing to the road I followed a track between fields of stubble to Salford whose church was largely rebuilt by G. E. Street, a prolific church builder who also designed the Law Courts in the Strand, although there are two interesting reset Norman doorways. There is ridge and furrow in the field behind the church and the Old Rectory is of stone but with more fashionable render on its main south front: an

interesting sidelight in country so rich in superb building stone.

The village is disappointing and I walked north towards Little Rollright. Here navigational problems were solved after much to-ing and fro-ing by ignoring the sign on the left to Little Rollright and carrying on along the track northward, passing a sign 'Top Lake', and then footpath signs rounding the hedge to head west to pick up the footpath following the ridge hedge northward. This drops down into Little Rollright, a village reduced to a few houses and a church set in a secluded valley with a moated site, old fish-ponds and village earthworks. It was originally cleared largely to run sheep, in part by the Dixons whose splendid seventeenth-century monuments occupy the north side of the chancel of this delightful church. Manor Farmhouse is dated 1633, the Old Rectory 1640. I climbed out of the hamlet back to the ridgeway and ended the walk.

Cotswold Stones

WILTSHIRE AND GLOUCESTERSHIRE

But Cotswold, be this spoke to th'onely praise of thee,
That thou of all the rest, the chosen soyle should'st bee . . .
Michael Drayton

Walk 8

DEEP VALLEYS OF THE WILTSHIRE COTSWOLDS

Corsham and Castle Combe, Wiltshire. 14 Miles. November 1989.
OS Pathfinder Sheet ST87/97.

Much of the wealth in this corner of Wiltshire at the south-east edge of the Cotswolds came from sheep, both their wool and its processing into cloth. The river valleys had numerous water-powered mills, for example medieval Castle Combe had five fulling mills and at least one gig mill where teasels on rollers raised nap on cloth. Difficult as it is to visualize the tranquil valley of the By Brook as a teeming industrial area, this wealth produced fine churches, mansions like Corsham Court and numerous good stone-built houses and cottages. The walk passes over excellent oolitic limestones, the best being the Bath Stone types while less good ones produced rubblestone and roof slates. As a result virtually every house is stone built and many are stone tiled, but clay tiles and slate are also common on roofs. This Box or Corsham stone reached its zenith in the mid-nineteenth century when massive mined workings poured out millions of tons of superb freestone, vast amounts being sent away by railway as well as used locally. This area had its open fields enclosed mostly during the later seventeenth and earlier eighteenth centuries.

I started the walk in Corsham, from the car-park off Newlands Road behind the High Street. The historic core of the town lies east of Newlands Road with nineteenth-century development west along Pickwick Road. The High Street has a curiously Lilliputian scale like a two-thirds scale model. That said, it is one long archi-

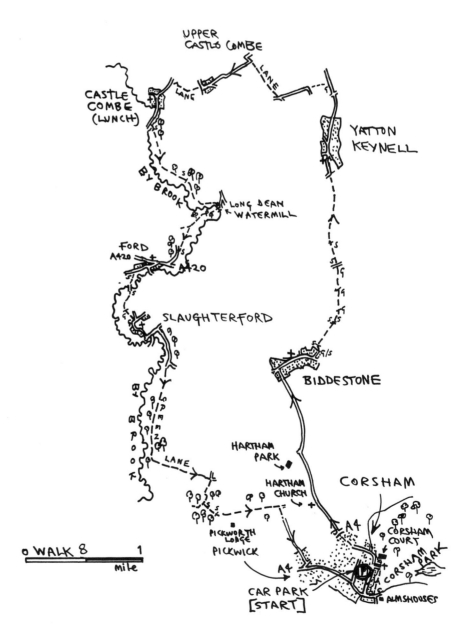

Corsham's stone-flagged pedestrianized High Street.

Almshouses and School of 1668 whose north front has seven gabled second-floor windows. Besides mullion and transom windows it has two elaborate achievements of arms below pediments, one over the north door, the other on the school range's two-storey porch.

On the opposite side I walked up the south drive to Corsham Court via a kissing-gate to the left of towering ball-finialled gate-piers. To the right Capability Brown's landscape park stretches into the distance, mostly oak and limes but one very large plane tree towards the church. On the east side of a small square the church has a curiously low tower and spire with three tiers of miniature lucarnes. On the north side beyond further large gate-piers flanked by hipped-roof stables and riding school is the south front of Corsham Court, a much altered house of 1582 with a resolutely E-plan appearance. It has two-storey bay windows with pediments to each and a two-storey porch with Tuscan columns and the upper storey gabled with mullion windows.

I walked down Church Street back to High Street, noting the much changed Town Hall, originally 1784 and open to the ground floor, but altered and heightened in 1882, and the famous Weavers Cottages. There are good houses in Priory Street but I walked north curving towards the A4 with Corsham Court's eighteenth-century stone-tiled farm and service yard on the right behind high walls overhung by a tumbling cascade of fantastically shaped yew hedging.

Crossing the A4 I walked up Hartham Lane passing Hartham Park Chapel by P. C. Hardwick, then Hartham Park with its restrained Wyatt Lodges which have deep open pediment gables and chaste ashlar elevations. The house is also glimpsed, Wyatt 1790s but much extended, and there is a small estate village mostly of the 1890s.

Continuing along the lane I turned right into Biddestone to shelter from the rain in its small Norman church. It has a thirteenth-century conical-roofed bellcote, a good south doorway and early nineteenth-

tectural historical feast with seventeenth-, eighteenth- and nineteenth-century buildings all melding into a coherent whole united partly by scale but also by universal stone. High Street is not quite straight so its delights unwind while the southern part is pedestrianized with stone flags and a sett central gully, green with weeds. The modern shopping centre on the west side is at least low-key and two-storey.

The High Street is closed by The Grove of 1737, a splendid five-bay house with thick glazing bar sashes and a complex centre-piece of superimposed orders. I turned left past the Methuen Arms and admired the large L-plan Hungerford

Tranquil Castle Combe seen from the time-gnarled village cross, amazingly a major medieval industrial centre when water drove the fulling mills to process the wool from the sheep on the surrounding hills.

century box pews and west gallery. Further east the Green is a memorable space with the seventeenth-century Pool Farm which has a range of mullioned windows, a gazebo and, in front, a seventeenth-century pond. On the north side Willow House (1730) is an urbane sash-windowed house.

Up a lane past the Post Office, I walked north through the fields, some pasture and then ploughed, to Yatton Keynell. Now soaked I sheltered in its church with cusped Perpendicular panelling everywhere: on the belfry, in the window reveals and in the arcades. North through the village noting a shaped gable end to a converted barn and a simple little Ebenezer Chapel (1835), I turned left into a field and then along a lane, right on to a green lane or byway, left again on to a pleasant lane with oak standards to Upper Castle Combe. This hamlet has some fine houses includ-ing the Manse. I carried on to descend the deeply cut lane into Castle Combe.

Castle Combe is a perfect stone village justly renowned and set in a secluded tree-lined valley. It is basically a single street with no jarring notes, the houses all having mullioned windows and stone roofs. The medieval market cross remains with a stone pyramidal roof and the church is superb. There is a large range of chest tombs south of the church and it has a fine fifteenth-century tower with crocketted pinnacles to each buttress set-off. Inside is a tall arcade and best of all the chancel arch has figures under canopies within the arch itself, most unusual and un-English. The north-east chapel has a good fourteenth-century effigy and a Victorian wheeled bier while the west tower has a tall arch and glorious fan vault.

I lunched and walked south past the Dr Doolittle filmset quay which canalized the By Brook and then crossed the river by a three-arch bridge to walk through Wiltshire Trust woodland above the valley to Long Dean with its two former water-mills and several good cottages. Crossing the brook I walked south-west to regain the road and into Ford, a pretty village marred by a busy 'improved' road. Its church by Ponting with its unusual tilehung gabled tower and octagonal shingled spirelet is usually locked; presumably no one expects visitors to an 1897 church. I crossed the river again and over the brow of the hill to Slaughterford, a perfect little village as good in its way as Castle Combe, its church isolated in a field like the hub of a wheel with the cottages round the rim.

Out of the village I walked south and then east along a lane above the east bank of the By Brook with fine views west and south-west. Eventually I turned right on to a metalled lane to descend into woodland, then left into a field and very steeply up to the plateau again, passing seventeenth-century Pickwick Lodge group which includes a high-walled garden. On past these on the farmtrack with a wooded valley dropping away to the left and, beyond, good views of Hartham Park with its three-storeyed porticoed west block and two-storey south range. I turned right on to Middlewick Lane and into Pickwick village.

Turning right on to the A4 Bath Road I walked to the junction to look at the Manor House, a seventeenth-century gem of seven bays with mostly cross windows and an elaborate shell hood on brackets above a bolection-moulded door-case: a memorable house in a day of riches. I walked back into Corsham down Pickwick Road lined with small early and late nineteenth-century villas – I was soaked but content.

Long Dean, a hamlet on the By Brook, in a leafy valley.

A foot-bridge by a weir crosses the winding By Brook near Ford in a gentle valley.

Walk 9

ALONG WINDRUSH HEAD-WATERS

Stow-on-the-Wold, Gloucestershire. 14½ Miles. July 1990.
OS Pathfinder Sheets SP02/12, SP22/32.

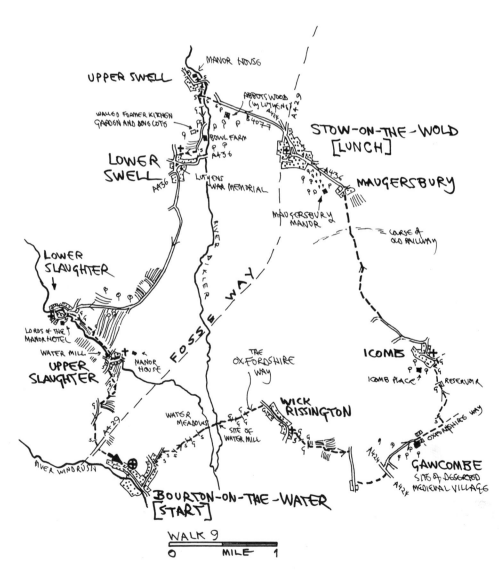

After the Roman invasion of Britain in AD 43 the legions and auxiliaries advanced across south-east England and within four years established a temporary frontier running from present-day Devonshire to Lincolnshire. Beyond this line were the unconquered British tribes, so the Roman military engineers constructed a military road to control the frontier. Now called the Fosse Way, much is still in use as main roads, lanes, green lanes or tracks. Soon after AD 47 the legions advanced north and the Fosse Way ceased to be the frontier but remained a major cross-country route. Today this stretch is subjected to a constant flow of traffic on its typically long straight Roman alignments.

As usual, most of the towns and villages turn their Anglo-Saxon backs on the Roman road, for roads were used by armies which, friend or foe, fed themselves by plunder. These villages are almost exclusively built in mellow golden Cotswold limestone and nestle in valleys cut into the oolitic limestone plateau by the headwater streams of the River Windrush. The only exception is Stow-on-the-Wold on top of the steep ridge where the Fosse Way climbs the watershed between the Rivers Windrush and Evenlode. So unusual is this village's situation that the latter part of its name is 'on-the-wold' meaning uplands. Until the eighteenth-century enclosures, sheep dominated the economy. From this wealth churches and villages were built.

I started in Bourton-on-the-Water, a beautiful town where almost all the shops are open on Sundays, dispensing food and souvenirs to countless visitors. Numerous

Gloucestershire's Venice: Bourton-on-the-Water's bridges criss-cross the Windrush. A rare quiet moment in this tourist mecca.

low bridges cross the River Windrush which bisects the town, so it is inevitably known as the Venice of the Cotswolds. Architecturally, there is much to admire, including the church behind the frontage houses. The fine tower (1784) by the local architect William Marshall, has a rusticated lowest storey and giant Ionic angle pilasters to the upper two, all surmounted by a lead-covered dome. Through the bustling town I turned left up Station Road, passing the gabled Bourton Manor in seventeenth-century Cotswold stone behind grand gate-piers.

Bourton is at the end of the Oxfordshire Way, a long-distance path from Henley-on-Thames. The first few miles of this walk follow this path, so navigation is no problem. I bore right on to Roman road where the OW disc waymarks start, to cross the pastures and water-meadows of the River Eye. At the road I turned right to walk through the village of Wyck Rissington which has a long green with attractive stone houses scattered on both sides.

A Cotswold landscape: the view west over Wyck Rissington.

Wyck Rissington church was substantially rebuilt in 1269, probably by Eynsham Abbey to whom it had been given in 1264. The east window is most unusual, having two pairs of lancets surmounted by concave lozenge windows and, above and between, a single lozenge window, all tied together by string-courses: a whiff of barbarism here and difficult to see as proto-tracery. The church is attractively located in a sloping churchyard with grassy hills rising steeply behind. The Oxfordshire Way leaves the churchyard at the east and then ascends, initially through ridge and furrow pasture, to the A424.

I turned left, then right, and at the sign 'Private Road Gawcombe' continued straight on down a lane flanked by exotic trees until it widened into modern land-scaped gardens. Gawcombe House, mainly seventeenth- and eighteenth-century stone and obscured from public views by extensive farm-buildings, is the site of a deserted medieval village. Beyond the farm at a footpath crossroads I turned left on to a grassy track beside a hedge to leave the Oxfordshire Way. At the end of the hedge I headed diagonally across arable to cross Westcote Brook on to a track which I followed, glimpsing the many-gabled Icomb Place, a medieval courtyard house of high-quality Cotswold stone. Beyond farm-buildings Icomb church has a saddle-backed Tudor tower. Inside the Norman thirteenth-century church is a fine effigy of Sir John Blaket (1431) under a wide cusped canopy with, for his convenience, a small window.

I walked through Icomb, turned right at the war memorial and left before the Old School. At the top of the lane I went straight on, then at a triangular copse on to a track which descends Maugersbury Hill and enters Maugersbury. The most conspicuous building is The Crescent of 1800 with arched windows and built on a semicircular plan. This attractive village with some good stone houses is separated from Stow by the park to Maugersbury Manor, a sixteenth- and seventeenth-century house with a three-storey porch and later alterations. I walked along the

road bordering the east side of the park and then into Stow-on-the-Wold itself.

Stow, originally called Edwardstow, was established by Evesham Abbey as a market town, Maugersbury having been the earlier settlement. The success of Stow, despite its windy and bleak situation, was based on its location at major road intersections. Its golden age came in the later Middle Ages with its two great sheep fairs: these survive as a Horse Fair. The town turns inward on its market-places, the north one being the larger. The church is west of the market hidden by later infill buildings and has a fine ashlar south tower of 1445–47, a landmark for miles even if near-invisible in the town. I entered the town and at the Royalist Hotel, dated 1615 on its porch, turned right up Digbeth Street to the square. There are many good buildings in a remarkably complete historic town, and St Edwards Café, a miniature Baroque front with giant fluted Corinthian pilasters and niches, is outstanding. After lunch I left the market place past the Queen's Head up High Street.

Across the Fosse Way I looked down a beautiful sheep-cropped valley towards the Swells, before bearing left onto the B4077, past the 1928 Walter Reynolds Homes of Rest. I descended the hill and, beyond gate-piers with acorn finials to Lutyens's Abbotswood of 1902, went through a gate into sheep pasture, crossed the River Dikler and turned right to Upper Swell, which has a near-perfect Norman church with rich ornate doorway and chancel arch. Immediately north the Manor House has a Jacobean two-storey porch with elaborate Tuscan broken segmental pediment door-case and the left-bay mullion and transom windows have king mullions. There are other fine houses and even a couple of large elm trees. I retraced my steps to walk south along the west side of the river, partly through parkland belonging to Bowl Farm which was built on the site of the manor house. A walled kitchen garden remains on the right and a dovecote rebuilt in 1917. Before the road I left the drive to head west across pasture

to Lower Swell church, a curious church where the exellent Norman nave and chancel are dwarfed by Buckler's 1852 north 'aisle' and chapel.

South through the village, passing Lutyens's refined war memorial with a flaming urn on a pedestal, I turned left at the sign 'The Slaughters' to follow the lane, soon taking the left fork on to a lane giving clear views across the Dikler

valley. With increasing amounts of ridge and furrow on either side I reached Upper Slaughter, a marvellous village, improved and added to by Lutyens and well worthy of the tourists thronging it. There is a castle mound and a church with unusual monuments in the chancel. After an excellent cream tea on the lawn of the Lords of the Manor hotel I walked east before turning right at a footpath sign to cross the River Eye and follow the path along its bank to Lower Slaughter, another very picturesque village with a brick water-mill complete with water-wheel. Everything else is stone and prettily built along the river bank. The Victorian church has a spire but the show-piece is the Manor House (1640) for William Whitmore by Valentine Strong, a member of a dynasty of local master masons.

Stone upon stone: a view in Upper Slaughter.

South out of the village, I turned left by pine trees into fields, and beyond a fence stile right to follow the hedge back to the road, soon turning left into fields to cross the Fosse Way (carefully) back into Bourton-on-the-Water.

Walk 10

WHERE COTSWOLDS MEET MIRY CLAYS

The Ampneys, Gloucestershire. 9 Miles. January 1990.
OS Pathfinder Sheets SP00/10, SU09/19.

The Ampneys are situated where the oolitic limestones of the Cotswolds dip below the Oxford clays to their south-east. This is proven by the weight of mud that accumulates on the boots in the stretch between Ampney Crucis and Poulton. It is mainly arable country although Harnhill preserves much ridge and furrow beneath its well-grazed parkland turf. The Cotswolds here are gentle in contrast to the more spectacular escarpment to the north-west. There is some drystone walling but mostly hawthorn hedges of planned countryside with oak standards. The villages and hamlets are almost completely built in the mellow golden-buff to grey local oolitic limestones which give them a homogeneous character despite numerous different architectural styles and periods. There is extensive use of stone roof-tiles as well as plain clay tiles, slates and thatch, for undoubtedly here the villages outshine the landscape through which the walk passes.

I started in the churchyard at Ampney Crucis, where the fifteenth-century churchyard cross finial is in remarkably good condition, having been walled up in the rood-loft entrance. Was it hidden here when Protestantism swept away icons and rood-lofts? The church in its beautiful setting has a grandiose tomb in the north transept to George Lloyd (1584) complete with fluted composite columns and pediments. Ampney Park behind is basically a large ashlar chimney-stacked stone manor house with many gables enlarged in the eighteenth and nineteenth centuries. I walked east down a yew-lined path to the road and turned right towards the main road passing The Lodge, the first of today's small houses of about 1700 with moulded stone cross-windows and stone-tiled roofs. I crossed Ampney Brook on a bridge of five small arches and continued south between drystone field walls with ridge and furrow in the left-hand field. Soon I turned left through a field gate and headed east then south beside hedges in muddy ploughed fields to Harnhill, although it would have been easier to follow the road.

Harnhill Park, surrounded by a lowish drystone wall, is corrugated with ridge and furrow which gives an idea of how most of the surrounding landscape would have been until the eighteenth century. The selions or individual strips vary from 9–11m between ridges and are very clear examples. I walked through it to the mainly Norman church whose south doorway

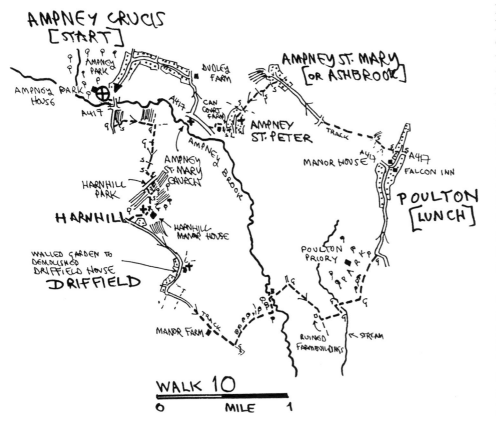

sixteenth century with three gables. South of the church the Old Rectory has a three-gabled front which was given a Gothick look about 1810 and is flanked by angle pilasters. I continued down the winding path flanked by high drystone walls to the road and turned left, noting shrunken village earthworks and ridge and furrow in adjacent fields and glimpsing the eighteenth-century front of the Manor House and its cupola-ed square dovecote.

I soon reached Driffield, a small village with a number of good houses, cottages and stone farm-buildings, some now converted into houses quite successfully. The church appears to have been rebuilt about 1734 and gothicized by William Butterfield. It retains a clue to its eighteenth-century origin in the classical tower cornice. There are some carved stones from the medieval predecessor reset and, inside, the Georgian pews and pulpit remain. East of the churchyard are earthworks which must relate to Lord Coleraine's great mansion sold for its materials in 1803, while south of the churchyard high stone walls are a remnant, presumably of the kitchen gardens. The Manor House opposite (originally a vicarage) has five bays of cross-windows.

Through Driffield I followed the lane round to modern Manor Farm and continued past its farm-buildings on to a green lane. At an oak copse I left it through a gate and skirted woods to a stream and plunged into the conifer copse to follow its bank north to a foot-bridge. This is probably not quite correct but the plantation and pheasant enclosures have entirely obliterated any clue to the footpath route shown on the OS map. Beyond the footbridge the route becomes clearer. Eventually, I saw Poulton Priory, a large stone house by Blomfield (1895) in vernacular style with mullioned bay windows, stone-tiled roofs and a large walled garden with gazebos.

Poulton is a long attractive village with many minor houses and cottages and is notable for work by Butterfield, who did the church and schoolhouse in 1873. These buildings are linked by dense yew

Ampney Crucis: the fifteenth-century cross of the name survives in excellent condition in the churchyard, having been walled up in the church for years.

tympanum is carved with a vigorous but somewhat crude St Michael killing a dragon. The Manor House, now a Christ-

ian healing centre, has its show front to the east with architraved sashes and parapet while to the west it is more vernacular

hedges, and by Ewan Christian, who designed the vicarage in 1868. At the road junction is a small green with a single beech tree and on the east side the Falcon Inn where I had lunch. On the west is the Manor House, a hipped-roof square stone house with cross-windows and dormers of about 1680 and now inhabited by a fortunate architect.

Continuing north I turned left to leave Poulton by the path left of the New Inn, then crossed a ploughed field to Ashbrook Lane, the old route to Ashbrook. At the road I continued into Ashbrook, a most attractive stone hamlet, then south across fields to Ampney St Peter, whose church is a curious amalgamation of Anglo-Saxon with enlargements by Sir George Gilbert Scott at his most inventive. The church is just past Iveson Manor (1908) by Gambier-Parry in a Cotswold arts and crafts style. Beyond the churchyard with its medieval cross and eighteenth-century tombstones is Eastington House in a small park. South

Poulton's four-square, hipped-roof late seventeenth-century Manor House is now occupied by a lucky architect.

is a most attractive grouping of stone houses round a small triangular green.

Ampney St Peter church lies isolated in the fields away from its village which migrated to Ashbrook half a mile away.

I continued west along a path north of Manor House, past a farm group to the main road.

I turned off to visit Ampney St. Mary's church, isolated in the fields and the mother church of Ashbrook. Apparently there is a deserted village site here but it has been ploughed out. The church is exceptionally interesting with an elaborate sanctus bellcote on the nave's east gable and a curious north door lintel carved with lions, snakes and a griffin, all grotesque and full of crude vigour. Inside is a rare carved stone screen and a collection of medieval wall-paintings. Recrossing the road, I walked into Ampney Crucis village, turning left at Dudley Farm, a new estate formed round the core of some barns and a farmhouse, a veritable hamlet. I followed the main street, which is a mile long and has many fine houses and cottages, before I turned right, back onto the path to the church.

Wessex Hills

DORSET, SOMERSET AND DEVONSHIRE

The zwellen downs, wi' chalky tracks
A-climmen up their zunny backs,
Do hide green meads an' zedgy brooks. . .
An' parish-churches in a string,
Wi' tow'rs o' merry bells to ring
An' white roads up athirt the hills.
                                 William Barnes

Walk 11

HILL-FORTS ABOVE THE RIVER STOUR

Hambledon and Hod Hill, Dorset. 14 Miles. January 1990.
OS Pathfinder Sheet ST81/91.

Dominating the route of this walk are the two great Iron Age forts crowning Hambledon Hill and Hod Hill on the chalk ridge between the valleys of the River Stour and its smaller tributary the Iwerne. Within their ramparts was evidence of settlement; mainly in the form of hut circles, pits and yards. Hod Hill was besieged and taken by the Romans in AD 44 and a fortress was built in its north-west corner. Their ramparts circle the hilltops but are most spectacular in the case of Hambledon Hill, where the bare turfed hill is tonsured in concentric rings. The River Stour winds close to Hod Hill and then meanders over the plain while the Iwerne flows through a formerly densely populated valley where several settlements have completely disappeared or been reduced to a single dwelling. Most of these were fairly small settlements and, in this instance, it would seem that the Black Death, the great bubonic plague epidemic that swept Europe in the fourteenth century, was responsible for tipping over these marginal settlements into oblivion, including Lazerton, Ranston, Steepleton and Preston.

There is a wide variety of building materials in this area. Greensand is predominant in the north part of the route, while the rest of the walk is on chalk. The tower of Child Okeford church, for example, is in fine-cut greensand. There is some imported limestone, notably Hamhill from Somerset, and a certain amount of chalk-stone as in the park wall to Ranston. Flint is common from the chalk and brick, but exposed timber-framing is rare. There are a lot of thatched roofs and the villages are attractive, although Child Okeford has greatly expanded in recent years.

I started the walk in Child Okeford whose church has a fine tower. Manor Farm north of the church has an eighteenth-century west elevation while the rendered south gables are inscribed 'W.T.D.T. Esq. 1841'. Opposite the war memorial cross, Monks Yard has one greensand bay amid the poorly pointed brickwork concealing sixteenth-century timber-framing. Turning right, I descended through Gold Hill, a mainly nineteenth-century hamlet including two pairs of greensand cottages dated 1854. Just before the derestriction sign I turned left on to a track which became a green lane. At the end I climbed a stile to walk through pastures first enclosed from commons after 1840 – to my left the Stour and to my right views of Hambledon Hill. At the road I crossed the weir bridge into Hammoon, noting shrunken village earthworks south of the road. The church is curious, for the chancel was

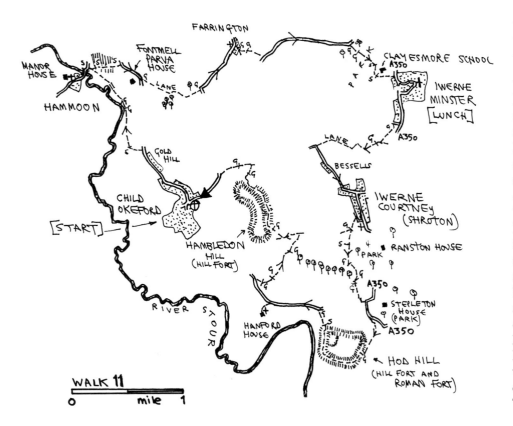

Tiers of ramparts on Hambledon Hill's Iron Age hill-fort dominate the River Stour and the Blackmore Vale.

seventeenth-century house of five bays in brick with stone dressings and a steep-pitched stone-tiled hipped roof. It was enlarged by George Evans of Wimborne who added roughly matching wings and distinctive arched timber gables in the 1860s, certainly not diminishing its quality. Opposite, I headed up a green lane, then on to a road that led to Farrington, a shrunken village originally independent but now absorbed into Iwerne Courtney parish. Here there is a small, apparently redundant, church and several attractive thatched houses, including Church Farm-house, a seventeenth-century two-bay stone house with gabled upper storey and mullioned windows but much extended. Beyond an eighteenth-century brick and thatch cottage I struck into fields and, reaching the road, walked east, passing Brickyard Cottages in front of a scrub-invaded brick pit.

At a lodge I turned into the grounds of Clayesmore School, formerly Lord Wolverton's palatial country house of 1878 by Alfred Waterhouse. It is huge and curiously gaunt in two stones, a local grey and a yellow Bath stone with grounds full of school buildings including a fine stone chapel of 1956. Waterhouse's stables have a vigorous tower over the archway with tourelles and buttressing piling up in fierce red brick. Wolverton certainly put his stamp on the village of Iwerne Minster which is full of black and white half-timber-ing and hot red brick. The church is a complex one with a good Norman north arcade, a greensand tower and recessed spire while the south-east chapel of 1880 by Pearson has a superb lierne vault. To the south of the church the Homestead looks like a converted barn with a jetty-like porch on dragon posts, but it dates from 1921 and was built as a village hall by Baillie Scott and Beresford, noted arts and crafts architects. Immediately west of this is the Chantry, a banded stone and flint house of two bays with central chimney and a south full height staircase-porch: a quintessentially Dorset seventeenth-century house. I wound through the village and lunched at the Talbot on the A350,

rebuilt in expectation of an aisled nave which never came and is therefore start-lingly out of axis. To the north of the church the thatched Manor House is an L-plan house with a mid-sixteenth-century front block with a two-storeyed porch, the arched entrance with Tuscan half-columns and entablature, a shaped gable and scrolled and obelisked eaves. To the right is a sixteenth-century bay window and the thatched roof makes a most attractive composition.

I retraced my steps across the bridge and then into a field with ridge and furrow to the road past the front of Fontmell Parva House, a fine four-square late

Cricket at Iwerne Courtney; beyond, a newly thatched ridge on a cottage.

another Wolverton black and white building.

Beyond Oakwood Drive I turned off the A350, across a field to Oyle's Mill, an eighteenth-century water-mill, now a house, and on to a green lane that forms the parish boundary and appears to utilize parallel boundary banks from an Anglo-Saxon estate. At the road I turned south and walked through the hamlet of Bessells.

Beyond, I reached Iwerne Courtney, its open fields enclosed by agreement in 1548, a long village with some good houses and at the south end a large half-H-plan thatched stone barn range. Beyond is the church, a remarkable Gothic survival building of 1610. On closer examination the chancel is recased but the bulk is seventeenth-century work by Sir Thomas Freke, a local whose family rose from

small-farmer status to gentry by serving the Crown. He provided the superb screen round the north-east chapel with its somewhat rustic wall monument (note the lumpy 'putti'). A slight retrace of my steps and I climbed on to the downs alongside the partly chalk-stone and partly limestone and flint park wall to Ranston, a house on the site of another settlement deserted by the early fifteenth century. Mostly rebuilt, the west front dates from about 1753 and has five bays with a pedimented centre and Corinthian pilasters.

I continued south, reaching the road at Stepleton House, set in a superb landscaped park that entailed diverting the road west around its perimeter. The course of the old road can be seen in

Late eighteenth-century thatched stable at Shroton Farm, Iwerne Courtney.

Jacobean Hanford House, all gables and chimneys, now a school.

the park and glimpses of the house show it to be a fine seventeenth-century square five-bay ashlar block with a dormered stone-tiled hipped roof and set-back eighteenth-century flanking pavilions. I climbed up to Hod Hill and walked around its outer rampart as far as the Roman entrance, descended the hill and walked

Stepleton House, a delightful seventeenth- and eighteenth-century mansion, nestles within its park whose creation involved diverting the main road in a wide loop.

past Hanford House, a splendid stone house of 1604–23 with three gables each side and a forest of ashlar stacks. It was built round a small courtyard, roofed over in the nineteenth century, and was the fruit of wealth amassed by Sir Robert Seymer as a Teller in the Royal Exchequer. Nestling in its lee is the church which was thoroughly altered in the seventeenth and eighteenth centuries.

Beyond, I scaled the hills, walked along the edge and then turned right to follow a fence alongside cross-dykes. Then I walked into a vast ploughed field across the site of a Neolithic causeway camp of circa 3000 BC. In the midst of this I

reached a grassy track and followed it uphill, then right on to Hambledon Hill. A bridleway skirts its northern edge, but you can climb into its centre where it is easy to imagine the Clubmen making their last stand against General Fairfax in 1645 during the Civil War. These Clubmen were 'poor silly creatures', according to Oliver Cromwell, who grouped together to defend their property against Royalist and Roundhead alike under the slogan: 'If you offer to plunder or take our cattle Be assured we will give you battle.' Beyond this great Iron Age monument I descended on to the fields and then down a deep sunken lane back into Child Okeford.

Walk 12

A VERY FAYRE CASTELL AND THE ISLE OF PURBECK

Swanage and Corfe, Dorset. 14 Miles. November 1989.
OS Pathfinder Sheet SY87/97/SZ07.

The Isle of Purbeck, cut off from central Dorset by heathland and the chalk and greensand ridge guarded by Corfe Castle, is renowned for its grey limestone and 'marble'. This marble, in fact a shelly stone which when polished resembles marble, was the basis for the area's medieval wealth and ran in a 2ft seam from Warbarrow Tout to Peveril Point. The industry was centred on Corfe where the 'marblers' or quarry owners lived and had their yards. It is difficult now to visualize

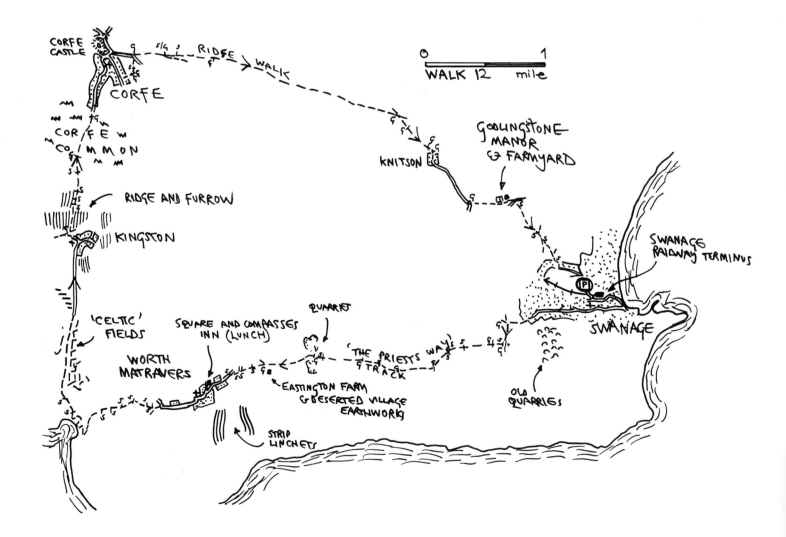

Corfe at its stone-dusty height. Although taxed as a borough by the fourteenth century it only received full borough status in 1576 and until the 1832 Reform Act had two MPs. The stone industry declined after the Middle Ages and was only vigorously revived in the eighteenth century when Swanage became its main port. The peak came in the nineteenth century under the Mowlem and Burt families. Mined and quarried from the surface and cliff quarries, by 1821 there were over sixty quarries in Swanage parish alone. Purbeck stone is still quarried at Acton and elsewhere, but the landscape south of the Corfe–Swanage road is pocked with grassy depressions, irregularities and changes of ground level. Much of the pasture is thin and sparse overlaying old excavations, for the Purbeck Marblers and Stonecutters charter gave them relatively unfettered rights to extract stone and, judging by the pock-marked landscape, they exploited these rights to the full.

The town of Swanage has much brickwork as well as stone in the older buildings, but other settlements, notably Corfe, Kingston, Worth Matravers and many isolated farmsteads are almost exclusively built in this grey stone. Most roofs prior to about 1850 are of Purbeck stone slabs, usually mortared to prevent water penetration between courses. A striking feature of the limestone hills is the drystone field walls which in many instances run unbroken from the Kingston–Swanage road to the sea. Several of these represent the boundaries between manorial estates, some of which were hamlets in their own right, such as Eastington where there are deserted settlement earthworks south of the farm, while others are represented solely by a farmstead or two, including Weston and Renscombe, or remain as hamlets within larger parishes such as Acton. The striking feature of these long narrow manors is not repeated north of this road, where they were squarer but more numerous, though now subsumed within larger parishes. Within modern Corfe parish there are many small hamlet or

Swanage Town Hall. This spectacular 1660s over-the-top façade was salvaged from the City of London by a local stone contractor in 1872.

farmstead manors including Lynch, Scoles which has a ruined chapel, Afflington, Woolgarston and Ailwood. A brief examination of the Ordnance Survey Pathfinder map will enable you to reconstruct the ancient boundaries of these manors which brings the Anglo-Saxon landscape vividly to life.

I started at the car-park in Victoria Avenue in Swanage, and passed the station which is the headquarters of the Swanage Railway, a preserved working steam railway. The parish church is worth a visit for the complex roof trusses (1860) by Wyatt. The town is rewarding and in the High Street the Town Hall is quite astonishing – until you realize it incorporates the rich

Caroline façade of the Mercer's Hall in Cheapside, London. This sculptural *tour de force* of the 1660s by Edward Jarman was rescued in 1883 by George Burt, a prominent citizen of Swanage and a major stone contractor. Opposite, Purbeck House, now the Convent of Mercy, was built in 1883 to Crickmay's designs by George Burt. A pig of a building, its elevations are perversely crazy-paved in Guernsey granite. I continued up the mile-long High Street, then left on to Priests Road at Parker's Stores, a yellow stuccoed building. This becomes Priests Way which heads generally west, mostly clearly waymarked, and flanked by quarries, overgrown or, near Acton, still working, and by miles of drystone walling.

I paused for refreshment at the unspoilt Square and Compass in Worth Matravers, ducks and hens in the yard, and looked south to the quite remarkably crisp and clear strip lynchets which line Seacombe and Winspit Bottoms. These medieval terraces are relics of thirteenth-century land hunger that resulted in such steep slopes being ploughed. Owing to its sloping site Worth Matravers is a most attractive village with good stone buildings and jumbles of Purbeck slab roofs, though the village pond looks contrived, as does the green telephone kiosk. The church is an exceptionally interesting Norman one with a decayed Coronation of the Virgin sculpture in the south door tympanum, a rare subject as early as 1130, good corbel tables and chancel arch. Westward I descended to Chapman's Pool where the geology differs and this Kimmeridge clay produces landslips. A steep descent and climb out of the valley was followed by a long walk up a tarmac farm road with Celtic field boundary banks on the east slopes.

Over the summit into Kingston the consummate Victorian church by George Edmund Street, the architect of the Law Courts, is sumptuous in Early English Gothic or Lancet style with a grand central tower and a profusion of, not surprisingly, Purbeck marble shafts and capitals inside. It was financed by Lord Eldon of the nearby (but private) Encombe House, and cost the then staggering sum of £70,000. It dominates views of Kingston from the north. The village was largely rebuilt in the last century by the Eldons in vernacular style. Unfortunately, most of the cottages have recently been badly repointed: ribbons of rock-hard cement mortar.

Down from the hill through ridge and furrow I crossed the heathland to Corfe with its castle dominating the village and situated on a hill in the gap in the chalk ridge, strategically and superbly sited. The castle was famously besieged in the Civil War and then slighted to produce today's picturesque, somewhat drunken ruins. The village (or decayed town) has many good buildings particularly in West Street. The church is mostly a Victorian rebuild, but the Perpendicular west tower has much fine sculpture, including gargoyles and niches. The Market Place is a memorable space with the Greyhound Hotel which has a projecting first-floor bay on three columns dated 1733. Several other buildings have these projecting first floors, in effect forming porches. On the south side the Town House has a most unusual but genuine eighteenth-century first-floor window with a leaded arched centre and curved sides, and belongs, in fact, to the mayor's robing room. Just round the corner is the Town Hall which has a stone ground floor and brick upper floor with arched stone architraved windows and only two bays, reflecting the declined status of the borough by 1774.

I walked south down East Street past Morton's House Hotel, a smallish E-plan house of about 1600, and then turned left to cross the trackbed of the old railway which the Swanage Railway hope to relay. Beyond Challow Farm I climbed on to the chalk ridge, hoping for the superb views normally seen from this fine ridge walk, but the mist had descended. Eventually, I dropped down to the hamlet of Knitson and walked south along the lane, then across fields to Godlingston Manor. Here there is first a Victorian model farmyard on an E-plan which has very steep gables and extraordinarily attenuated nar-

The route reaches the sea dramatically at Chapman's Pool with Houns-tout Cliff soaring beyond.

Corfe Castle: its ruins dominate the town.

Purbeck stone: a cottage in West Street, Corfe.

row dormers. The central arm gable elevation has stone mullioned openings totalling sixteen lights below a further eight in the gable. Beyond is the Manor House, partially of about 1300 as evidenced in the round tower on the left and the cusped arched doorway. It was altered in the seventeenth century when the hipped dormers were added and the right-hand crosswing was rebuilt after a fire in the nineteenth century. It is picturesque and a fitting climax to my walk. I then headed south-east along the banks of a small stream back into Swanage.

Walk 13

UNMANNERLY IMPERIOUS LORD

Milton Abbas, Dorset. 13½ Miles. January 1990.
OS Pathfinder Sheets ST60/70, ST80/90.

On many of these walks are landscapes of desertion, mostly medieval, and this one includes the earthworks of two villages cleared by their lords of the manor for sheep. It also has one of the most audacious examples of eighteenth-century patrician arrogance: Milton Abbas. Here Joseph Damer, Viscount Milton, later Earl of Dorchester, cleared a whole market town from his imperious sight to give Capability Brown a free hand in designing a landscaped park in which no lesser mortal or tradesman could be seen, smelled or heard. Up a nearby valley out of sight of his house he built a model village for the displaced, re-erected the town's almshouses and built a new church. Much photographed and very picturesque, the new village is a testament to the untrammelled power of eighteenth-century landowners. The presbytery, crossing and transepts of the medieval abbey at whose gates the town and its market had developed became the private chapel of 'this unmannerly imperious lord', a description of Joseph Damer given by the architect of his mansion, the great Sir William Chambers. This towering church dwarfs the Gothick-style house next to it, a house incorporating the sumptuous Great Hall of Abbot William Middleton of 1498.

This walk is mainly on the chalk and the predominant building materials for houses and cottages are flints, usually brick dressed or with brick bands alternating, but also found with stone dressings and brick bands, and, of course, cob which is usually rendered over. Other high-quality stone is used such as Ham Hill and Purbeck for Milton Abbey, and Portland for the Abbey house. Roofs are thatched, clay tiled or less commonly stone tiled. This

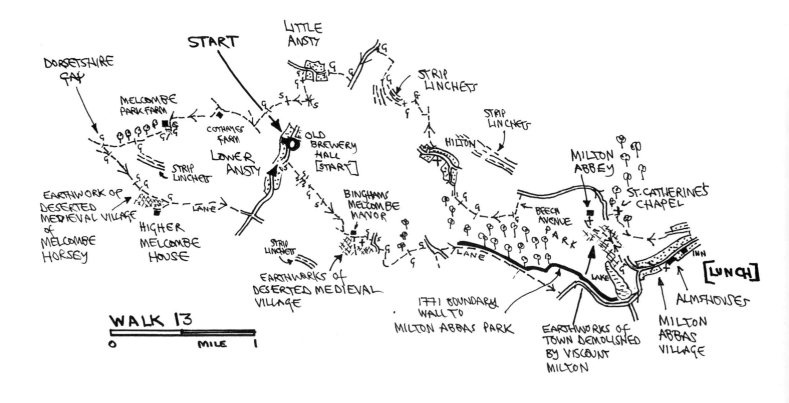

area was formerly farmed under the three-field system and medieval strip lynchet terraces remain on the steeper slopes, although elsewhere the strips have been eliminated by ploughing and later enclosure.

I parked by the Old Brewery Hall in Lower Ansty which was, according to a plaque, the original brewery of Hall and Woodhouse in 1777 and converted to a village hall in 1946. It is said to incorporate material from Higher Melcombe and certainly has some superior detail for a malt-house, including stone-jambed windows with keystones. I walked downhill and turned left on to footpaths along the south side of the quaintly named Mash Brook to Bingham's Melcombe manor house. This is a very fine stone-built courtyard house, mostly sixteenth century. It replaced the fourteenth-century hall house of the Binghams who bought the estate in the thirteenth century, consolidated it and expanded and moved into sheep. By 1400 they had cleared away the village and its earthworks – a superb set – remain south of the church. The Binghams are just one example of numerous wool families on the chalk

Looking back on Bingham's Melcombe, its church, the manor house hidden in trees and the earthworks of the village, deserted in the sixteenth century.

The walk starts here: the Old Brewery of 1777 in Lower Ansty lives on as the village hall.

downs and a counterpart of the Abbots of Milton who also ran enormous flocks of sheep. The house is mainly concealed by an entrance and kitchen range, by high brick or brick and flint walls and venerable sweeping banks of yew hedging. It is worth walking down the drive to look at the Purbeck stone eighteenth-century gate-piers, and for the good views of the village earthworks east of the drive. The church, in effect a chapel for the Binghams, is delightful and has good fragments of medieval stained glass, a screen of 1619 and even in the porch graffiti dating back to 1582. As I climbed out of the valley on to the chalk down, there were fine views back over Bingham's Melcombe nestling in its small wooded park and the village earthworks laid out like an aerial photograph.

Over the top I reached the road, turned right, then quickly left on to a metalled green lane. A flint wall appeared on the left, then a stuccoed mid-nineteenth-century lodge and a large plantation. This flint wall in varying states of decay is part of the five-and-a-half mile boundary wall built by Viscount Milton around his new park after 1771. I followed this wall more or less all the way to Milton Abbas, some of it in the woods mossy and bracken-coped, other stretches in the open and complete. At one point just before

Fishmore Hill there is a fine view across to the winding main street of Milton Abbas with its colour-washed, rendered and thatched-roofed cottages and wooded valley sides.

Past the lodge and the rusticated and swagged gate-piers is Capability Brown's wonderfully placed lake. I continued round the east side of the lake and temporarily ignored the village to walk down the footpath just before Luke Lodge to Milton Abbey. This emerges beyond the lake and passes amid the town earthworks on both sides, those to the left on either side of what were Broad and Fishway Streets being the clearest, while on the right closes and tenements climb the slopes. South of the church the High Street and Market Street are lost under the landscape gardening works. Following total destruction by fire in 1309 the Abbey Church was slowly rebuilt on a sumptuous scale mainly in Hamhill and Chilmark limestones, while inside the webs of the rib vaults are in cut chalkstone. At the west end is the start of an intended nave and at the east end the retrochoir has been demolished. Inside there are several good monuments, notably in the north transept a poignant tomb with Lord Milton looking down on his dead wife Caroline, the figures by Carlini (1775). The 'font' by Jerichau is bizarre, consisting of two life-size angels and an insignificant scallop shell for the water between their feet. To the north of the church is Chambers' mansion for Viscount Milton in a somewhat perfunctory Gothic revival style: Chambers was a dedi-cated classicist. Opposite, the church Tudor-arched windows show Abbot Middleton's astonishingly richly roofed Great Hall. The house, open in the Easter and summer holidays, is a school.

I retraced my steps into the village built for Damer's tenantry lining a generously verged street with church and almshouses halfway along. Beyond, is the Hambro Arms, named after the family that succeeded the Hamers and which serves excellent food. After lunch I climbed a path

Milton Abbas. The genuine medieval Gothic abbey church and Sir William Chambers' 1770s pale Gothic mansion await the storm.

The Dorsetshire Gap. Descending from the ridge towards Melcombe Horsey deserted village earthworks.

to the former rural district council housing and walked along the top lane, diverting into the woods to visit St. Catherine's Chapel, a Norman and presumably a wayside chapel. It is incorporated into Milton Abbey by means of a long flight of steps and a swathe cut through the woods.

I descended to the road and walked towards Hilton, getting good views of the Abbey which emphasized how much more majestic the church is than the white stone mansion lurking in its shadow. At a beech avenue I walked down to a stream and followed it into Hilton, noting superb lynchets on the northern hill slopes. The church has an elaborate north aisle with fifteenth-century windows and buttresses

of high quality, which almost certainly came from Milton Abbey after the Dissolution in 1541 when the monastic buildings were demolished.

From Hilton I walked to Manor Farm and then up a lynchetted coomb. Reaching the hamlet of Higher Ansty I continued across country to Melcombe Park Farm whose name commemorates the medieval deer park that occupied the north part of the parish. The countryside here is mainly pastoral with herds of dairy cattle in fields. These fields, now somewhat consolidated, are divided by hazel and thorn hedges with mainly oak standards, for we are on the edge of the lush Vale of Blackmore. Beyond the farm I climbed on to the chalk ridge which

gives spectacular views north over the Vale, and walked to the Dorsetshire Gap, a notch in the ridge. Descending, I headed southeast down a sunken way, then past fields to Higher Melcombe's deserted village earthworks. I briefly doubled back at the road to look at the outside of Higher Melcombe House which has medieval elements and a mainly sixteenth-century Tudor west range, but is chiefly notable from the outside for the former chapel built for Sir Thomas Freke by 1633. From here I walked east along the lane back to the road. Turning left, I walked through Melcombe Bingham (yet another variation of the name) and Ansty, passing attractive cottages to get back to the car.

Walk 14

ACROSS HAMSTONE HILLS

Montacute and Ham Hill, Somerset. 12½ Miles. October 1989.
OS Pathfinder Sheet ST41/51.

As the Fosse Way sweeps south-west bisecting Somerset, it comes within a mile or so of Ham Hill where a Roman garrison intermittently kept watch on this important route. Ham Hill is, however, more widely known for its building stone, an inferior oolitic limestone. Quarried since Roman times it is ideal for building work and has been used even for humble cottages as an ashlar or dressed stone. Every village on this walk is built primarily in this golden brown stone, certainly up to the First World War. Such was the value of the stone that the parishes of Stoke-sub-Hamdon, Norton-sub-Hamdon and Montacute vied for control of the hill top. Their boundaries criss-cross Ham Hill, giving each a stake in the quarries. Further east, between layers of limestone, Yeovil Sands produce characteristic lanes cut deep into the soft sandstone, overhung by hazel, sycamore and ash, with sandy cliff-sides up to 30ft high in places, making for very attractive walking.

I started the walk from West Chinnock, an attractive village with a long north-south main street, whose church was rebuilt in 1889 by Charles Kirk of Lincolnshire and has characteristically pious Victorian glass by Ward and Hughes. I turned right, uphill past Church Close, a nine-bay terrace of 1830, and then left over a stile to cross fields to Middle Chinnock, a perfect hamlet with a disappointing church but having a good Norman south door and Royal Arms of 1660. Opposite, the old seventeenth-century rectory with mullioned windows was extended into a double-pile house in

the nineteenth century. Walking north, Chinnock House of the early nineteenth century has architraved sashes and a pilastered Doric door-case. Beyond, Manor Farm has an older north range and a larger seventeenth-century chamber wing of two

high storeys and gabled attic windows. The first floor has two four-light mullioned windows to the high great chamber.

Retracing my steps, I turned left on to a lane which became a footpath, a concrete farm road and then the lane into East

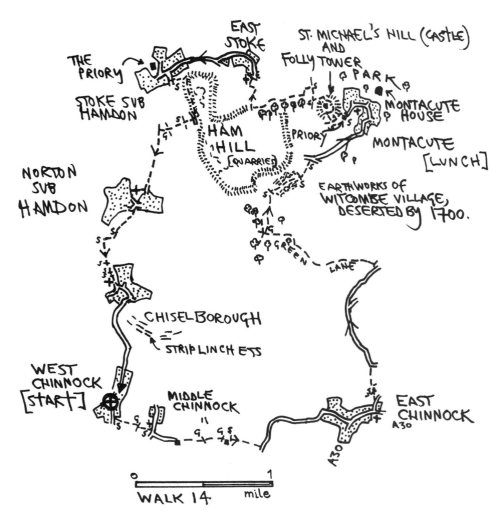

Remarkable stained glass in East Chinnock church by Gunther Anton, a stained glass artist who had been a prisoner of war in the area.

The earthworks of the village of Witcombe, deserted by the 1560s, fill a remote valley terraced by strip lynchets.

Chinnock, all the time with the limestone hills to the north beyond the willow-lined Chinnock brook. The hills are terraced by strip lynchets but these are obscured by invading scrub on the steeper slopes.

In East Chinnock, Weston House is particularly fine with four bays of mullioned windows and coped gables. There is much modern infill and even culs-de-sac, such as Weston Close, and nineteenth-century Portman estate cottages in red brick with yellow brick bands and dressings amid the hamstone houses. I turned left at the end of Weston Street on to the A30, roaring with traffic, and walked up the hill past the Portman Arms of the nineteenth century in Tudor Revival style. Inside, the tall-towered church has no arcades and a flat ceiling dating from a re-working in 1810. The remarkable stained glass by Gunther Anton, a prisoner of war here, is in Ottonian or Byzantine style and took him over twenty-five years to complete.

Opposite the church I followed the sign to Odcombe, then a path across the brow of the hill, to descend into stunningly beautiful sunken lanes cut into the Yeovil Sands and overhung by trees. After two miles I turned right on to a field path beyond Westfield Farm. The path crosses the earthworks of the deserted village of Witcombe in a remote valley with strip lynchets on the slopes to the west. The village disappeared soon after 1566. The path climbed out of the valley back to a road and I descended into Montacute via the aptly named Hollow Lane, flanked by high sandy cliffs.

Montacute acquired its Normanized Latin name *mons acutus*, or steep hill, to replace Anglo-Saxon Bishopston, a name preserved in the street north of the church. Around 1100 it became a borough, and by the thirteenth century East, Middle and South Streets and The Borough, a fine square, were laid out. It is a delightful small town and well known, its houses nearly all hamstone with mullioned windows. The Phelips Arms has unusual tripartite sashes in which the central sash is higher, while the Kings Arms at the end of Middle Street has Tudor tracery and a two-storey bay window.

Montacute House lies beyond its lodge and kitchen gardens, which are laid out for car parking and service buildings, in its park (National Trust: open daily, except Tuesdays, at 12.30p.m. until 5 Novem-

Hollow Lane leads down to Montacute, cut deep into the Yeovil Sands, a soft yellow sandstone. Only tarmac prevents the cutting from going deeper.

ber; grounds and car-park open every day). The superb E-plan hamstone house of the 1590s, three-storeyed with shaped gables and corniced between storeys, faces into a parterre with ogee-roofed plaisaunces or pavilions at each corner. The top-storey long gallery contains the Tudor collections of the National Portrait Gallery, a telling demonstration of how far English portraiture was behind Italy, most being little more than caricatures.

The church tower is tall with pierced quatrefoil stone panels to the belfry openings, while the Phelips monuments in the north transept and the Norman chancel arch relieve a somewhat stripped interior.

Left out of the churchyard and then right to pass in front of all that remains of the proud Cluniac Priory founded by the Mortains around 1102 is the Gatehouse of Thomas Chard, prior from 1514–32, with a high central arch, an oriel above and battlements. Dissolution in 1539 followed hard on the heels of this fine late flower-

Looking north-east from Batemoor Barn west of Montacute, towards St Michael's Hill with its tree-clad motte-and-bailey castle surmounted by the 1760 viewing tower and eyecatcher.

ing. Beyond, I climbed into the woods fringing St Michael's Hill, adapted into a motte-and-bailey castle by Robert, Count of Mortain, in 1067. Today the hill is crowned by a 40ft tower erected by the Phelips family in 1760 to take advantage of the spectacular views.

Down the hill, I walked along the edge of Ham Hill before descending into East Stoke and visiting its church: basically

Doves rise in front of the priory in Stoke-sub-Hamdon, in fact a fine medieval house and farmyard.

Norman with a curious north door tympanum showing Leo and Sagittarius flanking the tree of life and a paschal lamb. Inside, the nave walls have eighteenth-century painted texts in cartouche frames and a splendid Norman chancel arch of three enriched orders. In the churchyard are good eighteenth-century tomb chests and headstones and a fifteenth-century churchyard cross; I left via a four-centred seventeenth-century stone archway.

Out of the churchyard, right and then across the main road, I walked down Windsor Lane, noting East Stoke Farm (1698), radically altered in the 1860s and given extraordinary circular stone chimneys. Back on the main road I walked into Stoke-sub-Hamdon, much larger than East Stoke and known for its quarrying and also glove-making. During the nineteenth century, enclosure of Stoke's common fields accelerated, but the Great Field north-west of the village was still cultivated traditionally in the 1890s. There are several good houses, including the Fleur de Lys Inn of the fifteenth century with two splendid arched doorways, one relocated from the rear. Up North Street is the Priory, the house and farmyard of a college of chantry priests. Through a great archway with a blocked postern, I visited the great hall via a porch and screens passage. Round the two yards are barns, stables and a dovecote with five hundred nestboxes but no roof.

Scaling Ham Hill to the obelisk war memorial, I could pick out sheep grazing on Rixon Common to the north, and to the north-west and west the remnants of Shetcombe and Great Fields, still remarkably undivided as in open-field farming days. The quarry workings have blurred the great Iron Age hill fort. I walked south along its west rim before turning right to descend steeply to the green lane into Norton-sub-Hamdon whose tall narrow-aisled Perpendicular church is superbly enriched by various art nouveau fittings by Harry Wilson: a 1904 alabaster font, tower screen, tower vestry cupboards and, outside, a colourful tower west door. South of the church is a circular dovecote and beyond that a delightful stone village.

I turned right down Little Street and left on to a footpath and walked along the south bank of a stream, crossing it and then turning south to cross it again to head for Chiselborough. Its church has a bulbous spire above a central tower, a Victorian nave and a plain seventeenth-century chancel ceiled incongruously in insulation board. I walked back through the village to West Chinnock, initially along another deep-cut sunken lane.

Walk 15
WALKING TO CAMELOT

Cadbury Castle, Somerset. 12½ Miles. September 1989.
OS Pathfinder Sheet ST62/72.

Parking in Woolston Road in North Cadbury village I walked down the beech avenue to the parish church where I bought a booklet entitled *The Camelot Parishes*, a guide to eight churches and villages in the Camelot Team Ministry, an ecclesiastical co-operative including North Cadbury. I was in King Arthur country with a vengeance, for Cadbury Castle, a great Iron Age hill-fort on a spectacular limestone outcrop behind South Cadbury, has been associated for centuries with Arthurian legend. It is one of a number of sites claimed for Camelot and from 1966 Leslie Alcock excavated here to prove this one way or another. Impossible to unearth a legend of course, but he found that it had been refortified around AD 500 to play a

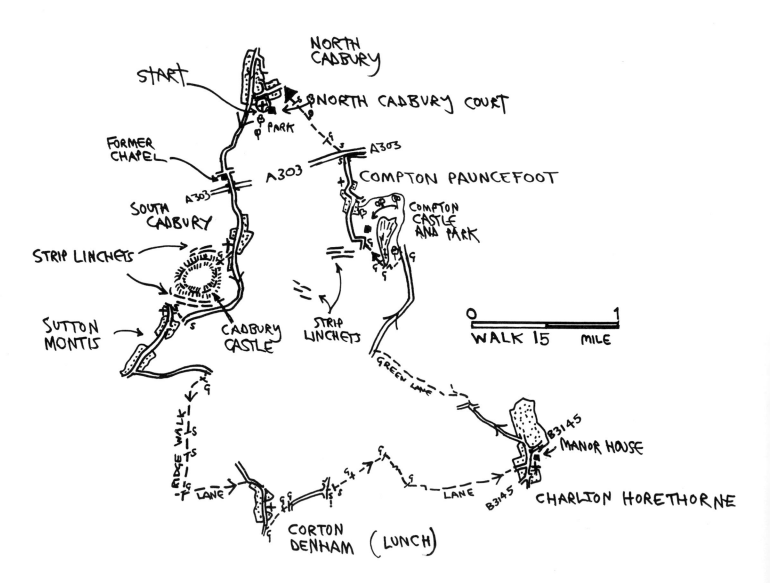

Before reaching North Cadbury church I looked beyond the splendid gate-piers with their ogeed fish-scaled finials to the mullioned and transomed splendour of North Cadbury Court, a stylish Elizabethan mansion with four gables. From its long flat front two bays project, the left-hand bay being an arched porch leading into the screens passage of the hall while the oriel bay is at its high end. Backing on to the churchyard is a long stone stable range (1715) with two-light mullioned upper windows, cross-windows to the ground floor and a mellow pantiled roof.

Through the 1910 lych-gate, the plain rear wall of the stable block is adorned by a bronze resin sculpture group of 1972 by John Robinson, which symbolically represents the Redemption. Passing this the church, built anew by 1423, has west-tower angle buttresses with no less than seven set-offs and stately two-storeyed nave porches. Its interior is spacious and flooded with light, for there is little stained glass in the large traceried windows. In the tower are effigies on a tomb chest of Lord and Lady Botreaux, the builders of the church. The bench ends, dated 1538, have an astonishing variety of subjects carved on them, including St Michael, wyverns, caricature portraits, a pack-horse, a windmill, and a large church.

Back at the Woolston Road, I turned right to buy iron rations at the Post Office and General Store which occupies the ground floor of a stuccoed double-fronted early nineteenth-century house. In the tiled hipped roof are three thermal or semicircular dormers. I returned to High Street and then walked north, then on to Cutty Lane and a footpath, then a lane past a Wesleyan chapel of 1848. Heading south past the hamstone Butterfield-style school of 1875, I walked down Cary Road with more good stone houses and the colour-washed stone Catash Inn, and continued on down Parish Hill. Ahead, Cadbury Castle, fringed tonsure-like by trees, dwarfed the spiky silhouette of South Cadbury church tower.

The A303 is being made into a dual carriageway and the small thatched Per-

A fanciful gravestone in North Cadbury churchyard where the walk starts.

role in British resistance to Anglo-Saxon invaders sweeping west.

The countryside is dominated by Cadbury Castle with limestone hills running east and south, cut into by deep coombes and valleys. To the west is the flatness of the Somerset Levels. The delightful hamstone villages have fine churches, set partly in pastoral landscapes of well hedged fields and partly amid great arable sweeps.

pendicular former chapel at the old cross-roads peers down into the roadworks. Chapel Road leads into South Cadbury. Opposite the church the former rectory is a large eighteenth-century L-plan house with stone-architraved windows, but ruined by plastic windows with transom lights replacing many of the sliding sashes. The west tower of the church and the wall painting of Thomas à Becket are note-worthy; the garish Victorian encaustic tiles on the chancel floor are not. From the north door one can see the sashed south front of North Cadbury Court (1790), a complete contrast to its Elizabethan north front.

Manor Farm (1687), thatched with some stone mullioned windows, is oppo-site Castle Lane which leads to Cadbury Castle. At the top I walked round the inner rampart which has a fair amount of stone in it. Could this be the remnants of Ethelred the Unready's defence works? Indeed, from 1009–19 there was a mint here. Most coins went to Danegeld, Ethelred's taxes raised to buy off Danish invaders – thus most are in Danish museums. Vespasian is supposed to have cleared the fort around AD 70 when it had been a sizeable town. From the ramparts there are spectacular views. The southern slopes have massive lynchetting with in-terconnecting ramps and, beyond, Sutton Montis has its houses interspersed by cider orchards. There are overgrown stonepits east on Littleton Hill and more lynchets beyond. South-east, Whitcombe Farm occupies the site of a deserted village.

Away from the castle I walked along lanes to Sutton Montis with excellent views of the strip-lynchetted complex of the southern slopes. Sutton Montis church is more rustic with a squat tower and, incongruously, a Doric-columned pedimented porch. Inside, the Jacobean pulpit has an eighteenth-century octagonal ogeed tester. Abbey House to the north-west is a sixteenth-century house with a through-passage plan and Tudor-arched windows, while east of the church Parson-age Farm has a mullioned windowed north front. Heading south through the village, which has intermittent clusters of ham-stone houses and cottages, I turned left north of Home Farm, a vigorous 1889 Victorian house. Then I turned right up Kember Hill into a short stretch of hedged lane, and continued uphill through the sheep on to Corton Ridge. Eastward, the slopes of the Beacon are terraced by medieval lynchets, and Corton Denham church tower rises above its tree-lined village, a felicitous Victorian scenic com-position. The views west over the flat-lands seemed infinite.

Looking south from the ramparts of Cadbury Castle hill-fort towards Parrock Hill, the next hill on the route.

The view south-east from Corton Ridge across the Somerset Levels.

Walking down Ridge Lane into Corton Denham, I lunched at the Queen's Arms which, it should be noted, closes at 2.00 p.m. Corton Denham House, the former, mainly eighteenth-century rectory turns its back on the village, but the church by C. Barker Green (1870) is superbly situated. Lord Portman paid for it (his brother was vicar) and the Belgian stained glass by Capronnier is excellent.

I walked south and left the road for the footpath up the hill which became a lane at the top. Then I crossed a road to battle through a dense hedge. A walk through fields eventually led to Cowpath Lane, a field access route from Charlton Horethorne. The church tower has pierced stone belfry openings of Somerset type and a heavy arts-and-crafts-style lychgate of 1888. North of the church the Manor House is a large seventeenth-century stone house of five bays with mullion and transom windows. The north front has a two-storey porch with arched entrance and fine panelled gate-piers with urn finials. The Green is unified by a number of large horse chestnut trees and on its west the King's Arms is an eclectic Victorian mess.

Out of the village down Harvest Lane and then Green Lane I reached the road and turned right. Soon I went through a gate into the woods of Compton Castle, noting a quarry littered with hamstone blocks. At the foot of the hill the lakes have been domesticated for ducks, but the grottoes are a picturesque assemblage of unworked stone posts and lintels from which water cascades. Beyond in its well landscaped park in the tree-lined valley sits Compton Castle, a Gothick 'castle' of 1825 with towers, turrets, battlements and traceried windows: not a very distinguished design.

Out on to the road the lodge and archway are in similar castellated vein. Left, down New Road, I passed The Crescent, five big cottages in a crescent dated 1808, and other fine houses, to reach Compton Pauncefoot church. The Old Rectory south of the church is a formal eighteenth-century composition with the centre bays set forward. East of the church Manor Farm is more austere with three bays of box sashes and a central Doric portico. Compton Pauncefoot church has a superb recessed octagonal spire and inside there is more glass by Capronnier with its strong jewel-like blues and reds. Walking north I crossed the A303 and then arable fields and pasture with large parkland beeches and limes back into North Cadbury.

Walk 16

WHERE THE FOSSE WAY RUNS DOWN TO THE SEA

Axminster and the Fosse Way, Devonshire. 14 Miles. September 1989. OS Pathfinder Sheets SY29/39, ST20/30.

The Fosse Way, after its long straight run from Lincoln, descends via the Axe valley to the sea at Lyme Bay through the far south-east corner of Devonshire. The valley bottom is wide and the river meandering but the hills on either side are classic Devon: small irregular fields, deep-cut winding lanes with high hedge banks and villages and hamlets with whitewashed thatched cottages. This is the landscape of farmsteads away from village centres, of small common fields and of 'assarting' into the wooded slopes and heavily wooded summits. Assarting was a technique of clearing fields from woodland, normally used independently rather than communally by farmers. It produces characteristic patterns with field edges zigzagging into wooded slopes.

This countryside makes for most attractive walking but, because there was always a dense network of lanes, footpaths are not common and, where indicated on the OS Pathfinder map, are often still difficult to locate on the ground. This walk is consequently mostly on quiet lanes, except for the half mile along the busy Fosse Way itself, the A358, where care is needed.

Many people associate Devon with 'cob', that is earth walling plastered over and whitewashed, and there is indeed some on this walk. However, the more common material in this area until the mid-nineteenth century is undoubtedly stone of various types. The Beer quarries near the coast produced a greatly prized hard chalk-stone which is best seen as carved stonework inside the churches on this walk. Then there are various mostly golden limestones, greensand, cobbles, flints and chert, a very hard siliceous stone found extensively and used for the outside of Axminster church. Cottages are usually in whitewashed and rendered rubblestone,

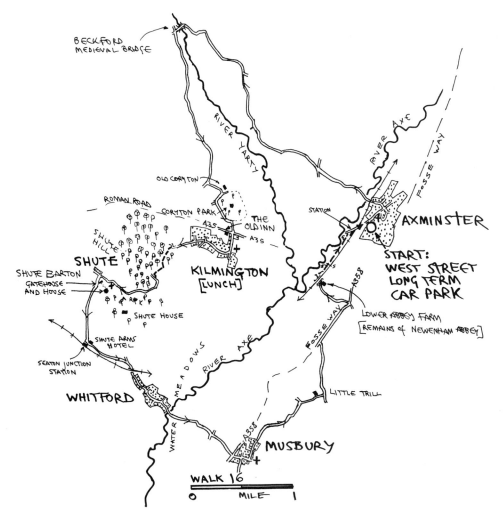

Axminster, home of the carpets: a typical Devonshire market town with colour-washed rendered walls and slate roofs.

while roofs are mostly thatched or slated. In the eighteenth century brick became fashionable but whitewashed render was always popular.

I parked in West Street car-park, Axminster, an unpromising part of the town. The small Devon town is not very impressive with its run-down buildings and poor renovations (when made). From West Street I emerged into Trinity Square, the tree-lined churchyard on the south side and to stuccoed or roughcast Georgian fronts on the other sides. On the east side the Conservative Club is a three-storey limestone building with segmental-headed windows, some sashed but mostly three-light cast-iron casements. This was the famous Axminster Carpet Factory established in the town by Thomas Whitty in 1755. It closed in 1835, but this building only dates from 1827.

The churchyard with its raised ground level dominates the square and the church is a good solid town church with a room over the porch reached by external steps. Inside there is an incongruously domestic touch in that the reordered nave has modern Axminster floral pattern carpeting: understandable but decidedly odd in effect, as are the plain 1834 clerestory windows.

Out of the church I walked north into Victoria Place with Georgian stuccoed fronts prettily following the curve of the road. Dominating the north side is the eighteenth-century The George Hotel with box sashes in a painted brick façade and a Venetian-windowed assembly room over the carriage arch. I walked down South Street, a minor street architecturally, to Silver Street which has some good houses, including Law Chambers next to the old carpet factory, an urbane house with tripartite sashed bows and faced in yellow mathematical tiles. Retracing my steps, I turned downhill from Victoria Place past the Market Square which has a brutally altered market house of 1830.

Castle Hill has mostly small-scale domestic cottages, many of them insensitively 'improved'. At the Market Square end several good houses exist, including Castle Hill House, Georgian with a Venetian window, and, opposite, Gloucester House, another yellow mathematical-tiled early nineteenth-century front. At the foot of Castle Hill is the Old Brush Factory (1827), three storeys high with cast-iron windows and, behind it, further early factory buildings. Beyond the railway I crossed the three-arched stone bridge, pausing to look back at the town

with its church tower rearing above a satisfying huddle of mostly slated roofs.

Soon I climbed out of the valley into winding lanes before crossing the River Yarty on a modern concrete slab bridge, but beside it is a narrow single-arch packhorse bridge, probably sixteenth century, called Beckford Bridge. The lane now runs along the west slopes of the valley reaching Old Coryton Farm behind a rubblestone garden wall. This is a redbrick house (about 1700) with cross-windows, somewhat run down with several windows blocked. The road then skirts Coryton Park which itself diverted the old road to its perimeter. Only one wing of the Palladian mansion remains, built in 1756. The south entrance gate-piers survive with entablatured caps surmounted by absurdly small concrete ball finials, literal pimples on a gatepost.

The lane crossed the A35, the old Roman Road, and I lunched at The Old Inn. I walked down Whitford Road to the church which has two Georgian wall monuments. Out of the church I turned right and wound through The Street with pleasant Devon whitewashed cottages and

Beckford Bridge, a medieval packhorse bridge over the River Yarty.

Shute. This impressive Elizabethan castellated gatehouse and screen is built in chert and greensand.

modern development. A rare stretch of footpath through woods brought me back to roads which skirted the north side of Shute House Park, an eighteenth-century improved medieval deer-park. Shute church has, in the north-east chapel, a large 1741 statue memorial to Sir William Pole of Shute House, 'Master of the Household to Her Late Majesty Queen Anne of Ever Glorious Memory': utterly secular in feeling and better suited to a public park.

Beyond the church is the gatehouse to late sixteenth-century Shute, built in chert with greensand. It has three storeys and is battlemented with octagonal turrets and large mullion and transom windows. Attached are nineteenth-century pavilions in similar style, a most picturesque composition. Within is Shute Barton, the remnants of Shute House's predecessor, largely demolished in 1787 (National Trust: open April to October, Wednesdays

and Saturdays, 2.00–5.30 p.m.). This, also built of chert and greensand stone, consists of an altered fourteenth-century hall house, enlarged in the fifteenth and sixteenth centuries. The kitchen fireplace arch and the high-quality arch-braced roof are of particular note, but the whole ensemble is picturesque, architecturally mystifying and highly evocative.

From here I followed the road south to Seaton Junction with its Tudor-style railway station of 1859, in orange brick with stone dressings. Continuing south-east, Shute House (1787), today apartments, can be seen in its park. It has three storeys with parapets and single-storey wings largely hidden by trees. Passing under the railway bridge, I arrived in Whitford, an attractive village with several sixteenth-century houses with large lateral stacks. Across the River Axe I saw water-meadow earthworks on the left. Into Musbury, I crossed the Fosse Way into The Street and then up Church Hill to the church.

The church is notable for the Drake monument of 1611, a curious composition of kneeling couples in line ahead separated by reading desks and two-light windows through which they peer for ever. Back down Church Hill I turned right into Doatshayne Lane, which becomes a pretty lane winding through small fields. Beyond Little Trill, an eighteenth-century house with its farm-buildings converted into holiday cottages, I turned left and followed the lane down to the Fosse Way. After a hair-raising walk along the Way to Abbey Corner, I was able to turn left to walk down to view, hopefully, the remains of Newenham Abbey. This had been a Cistercian House founded in 1257 by Reginald and William de Mohun. However, there is nothing visibly medieval at Lower Abbey Farm from the public footpath. Beyond this, I went under the railway and through water-meadow earthworks along the River Axe to the road, over the railway with the Tudor-style station in painted brick and with stone dressings, and back into Axminster.

A cob cottage in Shute village is quintessentially Devonshire.

By Trout-Rich Rivers

WILTSHIRE AND HAMPSHIRE

Fly fishing may be a very pleasant amusement; but angling or float fishing I can only compare to a stick and a string, with a worm at one end and a fool at the other.

Samuel Johnson

Walk 17

THE SPIRE ABOVE THE WATER-MEADOWS

Salisbury and Wilton, Wiltshire. 15 Miles. January 1990.
OS Pathfinder Sheets SU02/12, SU03/13.

Besides the medieval planned city of Salisbury, its hill-fort predecessor at Old Sarum and the ancient capital of Wessex at Wilton, this walk is shaped by the seventeenth-century water-meadow system of the Avon and Nadder rivers. This system still functioned after the last war and was an essential part of the corn and sheep regime of this part of Wiltshire where sheep dung was crucial to corn produc-

tion. The number of sheep kept dictated the fertility of the arable with sheep being 'folded' by night in the cornfields. The more sheep and indeed cattle the higher the dung yield; good grazing was therefore vital. Flooding the meadows assisted by depositing nutrient silts and insulating the grass. This stimulated rich early growth when the downland grass was still sparse and later in the year helped to

improve hay crops. The water was distributed over the fields by carrier streams and removed by drainage channels, all governed by sluices, looking on occasion remarkably like ridge and furrow. The Harnham and Nadder water-meadows were created by the Pembroke estate at Wilton from the early seventeenth century onwards and were in use until fairly recently. Recent floods gave some idea of

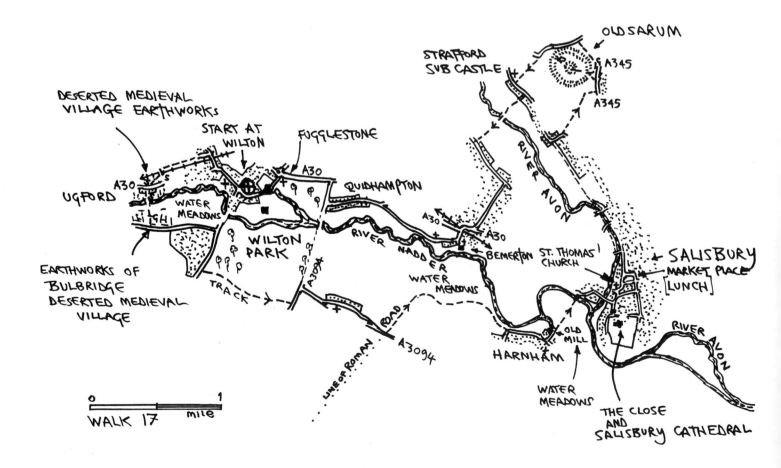

their appearance in late winter when the floated meadows were functional.

I set off from the market-place in Wilton, a market town somewhat blighted by heavy traffic. The ruined nave of the old parish church occupies its north side, although the chancel remains with its Gothick east window and plaster vault of 1751 (you can get the key at Wilton Hardware Shop). I walked along West Street with its quite unexpected church of St Mary and St Nicholas built for Sidney Herbert by Wyatt and Brandon (1841–45) in Italian Romanesque style, complete with a tall campanile. Inside is a remarkably rich collection of stained glass from the twelfth to nineteenth centuries collected by Sidney Herbert. Beyond St John's Hospital, part fourteenth century, I turned right by the Bell Inn and then left under the railway bridge.

The road became a footpath, crossed the railway and then headed diagonally across a pasture to Ugford, now a few fine houses, one timber-framed, and clear deserted village earthworks. I crossed the Nadder water-meadows on a footpath to Bulbridge, another deserted medieval village with the earthworks ploughed and flinty but still discernible. Beyond the Pembroke estate model farm I turned left on to the road and eventually right to walk alongside the eighteenth-century stone and brick walls to Wilton Park. These turn east; I followed them past Home Farm with expansive views south over rolling chalkland and north into the landscaped park of Wilton House. At the road I turned left to follow the nineteenth-century brick park wall, then right to Netherhampton which has a flint and limestone chequered church rebuilt by Butterfield in 1876. This small village has a Baroque stone-fronted Manor House of about 1720 with segmental arched sashes in five bays, urns to the parapet and two bay wings, all set behind wrought-iron railings flanked by urn-topped brick piers.

Beyond Netherhampton I turned left on to a track that follows the 'agger' of the Roman road from Dorchester. The path leaves this by the river to head east beside

Rustic-baroque: Netherhampton House of 1720. Elegant swept parapets, urns and arched windows of a country manor house.

the willow and alder-lined water-meadow carriages or feeders to reach Middle Street at Harnham beside the Nadder. The road leads into West Harnham with its mainly Norman church and then down Town Path to the mill. This is a fifteenth-century fulling mill in chequered stone and flint. The brickwork replaces louvres which ventilated the mill, now a restaurant and a rare survival of the medieval cloth industry of the Avon and Nadder valleys.

Continuing along Town Path I walked across Harnham water-meadows with the great spire of Salisbury Cathedral to the right, somewhat coarsened by its girdle of scaffolding. These are the famous views that Constable painted and one of the most exciting walks into any city.

Salisbury basically consists of a walled cathedral close, which retains all four original gateways and a stunningly beautiful collection of medieval and later houses, and a town laid out on a grid pattern known as the Chequers. All this dates from the 1220s when Bishop Poore moved from Old Sarum and laid the cathedral foundation stone. The city of New Sarum received its charter in 1227 and almost certainly by then the Chequers were laid out. The cathedral is mainly Early English

and was built in one long campaign from 1220 to 1266, with the tower heightened and spire added in the 1330s. It has a

Harnham Mill was built about 1500 as a fulling mill but by 1700 it had become a paper-making mill. It is now a restaurant.

Old Sarum. Looking through the rampart of the Iron Age hill-fort towards the Norman castle mound.

splendid collection of monuments but is somewhat sterile inside thanks to over-enthusiastic restoration by Wyatt and then Scott. In the Close, one of England's best, the Museums and Mompesson House (National Trust) can be visited.

On this walk one can only superficially view this wonderful city, but the route takes in some of its best buildings. From Town Path I walked east past the Infirmary whose core is by John Wood of Bath (1767–71) and over Crane Bridge, right at the traffic lights and into the Close. I left the Close by St Ann Gate at the east, left up St John's Street, then Catherine Street, into Queen Street, left into Market Place, a very well-proportioned space with no jarring notes and Sir Robert Taylor's 1780s Guildhall with tuscan portico. I went down the alley to its right and then along pedestrianized Butcher Row past the fifteenth-century Poultry Cross on to Silver Street. Turning right again to the church of St Thomas, the townsmen's church with its famous Doom painting, I continued along the path north into the Cheesemarket with a three-arched façade to a modern library, in fact the shell of the 1858 Corn

Exchange. Northwards up Castle Street beyond Hussey's Almshouses I turned left on to Mill Stream Approach. I have mentioned few buildings for lack of space but a perambulation with Pevsner's *Buildings of England* Wiltshire volume is recommended. There are many buildings with mathematically tiled fronts, for example in Catherine Street, grand Georgian fronts, timber-frames including Beach's Bookshop, and a wealth of superb architecture to make Salisbury a very rewarding city.

Over the Avon I turned right on to the riverside walk and headed north under the railway and ring road, turning right into Ashley Road, then left up Hulse Road and on to the footpath to Stratford sub Castle. At the road I turned right then straight on up the Portway track to Old Sarum, an Iron Age hill-fort with a Norman castle on a motte, and the foundations of the first cathedral before it moved downhill away from the Royal garrison. The ramparts give exciting views over Salisbury and its surroundings. Back out of the entrance I walked north to skirt Old Sarum and descend to Stratford sub Castle whose church has a good tower (1711) and many fine

fittings. I went down Mill Lane into the Avon water-meadows and climbed out to Devizes Road, continued left along it for a while and then right on to Roman Road. At the main A36 I crossed the railway and turned left into Church Lane to Lower Bemerton church and rectory where the poet George Herbert was rector from 1630 until his death from consumption in 1633. Westward I passed Wyatt's St John's church (1860) and then a model farmyard built in Russian style for Catherine Worontsow, Countess of Pembroke, to allay her homesickness.

I continued along the road with the Nadder and water-meadows on the left into Quidhampton, then north and west alongside the walls to Wilton Park, past Fugglestone church and south to Wilton House, the great courtyard mansion of the Herberts, Earls of Pembroke. It has a complex building history, but is justly renowned for the single and double cube rooms in the south range by Isaac de Caus, advised by Inigo Jones and John Webb. The grounds are splendid, but many cedars have gone in recent gales. I then continued past the Pembroke Arms and through Kingsbury Square into Wilton Market Place.

Walk 18

IN WARDOUR VALE

Tisbury and the Nadder Valley, Wiltshire. 17 Miles. February 1990.
OS Pathfinder Sheets ST82/92, ST83/93, SU02/12, SU03/13.

This part of south-west Wiltshire is characterized by flat-bottomed river valleys and rolling well-wooded hills. The villages and farms are mostly built in two stones: one a greyish or buff limestone from the Purbeck and Portland beds, called in this area Chilmark or occasionally Tisbury stone, and used to build Salisbury Cathedral; the other a greensand which actually is distinctly greenish. On this walk one can see several quarries and stone pits, mostly overgrown. Being on the northern edge of Carnborne Chase deer can often be seen by quiet walkers.

Parking in Tisbury I walked to the large cruciform church whose tower's upper stage is a 1762 replacement for a spire struck by lightning. Inside the spacious church, the aisle roofs are flat with moulded and decorated beams dated 1535, 1560 and 1616 while the nave wagon-roof has angels on pseudo-hammer-beams. There are many tablets to the Arundells of nearby Wardour Castle and, unusually, the nave pews are all Jacobean. The church offers a richly rewarding visit, located north of the young River Nadder which I crossed. Beyond the station I followed a footpath eastward alongside the railway and above the Nadder water-meadows, before turning north to Place Farm, a quite outstanding

fourteenth- and fifteenth-century monastic grange erected by the nuns of Shaftesbury Abbey. It includes inner and outer gatehouses, a house with seventeenth-century extensions and a spectacularly long tithe barn of thirteen bays with an enormous thatched roof. All is built in a warm and mellow Tisbury stone which has survived, happily.

I returned south towards the railway and through a water-mill complex to walk alongside the railway, first to its north then to its south, passing a large overgrown quarry. At Upper Chicksgrove I turned right at the level crossing to head south, then east along a farm track to

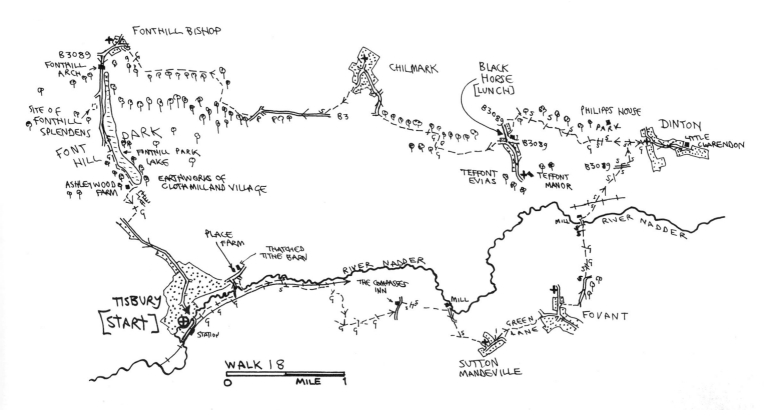

Chicksgrove hamlet. Opposite Compasses Inn with a thatched roof, I turned on to a lane, then across plough-land to a clump of isolated oaks, remnants of a hedge, before descending to the ruinous eighteenth-century Sutton Mandeville Mill, a brick water-mill last worked in the 1940s. South along a lane, then diagonally uphill across arable and over a curious stile consisting of an upside-down sink to continue east to Sutton Mandeville. The church has a greensand churchyard wall and tower, but the rest is Chilmark limestone and inside it is very heavily restored. In the church-yard is a fine stone-pillar sundial dated 1685.

Out of the churchyard and left at the road I walked along until bearing left into a lane signposted Glebe Cottage. Beyond the cottage this becomes an attractive green lane with fine views south. In Fovant I turned left into Church Lane,

passing first the Manor House, a thatched three-bay house with tripartite sashes, and then Fovant House, the old rectory, a formal late eighteenth-century ashlar house with sashes, a central pedimented door-case and Venetian window. The best feature of the church is the tower built for George Rede, the rector who died in 1492, with a pierced crenellated parapet. Immediately north is a fine greensand model farmyard, partly converted to hous-ing.

I retraced my steps to a footpath sign, crossed the river to the road, then left at the bend over a stile. A walk though fields led to Mill Farm on the Nadder with good water-meadows along the valley floor. From here I headed diagonally across the field, over the railway and through plough-land to the main road. Across this I headed for Dinton with Philipps House a way further on the left in a park, a nine-

bay country house by Jeffry Wyatville of 1813–16 in ashlar, with a giant Ionic pedimented portico. It is owned by the National Trust. Heading east, I passed in front of Hyde's House, birthplace of Edward Hyde, the royalist historian and chief minister to Charles II. The façade is of a later date, an early eighteenth-century remodelling with a pedimented centre and architraved sashes: a most happy design. Beyond, I entered the churchyard with its large aisle-less cruci-form church. I walked through the village to look at Little Clarendon, a big sixteenth-century stone yeoman's house also owned by the National Trust.

Back past Philipps House, I continued through pastures and then woods along a track, and left in the woods to descend a steep sunken lane into Teffont. I turned left and lunched at the Black Horse, before continuing south through the

Mill Farm in the water-meadows along the River Nadder.

Philipps House at Dinton, Jeffrey Wyatville's 1816 mansion for the Wyndham family, sits in its parkland.

attractive stone village to Teffont Evias church which was mostly rebuilt by Charles Fowler (1824–26) for John Mayne of Teffont Manor. It has a tower with a suburban spire (but is none the worse for that) and is full of interest inside with a large collection of Dutch and Flemish glass in the windows and elegant spindly early nineteenth-century Gothick detail, including poppy-head pews. Seventeenth-century Teffont Manor behind is a curiously flat four-bay battlemented house which was remodelled in the early nineteenth century. Behind are two battlemented towers, one a three-sided sham; both are beautifully situated in a landscaped valley.

Northwards, I turned left opposite a post box to climb out of the village and headed west along a hedgeless lane through pastures. Beyond a copse I turned right into a field, then left to walk first beside and then within woods to the road into Chilmark, an attractively situ-

Henry Ley and his two sons lie side by side in Teffont Evias church.

The great archway into Alderman Beckford's Fonthill Park was probably designed by Inigo Jones but built by John Vardy in 1756, a century later.

ated stone village, its church on rising ground, cruciform with a central vaulted tower and recessed spire. Downhill, the seventeenth-century Manor has three ranges round a small court closed by a wall curved down to ball-finial gate-piers. I walked south, then right into Claylands and past council cottages to head uphill across plough-land to a road. This is a lane running along the ridge with good views on both sides. Beyond a complex junction and a derelict chapel of about 1900, I turned right at a bridleway sign on to a track through woods, soon bearing right at another bridleway sign to descend towards a valley, then right through a beech stand and west out of the valley, emerging on to a grassy track beside plough-land.

This emerges in Fonthill Bishop, a small village clustered around a green with a mainly Early English church where Sir Christopher Wren's father was rector in the 1620s. The village is at the gates of Fonthill Park, for beyond the village centre I turned left into it, initially between screen walls with gigantic urns on vermiculated piers and then through a splendid archway which incorporates lodges. This massive structure, encrusted with vermiculation, including huge bearded face-mask keystones, is on a Piranesian scale: a fitting entrance to Alderman William Beckford's great park around his mansion, 'Fonthill Splendens'. Formerly attributed to Inigo Jones, the archway is now thought to have been designed by him for elsewhere, but built here a century later in 1756 by John Vardy. Through the archway the long lake of Fonthill Park stretches away to the left, and to the right, beyond the road junction, is the site of Fonthill Splendens, built in 1756 by Hoare but demolished in 1807. William Beckford's more famed Fonthill Abbey was away in the woods to the southwest and private, a fantastical Gothic mansion started in 1796 and designed by James Wyatt with a central tower 250ft high. This badly built romantic house of folly mostly collapsed in 1825.

I followed the road beside the lake with parkland rolling away to either side and much tree planting along the banks. At a lay-by I climbed a stile and walked through woods beside the lake as far as its dam and at Ashleywood Farm (1861) I continued south, noting across the river the clear earthworks of an abandoned Huguenot weavers' settlement, set up in the seventeenth century around a water-mill. Out of the woods I followed a green lane round to the road, turned left and walked into Tisbury. This small town has many attractive stone cottages and houses; just before the church is the Wiltshire Brewery, rebuilt in 1885.

Walk 19

CHALKSTREAM TROUT AND WATER-MEADOWS

Alresford and the Itchen Valley, Hampshire. 15 Miles. April 1990.
OS Pathfinder Sheet SU43/53.

This walk mainly follows the river valley of the Itchen which, besides chalkstream trout fishing of high quality, has extensive areas of watercress beds, particularly around Alresford, and remnants of water-meadow channels. The villages above the flat valley floor are characterized by winding lanes lined by mainly seventeenth-century timber-framed houses with brick or rendered infilling panels and eighteenth- and nineteenth-century houses and cottages in brick, brick and flint or colour-washed render. This is rolling small-scale chalk country and the scenery is remark-

ably varied and intimate. Away from the valley the scenery is more expansive, mainly arable chalkland. The route allows several river crossings to produce shortened routes or two separate walks, one based on Easton, the other on Alresford.

I started in Easton which has a late Norman church with an apse and a curious west tower but is somewhat untrustworthy as Woodyer gilded the Norman lily in the 1860s. At the corner I turned right and then left past The Cricketers, a pub with colour-washed render or brick infilling panels to its timber-frame, to walk

through the village which has a good range of typical Hampshire houses and cottages. At the end of the street I turned left, passing more timber-framing and the Cricketers pub with planted framing and pink colour-wash. At the bend is a good group of thatched cottages, including the Old Post Office (1834) and Bacton House, also thatched but more formal with sashes and a central oriel.

Easton petered out eventually and soon the lane climbed into woods which mark the beginning of Avington Park, passing a most picturesque yellow colour-washed

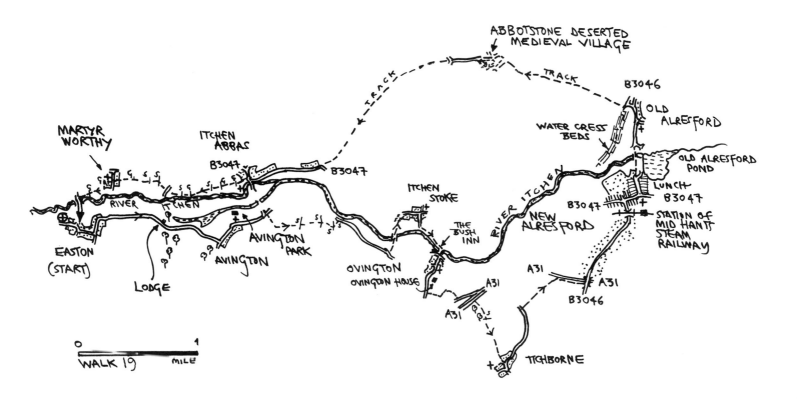

brick lodge with a full-height trellis-arched verandah of five bays. Over the brow Avington Park House in its superb parkland comes into view with a long lake winding past, formed from a tributary of the Itchen. The mansion has a painted timber central portico with four columns and a pediment flanked by four bays on each side, divided into pairs by pilasters and dating from about 1710. This seems a slightly restless composition, for the white portico appears cramped in relation to the generous bays of the side wings. Within the house are remnants of Tudor work but most of the house was built for the Bridges family who came into the estate in 1665. At the junction I turned left past the walled kitchen gardens of the house to the village with thatched cottages on one side of the road and a terrace of brick and flint estate cottages with a pedimented centre on the other.

The church is an elegant Georgian brick box of 1768–71 with arched windows and patterned leaded fanlights. Inside, all is Georgian with a complete set of panelled box pews and a pulpit with ogee-roofed tester on fluted Corinthian pilasters. The reredos is also very fine with Doric columns and pilasters and an open segmental pediment to the centre while the west gallery has a delightful chamber organ.

I continued east with views of Avington Park House and its two fine Victorian conservatories. Just beyond the junction I turned right at a footpath sign on to a track that skirts the edge of the east park, south and then east, descending to the road to Yavington, a shrunken village with a farmhouse, a cottage and Yavington Mead, a red-brick house of about 1730 with box sashes and a modillion eaves cornice to its steep hipped roof. Beyond this I turned left on to a footpath, actually an overgrown sunken way, that led across the water-meadows and the river into Itchen Stoke, a village with thatched cottages and brick and flint nineteenth-century cottages built for Lord Ashburton of Northington Grange. The remarkable church, built by the then vicar's brother Henry Conybeare in 1866, is a small-scale

Looking back at the pretty trellis-arched verandah-ed Lodge to Avington Park.

version of La Sainte Chapelle in Paris; the light filters in through stained glass of a very creditable early thirteenth-century style.

I headed south of the river and turned left to walk along beside it, then crossed it into Ovington, pausing for a drink at the Bush Inn. This is another very attractive village whose Victorian church has a timber belfry and shingled stumpy spire. Beyond the walls of Ovington House, a two-storey brick house of about 1790, I turned left to skirt its grounds and climbed up to the A31 Alresford Road which I crossed and headed for Tichborne. This is a village made famous by the Tichborne Claimant, an imposter who tried to claim the Tichborne estate in the last century. It is a very fine village with many good cottages in timber-framing, including the Old Post Office of about 1600 which is jettied. The late eleventh-century church, quite superb and on a rise above the village, is in flint with stone dressings. Its double-splay chancel windows and gabled aisles were done later. The tower in brick is of 1703. The inside is whitewashed with Jacobean box pews and communion rail.

The chief interest is the Tichborne chapel with its monuments, including Richard Tichborne, a child effigy of 1619 propped sideways in girl's clothing, who died at 'one yeare six monthes and too daies'.

Through the village with glimpses of Tichborne House and parkland alongside the road, I turned right over the stream to pass Vernal Farm along the track towards New Alresford. I had to walk alongside the bypass before crossing it at the B3046. I lunched at the Cricketers before walking up the hill and into the town, passing the preserved Winchester and Alton Railway, originally called rather quaintly The Watercress Line. At the top I turned right into West Street. The character of the town, as in so many other cases, is predominantly Georgian and early nineteenth century with brick and stuccoed fronts of high quality and character, often concealing timber-framed earlier buildings, although fires in 1610, 1620 and 1689 depleted the stock. The church behind the main street is disappointing apart from the gravestones of French Napoleonic prisoners of war. Broad Street at the junction of East and West Streets is the oldest part of New

Michael Tichborne's monument in Tichborne Church. He died in 1621 at the age of eighteen months, having drowned in a puddle after being cursed by a gypsy to whom the Tichbornes had unwisely refused to give food.

Alresford, its layout dating from about 1190 when Bishop Godfrey de Lucy founded the town, originally called Novum Forum or new market. It is a very beautiful street planted with limes and descending the hill to the river. The town flourished with wool and corn mills and a timber-framed cottage by the river was built as a fulling mill. De Lucy also made Old Alresford Pond, now 30 acres but originally two hundred, as a giant header pond to power the town's water-mills.

Beyond the watercress beds I reached Old Alresford whose church was rebuilt in 1753 and tower added in 1769. Unfortunately it was Gothicized in 1862 and transepts were added. To the south the Schwerdt Mausoleum (1839) in classical style contains an Italian relief of the Madonna of about 1500. East of the church Old Alresford House was built

New Alresford looking from Bishop de Lucy's market-place, laid out in 1196, towards the church behind the frontage buildings.

Near the end of the walk: Easton church from across the River Itchen.

from prize money in about 1752 by the great Admiral Rodney. It is a large brick house of great quality. North to the village green, passing the largely concealed Old Alresford Place with giant brick pilasters and parapets, I headed west beyond Alresford watercress beds, climbing out past Manor Farm to walk along the green lane over the chalk hills. It becomes a tarmac road at the deserted village site of Abbotstone which has excellent clear earthworks of house platforms, a moated site and crofts. The village flourished until the early fourteenth century, being taken over by sheep in the sixteenth century, and its church utterly collapsed by 1589.

I continued along the green lane, eventually descending into Itchen Abbas, to walk through it to the Plough pub where I turned left and visited the gruesome 1860s Neo-Norman church by William Coles, which incorporates two genuine Norman arches. I continued west along footpaths, effectively within the parkland of Avington House, through Chilland to Martyr Worthy which has a church with a Norman nave and Victorian Norman apse. Leaving the church I headed for the river and followed the path along the bank, then crossed the river to walk back into Easton.

Walk 20
SELBORNIAN SCENES

Alton and Selborne, Hampshire. 14¼ Miles. February 1990.
OS Pathfinder Sheet SU63/73.

Alton is an attractive town eclipsed by the world-renowned Selborne to the south. Selborne was the home of Gilbert White, the eighteenth-century antiquarian and observer of nature whose letters to friends were published by his brother Benjamin in 1789 as *The Natural History and Antiquities of Selborne*. Reprinted many times, it is a classic example of the close observation of nature. White's house, now a museum, is visited from all over the world. It is particularly enjoyable to walk around the parish and see the things he described little changed; the great zigzag path up Selborne Hanger instigated by Gilbert and his brother John is included on the route.

Selborne lies on the greensand while the Hanger marks the boundary with the chalk which continues roughly north to pass east of Alton. The most obvious sign of this is the way in which the beech trees predominate on the chalk, while on the greensand oaks are the commonest tree in the hedgerows and copses. Flint is common as is malmstone from the greensand, a pale buff or grey sandstone. Darker greensands also occur, including iron-rich toffee-coloured ones, used for 'galleting', that is as chips pressed into joints in stone walling. As White says, 'strangers sometimes ask ... whether we fastened our walls together with tenpenny nails'.

I parked in Alton's Victoria Road Long Stay Car-Park, reached from Normandy Street, and walked west into Church Street, emerging north of brick almshouses (1653), turning right to St Lawrence's church. This church has a shingled spire above a Norman crossing tower engulfed in fifteenth-century re-

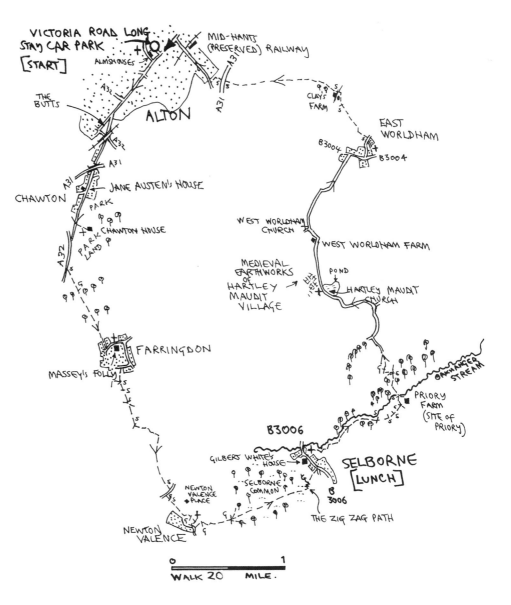

building where, unusually, the south aisle is roughly the same width as the nave. The best furnishings are the seventeenth-century pulpit with a free-standing arcade in front of the panels and the altar rails of 1680 made from staircase balusters from Bishop Ken's house at Winchester. These suited better before Victorian restoration

The south view of Alton church, mostly rendered and fifteenth century, around a Norman central tower capped by a Victorian broach spire.

swept away the box pews and galleries.

The High Street undulates and winds most attractively. However, there is much to regret from the 1960s and 1970s, including numbers 34A–E and 80–92 – three storeys with bands of windows above tiled panels and flat roofs – as well as other buildings set back from the old building line to disrupt the rhythm. There are excellent townscape buildings though, including number 6, now Stevens and Bolton, six bays of segment-headed sashes and Venetian ground-floor windows; number 36 of 1926, Lloyds and Barclays banks, all Neo-Georgian; and the Midland

Bank, a fine eighteenth-century five-bay house with the three centre bays pedimented and set forward. A diversion into Market Street leads to Market Square with the 1813 Town Hall, a dignified slated hipped-roof building with tall first-floor sashes and arcaded ground floor, now shops. Further west the style deteriorates somewhat and then the road opens out to the Butts, a triangular green with rendered cottages on the north-west side where archery was practised. I bore left along the green, under the railway bridge and down Winchester Road to pass under the A31 bypass into Chawton, a village

which has several good timber-framed thatched cottages. At the former main road junction, mercifully now a backwater, is Jane Austen's house, a modest early eighteenth-century brick house. This was formerly an inn bought for her, her mother and sisters by her brother, the adopted son of the Knights of Chawton House. It is now a museum which includes her writing table.

Chawton House and church are isolated south of the village beside the Lavant Stream. The church, rebuilt by Blomfield in 1871 has incongruous Suffolk flint flushwork decoration to the tower parapet. In the chancel is a high-quality monument to Sir Richard Knight of 1679 in full armour. The house of 1588 and 1630 presents a three-storeyed porch to the west drive and is mainly flint and stone dressings with the 1630s parts in brick, all with mullioned and transomed windows but largely hidden by trees. The stable block opposite the church is dated 1593 and is now a house.

Continuing south, the old road merges with the new. Then beyond the parkland, I crossed flinty fields to a track over the hills into Farringdon, the last part down an avenue of wind-racked Wellingtonias and yews. It is an attractive quiet village with much timber-framing. The church, beyond an ancient hollow yew, has a seventeenth- and eighteenth-century brick porch, and an unspoilt twelfth- and thirteenth-century whitewashed nave. The village hall is a crazy linking together of moulded terra-cotta and fiery red brick, a high Victorian extravaganza of appalling tastelessness. Built, literally, by the rector T. H. Massey

Massey's Folly, Farringdon: a virtuoso display of bad taste in fiery Victorian brick. Built, literally, by the rector around 1875.

Selborne Common. Ancient oak woods and hazel coppice where Gilbert White walked and was struck with delight.

himself from about 1875, it is unsurprisingly known locally as 'Massey's Folly'.

South across country to Newton Valence, reaching the road I turned right, then left by an octagonal former lodge to continue south-east through the park of Newton Valence Place. Newton Valence church peers out behind another ancient yew and the Manor House has eighteenth-century ranges in malmstone with galletted joints and a large south block in 1787 yellow brick with modillion eaves cornices. Back at the road, I turned left by the pond into green lanes and then across Selborne Common, taking the middle route along a wide grassy drive through ancient oakwood with some hazel coppicing and beeches. This leads into Gilbert White country, emerging at the east end of Selborne Hanger. From here I looked out over Selborne nestling below before descending White's zigzag path down the precipitous scarp and into the village.

Many of Selborne's houses are in grey malmstone which is difficult to distinguish from chalk-stone. The Wakes where Gilbert White lived is now a museum incorporating collections relating to the Oates family whose most famous scion died on Scott's 1912 Antarctic expedition. The Old Rectory on the north side of the Plestor or green is Victorian and replaces the one in which White was born. The church has splendid late-Norman arcades with pointed arches. The 1856 chancel arch and much restoration is by William White, Gilbert's great-nephew. It is a very worthwhile village to visit, somewhat tourist-oriented, but consequently good for lunch as well as souvenirs without any of the commercialism of, say, the Brontës' Howarth.

I headed east within a hanger, or beeches along a slope, above Oakhanger Stream to Priory Farm, an eighteenth-century stone house on the site of the Augustinian priory founded in 1233. I was now in greensand country with more oaks in the hedges and I continued north to isolated Hartley Maudit church opposite a

Gilbert White's view over Selborne from the Viewpoint Stone at the summit of the zigzag path down from Selborne Hill.

large pond. To the west and north are the earthworks of a deserted medieval village. Rendered inside and out, the twelfth century church has good seventeenth-century wall monuments in the chancel. Further north is West Worldham Farm (1652), a stone and brick lobby-entry-plan house with a massive axial stack. Then still further on is its single-cell church, ruinous until 1888 but restored and partially rebuilt by Winchester Col-

lege. Beyond this, the lane reached East Worldham, many of whose farms have large steep-roofed square oast-houses amid their farm-buildings. At the Horse-shoes pub I turned right on to the B3004, then left at the sign to the church, a spacious thirteenth-century aisle-less barn-like church with high-quality north and south doorways, many lancets and a chancel with marble shafts to the lancet window rear arches.

From the church I passed council cottages with pre-cast concrete plank walls and followed the waymarked route of Hangers Way, black arrows on a white ground, into open country – first past Clay's Farm, with a pair of oast-houses converted into a dwelling house, then Monk Wood, and across arable prairies with a footpath sign in the middle like a solitary scarecrow, to cross the A31 bypass into Alton.

Along Saxon Shores

SUSSEX AND KENT

Green Sussex fading into blue
With a grey glimpse of the sea.
Alfred, Lord Tennyson

Walk 21

THE VIEW FROM THE DOWNS

Lewes and the Ouse, Sussex. 17 Miles. August 1989.
OS Pathfinder Sheets TQ40/50, TQ41/51.

Visible for much of the walk, the county town of Lewes with its castle makes its strategic importance obvious, perching on the chalk ridge above the gap where the River Ouse cuts through the chalk hills. It was an Anglo-Saxon 'burh' and, after the Conquest, William de Warenne built his double-motted castle here. The valley widens south of Lewes into The Brooks, a flat polderland, before again being hemmed in by the South Downs.

In the Tudor period the Ouse was par-tially canalized, Newhaven founded and a start made on redraining The Brooks which had been inundated by the great floods of 1421, following centuries of slow reclamation. The bulk of the present polder landscape of The Brooks actually dates

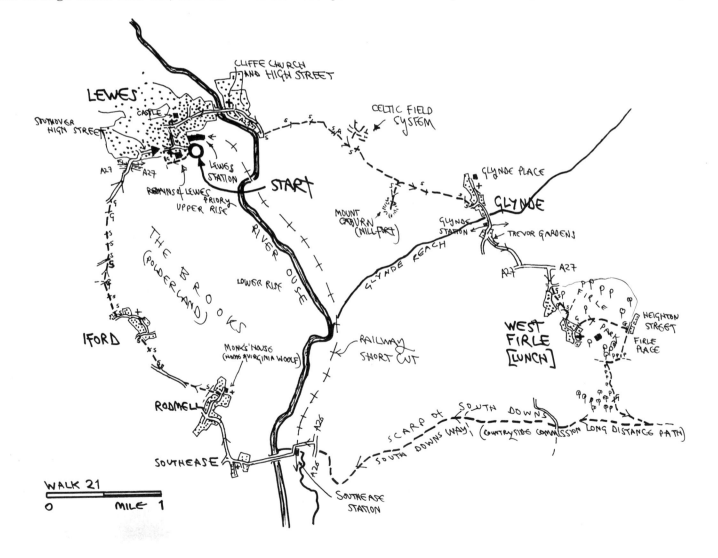

from the eighteenth century when the Ouse was further channelled and improved. The parishes on the west bank have their village centres above the flood plain, with downland to their west and to their east their share of The Brooks and Iford, including the 'islands' of Upper and Lower Rise which rise from the former marshes. By this means they obtained a good mix of land types, a similar if less clear distribution also being found on the east bank.

By using the railway between Southease and Lewes, this route can be split in two, but the 17-mile walker will set off in Lewes from the car-park in Mountfield Road near the station and next to the football ground. Leaving the car-park at its south-west corner, I passed the ruins of William de Warenne's great Priory of St Pancras, which had a church larger than Chichester Cathedral and a turbulent relationship with the bishops. The railway line cut through the ruins in a bizarre way, but the remains are still impressive. From Cockshut Road I turned right into Southover High Street, passing St John's church and the urbane Priory Crescent of about 1840, a formal bowed terrace with centre-piece and end pavilions worthy of a London Square. Then I turned left at the florid King's Head of 1888, soon passing Southover Grange (1572) in Caen limestone salvaged from the Priory, I climbed the cobbled lane of Keere Street. At the top is the 'Fifteenth Century Bookshop', a rambling timber-framed and much jettied building.

Along the High Street there are many fine buildings. Much use has been made of mathematical tiles to refront older buildings and there are numerous full-height bow windows, just like the cosier parts of Brighton. Note the black-glazed mathematical tiles, for example Bartholomew House or numbers 88 and 90, the round tower of St Michael's church and the fashionable grey header-bond brickwork of Numbers 152–55. Although refronting is common, there was also rebuilding, for example several old houses had to be cleared away for Castle House, number

Lewes: black mathematical tiles on the house on the left in Castle Precincts which leads to the fourteenth-century Barbican gateway to the castle.

166, with its ammonite-voluted pilaster capitals. The quality and variety of good buildings are endless and include the Castle, its Barbican, several museums and the cobbled Castle Precincts, while views from the top of the castle reward the climb.

Past John Johnson's County Hall (1812) in Portland limestone, High Street descends towards the river with two large 'gentleman's seat' five-bay, three-storey Georgian houses in grey header brick with red brick dressings on the right – School Hill House and Lewes House – while opposite is a good stuccoed group and round the corner in Albion Street a stuccoed terrace. Boots is an adequate 1970s infilling, all lead-dressed projecting windows and mansards. Beyond is the eighteenth-century Dial House in pale stone, a pedimented centre flanked by shallow bows, but raised a further storey. Over the bridge I arrived in Cliffe, again with some good houses and at the west end Harvey's Brewery with the church at the east.

I crossed South Street into Chapel Lane to climb out of the valley, soon passing a stone bench in a recess inscribed 'I will give you rest'. Climbing to the top above the chalk pits I passed behind the golf clubhouse out on to a path along the contours, before dropping downhill to Oxsteddle Bottom with its dry dew-pond. Out of the valley I diverted south on to Mount Caburn, an Iron Age hill-fort greatly strengthened in about AD 40 against the Romans. From here were spectacular views of the South Downs bluffs marching east and south-west to The Brooks, whose intricate pattern of four-, five- and six-sided fields bounded by drainage ditches is as clear as in an aerial photograph.

Back on the path I continued east and descended into Glynde, an attractive village with steep-roofed timber-framed and Georgian houses. Some of the latter are

The path descends from the Iron Age hill-fort of Mount Caburn through the stubble towards Glynde.

pink-washed plaster or tile-hung. Glynde Place is beyond both the Palladian church (1763–65) by Thomas Robinson, and its formal pediment-archwayed stables with their blue-painted cupola. Built in the 1560s in flint and Caen limestone with brick octagonal flues, the house is most picturesque and its south front can be seen from the churchyard (Open June– September, Wednesday and Thursdays, 2.15–5.00 p.m.). Internally, it was remodelled by Bishop Trevor in the eighteenth century. The church retains its Georgian fittings but is let down by Kempe's heavy-handed Holbeinesque stained glass.

Southwards over the railway and left past Trevor Gardens, estate cottages in a climbing terrace, and to West Firle, I entered its park past the Lodge and out again to the Ram Inn for lunch. Walking through the village past a house clad in black mathematical tiles and on the right a

Glynde Place's 1760s stables: a splendid Palladian composition with a judicious use of brick and flint for architectural emphasis.

Firle Place. The Gage's Georgian façades look out over rolling tree-lined parkland.

most successful farm-building conversion into a house, I reached the church with its Gage family monuments and John Piper-stained glass. Following the metalled track to the right of Firle Stores I soon re-entered Firle Park to walk east to Heighton Street, a deserted village site with two or three old houses surviving.

Firle Place was built for Sir John Gage before 1557 and altered in the mid-eighteenth century by giving it Georgian stone façades. The house is still owned by the Gages (Open from June to September; Sundays, Wednesdays and Thursdays, 2.00–5.00 p.m.). From Heighton Street I headed south to climb up to the South Downs Way and, turning right, followed it west to drop down Itford Hill to the Ouse valley. Up on the top there are views south to Newhaven and the sea. Itford Farm is all that remains of a deserted village and is a complex mainly sixteenth-century house with a substantial rear stack.

Across the railway and the river with water-reed-filled drains, I reached Southease which has a small triangular green with the church on the north side. This has a Norman round tower, one of three in Sussex, and faded wall paintings. I then walked north-west through the villages above the marshes. Rodmell has a long main street and modern housing interspersing older buildings, including the Old Rectory with its charming Gothick-like front of about 1860 in coursed knapped flint with stone dressings. Just before Monk House, a painted weather-boarded house lived in by Virginia Woolf who drowned herself nearby, turn right to the church through the school playground. The Norman church is delightful and cosy but disfigured by a horridly brutal Neo-Norman Victorian chancel arch; the pulpit and lectern are not much better. Iford is dominated by working farms and its church has a Norman central tower. Like Southease it is smaller than it was, its

north aisle demolished in the fourteenth century.

From Iford I followed paths back to Kingston Road, across the Lewes bypass and into Southover where mathematical tiles are again much in evidence; this time also in yellow as in Southover Old House which also has wooden-imitation rusticated quoins. Southover has many good houses in stucco, tile-hangings, brick and grey brick. Exposed timber-framing is found, as in Anne of Cleves House, now a fascinating museum and of Wealden type, while jettied numbers 17–19 are plastered over. The High Street is terminated in views looking west by the groups around the Swan Inn where the road curves: a most attractive streetscape. Back past St James's church with its brick tower dated 1714 and to the east a fragment of the medieval gateway to St Pancras Priory, and then once more past Priory Crescent, I returned to the carpark.

Walk 22

ISLANDS ABOVE THE MARSH

The Isle of Oxney, Kent, and Rye, Sussex. 16 Miles. February 1990.
OS Pathfinder Sheet TQ82/92.

Scenically, this walk contrasts rolling sandstone country along the edge of alluvial flatlands which include the Rother Levels and Walland Marsh. The Isle of Oxney has the Rother and Reading Sewer Levels to the north and south and Romney Marsh to the east, while the ridges north of Rye end abruptly at 25m-high cliffs above the Rother. Rye itself is on an 'island' or outlier to the south of this sandstone ridge. The marshes are criss-crossed by drainage channels, most spectacularly on the East Guldeford Levels which are almost entirely sheep-cropped pastures with irregular ditches of mainly medieval date. Elsewhere, arable and deep-cut drainage ditches blur the older patterns, but all over the hills and Levels is extensive sheep grazing, particularly good on Oxney, and although the hills nowhere exceed 65m there are superb views across the flats.

There has been much canalization of rivers and streams, but the most interesting work is the Royal Military Canal which runs from Winchelsea to Hythe along the edge of Romney Marsh. It was built between 1804 and 1806, mainly as a defensive line against potential French landings on the Marshes, and was backed by a Military Road. The aim was to have floating batteries and quick troop movements by road or water, as well as gun positions on the banks. It also acted as a trade route and earned revenue through canal and road tolls. The canal was never tested in anger but remains a fascinating piece of Georgian military engineering.

The Isle of Oxney is shared between

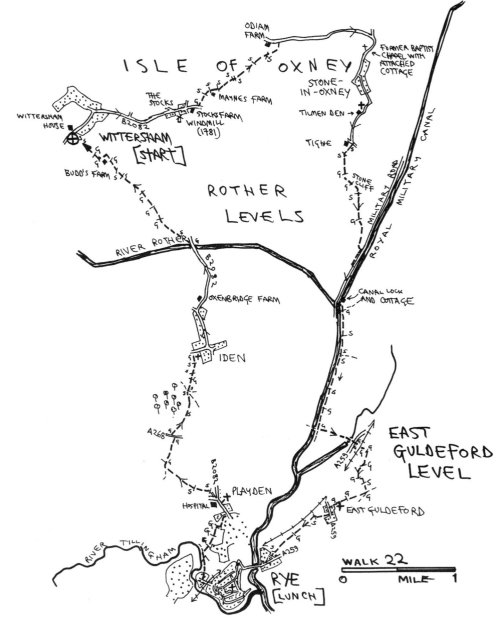

Wittersham and Stone-cum-Ebony parishes, and I started the walk in Wittersham, a most attractive village with tile-hung and weather-boarded houses, much of it concealing timber-framing. The large church has a five-bay nave, wide aisles with fourteenth-century crown-post nave, south aisle roofs and a tall west tower of about 1500. North of the church, Wittersham House was built by Lutyens for Alfred Lyttelton, 'athlete, lawyer and statesman' as the memorial in the church states, in 1906–09. It is a good Neo-Georgian house with pantile roof, deep moulded eaves, sash windows and a clipped yew-hedged garden. Lyttelton recommended Lutyens as architect for Hampstead Garden Suburb in London so it is no surprise to find roughcast and tilehung cottages in Wittersham.

At the Ewe and Lamb pub, an appropriate name here, I turned right along Stocks Road which follows the ridge and gives good views southwards. At Stocks there is a weather-boarded post-mill dated 1781 and Stocks Farm, a fine sixteenth-century house of hall and crosswing type, refronted in eighteenth-century fish-scaled tiles and tripartite sashes. Beyond the junction I turned left to walk through sheep pastures and down the north side of the Island to the road. I followed Lower Road to the Appledore Road and turned right, soon passing the former Baptist Chapel, two bays of weather-boarding with sashes attached to a seventeenth-century timber-framed cottage. Already on Lower Road I had passed isolated medieval and seventeenth-century farmhouses, and at the left turn up to Stone-in-Oxney church is The Cottage, a hall with jettied crosswing. More old houses give way to fields and a winding climb to the church, now on the Saxon Shore Way, a waymarked path round the shores of Kent. These low hills are mostly treeless and draped in pastures. The church of sandstone rubble and ashlar dressings is splendidly situated with a very fine timber-framed wealden house to the south. Inside the church there is a good crown-post roof, all the more interesting since the ceilings remain against the rafters as in the fourteenth century; all too often crown-posts and structural members are indistinguishable in a mass of bare rafters.

I continued up Church Hill and straight across the junction into fields beside Tighe, a big seven-bay lobby-entry-plan house in late seventeenth-century brick. The path descends Stone Cliff through pasture to the arable lands of the Rother Levels. The path reached the Military

Stone-in-Oxney: looking past a superb fifteenth-century wealden house to the church.

Road at the boundary between Kent and Sussex, marked by a pillar on a stepped plinth. The road runs behind the Royal Military Canal and I followed it to the junction with the canalized Rother, where I crossed the Canal beside a sandstone-ashlar lock cottage dated 1824 whose lock has only one pair of gates. I then walked south alongside the Canal and at a lane I turned left, crossed Union Channel to the A259, then the railway line and into the East Guldeford Levels, ancient sheep pasture of high quality and quintessential Romney Marsh. I headed south and then west to East Guldeford Church, a brick barn of a place consecrated in 1505 much remodelled about 1820 but interesting for the pale bricks made from local river mud. At the road I continued west through fields parallel to the railway which led to an estate, then the A259 and over the Rother Bridge into Rye.

Rye sits on its hilltop with the short octagonal spire of the parish church at its apex. It is a remarkable town and in many ways decidedly un-English in feeling with narrow streets and huddles of tiled roofs washing up to the church. It was one of the original five or Cinque Ports, which in return for tax concessions and some autonomy were, in the Middle Ages, required to supply ships for use of the king and defend the coast. The Ports often abused these privileges and indulged in piracy and smuggling. Those days are very much over and the town is not surprisingly a tourist 'Mecca' and crowded virtually all the year round. It was originally walled and the 1329 Landgate remains as well as the Ypres Tower, the keep of about 1250, and several stretches of wall. Within the historic core are a stunning number of superb old buildings, cobbled streets and literary associations in plenty. Here Henry James lived and wrote and E. F. Benson wrote the Lucia books and was Mayor. In the parish church the great west-window stained glass was given by Benson who appears in his mayoral robes with his dog. The church is splendid, spacious and well worthy of the town. I lunched and wandered the streets of what must be one of the least altered towns in England with a quite exceptional number of buildings surviving from before 1850.

I left the town along Ferry Road beyond large warehouses, some converted to other uses, crossed the railway and on to a footpath to the right of the Queen Adelaide. It followed briefly the River Tillingham which gave Benson the name for his fictional town of Tilling. I soon climbed out of the valley, passed through a cemetery and crossed the B2082 to Playden church. St Michael's is basically of about 1200 with a central tower, graceful

The Royal Military Canal at its junction with the River Stour. Looking back to a lock of 1824 and, beyond, the lock-keeper's cottage.

shingled spire and low eaves. Inside, the north-chapel timber screen of about 1300 is of rare quality. Back at the road, I crossed it and, by a sign to Cornworthy, climbed a stile and descended through fields to a bridleway, heading north, eventually reaching Iden church. This has lost its south aisle and is sparse inside. The north aisle is curiously out of alignment and the arcades have alternating brown and white stone voussoirs. I left the churchyard and walked through Iden village, left at the

Rye church tower's clock has an ornate eighteenth-century architectural framework, including Quarter Boys to strike the quarters (now fibreglass replicas). The clock mechanism cost £30 in 1562 and still works.

junction on to the B2082 to head north. Beyond a bend Oxenbridge Farm is a fine colour-washed rendered wealden house, extended by a bay, and thatched. Soon the road descends to the Rother Levels in a tree-shaded sunken way.

Across the River Rother I turned north-west to head diagonally across ploughland, then pasture and uphill to pass Budds Farm, a grand late seventeenth-century brick house of eight long bays with leaded cross-casements, bracket-eaves cornice and an old tiled roof with dormers. It is a complex house of two builds and has a gabled three-storey porch with a brick pediment to the arched doorway. Beyond gate-piers I skirted the grounds and then turned north-west through a gate to walk into Wittersham.

A famous view: the cobbled Mermaid Street leading steeply down to the Quay.

Walk 23

STRANDED IN THE SILT

Sandwich and Richborough, Kent. 14 Miles. July 1990.
OS Pathfinder Sheets TR25/35, TR26/36.

When in AD 43 Aulus Plautius' Roman invasion force landed at what is almost certainly now Richborough, this was a promontory on the south side of the Wantsum Channel which separated the Isle of Thanet from the mainland. The sea is now two miles further east, but even in Roman times shingle banks were forming and these created a sheltered harbour for the Roman fleet. After the conquest Watling Street, the great Roman road to London and Wales, started at the quayside and passed through a gigantic archway, the symbolic gateway to Britannia. In the third century Richborough became one of a chain of fortresses known as Saxon Shore Forts protecting the coast against Germanic invaders. From this period the great walls over 20ft high survive around three sides of the square, the east wall having disappeared through the combined efforts of erosion and the South-Eastern Railway.

South of Richborough and another sea-less port, Sandwich was one of the powerful group of medieval ports known as the Cinque Ports which had tax exemptions and other privileges in return for providing ships for the Royal Navy in wartime. Sandwich was one of the most important and the official port for exports of wool in the thirteenth century. However, as the Wantsum Channel silted up and Thanet joined the mainland, it declined. Small coasters can still reach Sandwich Quay up the tortuous Stour but most boats seen now are pleasure craft. Consequently, much of this walk takes place on what was sea-bed in historical times, although to the south around Eastry the route is on chalk where the North Downs dip below the later sands and alluvia. Building materials are therefore brick, timber, flint and pebbles.

I started at Woodnesborough church whose tower is unusually topped by a timber balustrade and a central ogee-roofed cupola. This eighteenth-century addition can be seen for miles on the ridge and even survived Ewan Christian's over-zealous 1880s restoration. Inside there is no clerestory, just two Victorian dormer windows artlessly placed (but ignore the mawkish 1978 stained glass by F. W. Cole if possible). Out of the church I walked south to Eastry along the course of the Roman road that linked Dover with Richborough. In theory a straight alignment, it

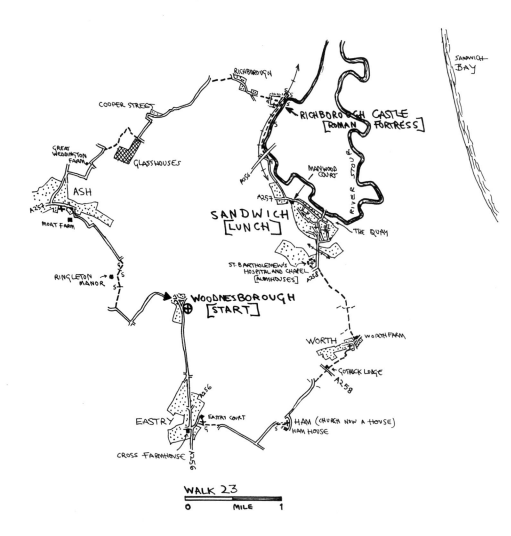

WALK 23
0   MILE   1

wanders slightly as the result of centuries of post-Roman unsurfaced use. It passes through market gardens, arable and occasional orchards to climb on to the chalk at Eastry.

Eastry High Street has a number of eighteenth-century brick houses, mostly painted and with doors on to the pavement. At the corner of Mill Lane, Cross Farmhouse is jettied and timber-framed with an original four-light arched window. Fine houses continue downhill in stucco, painted weather-boarding and brick. I turned left down Church Street to the church, a big Early English thirteenth-century building with an elaborate west tower, having a trefoil arcade in front of the ringing chamber windows and odd circles and ovals let into the buttresses. The austere lancetted exterior prepares one for the elegant nave arcades in the cool whitewashed interior. Over the chancel arch are five rows of seven thirteenth-century medallion wall paintings which would have been behind the Rood – a rare survival. Good monuments include that to Captain John Harvey about 1794 with John

Sandwich's St Peter Street looking downhill to the sixteenth-century Barbican gate, later converted into a toll-house.

Eastry: The Church Militant. A scene from the sea battle of the Glorious First of June, 1794, below the wall monument to Captain John Harvey who was killed during the battle.

Bacon's relief of a naval battle. Immediately north-east of the church Eastry Court has a long ten-bay brick west front with box sashes and an Ionic fluted-pilaster doorcase and parapets. This refronts a rambling mainly sixteenth-century house, best seen from Farthingate where the complex of tiled roofs is most clear.

I continued east out of the churchyard on a footpath to descend a field diagonally to Farthingate and turned left into the lane down Hay Hill. Just beyond the Blazing Donkey pub whose whitewashed walls are decorated with painted flowers, creepers and even a donkey, I turned left to pass a derelict ivy-clad seventeenth-century Hay Farm. Within a row of tall beech trees on the right I climbed a half-hidden stile and crossed pasture to skirt left of Ham church, with L-plan Ham House in eighteenth-century brick to the right. The bell-coted thirteenth-century church is now a house and stained glass studio and Ham House has an early nineteenth-century stuccoed south-east front. I continued north to rejoin Hay Lane and crossed water-meadows, turning on to the footpath right of a bungalow and waymarked 'White Cliffs Country: Sandwich Walk'. Across the A258 a charming stucco *cottage orné* is the lodge to Upton House which

has a Greek fluted doric portico. The path reaches Worth churchyard and the mostly Victorian rebuilt church with a quirky shingled spire. North of the church The Street has some good houses. I followed the path left of the pond and, beyond Worth Farm, in brick of 1675 with Dutch-shaped gables, I turned left on to a tarmac footpath, waymarked simply 'Sandwich Walk' and headed north to Sandwich through water-meadows.

At the road I turned right and then left at a sign for St Bartholomew's Chapel which was built soon after 1217 to serve St Bartholomew's Hospital and is surrounded by almshouses. These are not the normal high-flown architectural designs concealing sparse accommodation, but vernacular eighteenth- and nineteenth-century brick cottages which were built when needed, each with the name of the brother or sister in residence, and forming a small village. I continued north over the level crossing into Sandwich and then right along Town Walls, descending to St Clement's church with its big central tower enriched with two tiers of Norman blind arcading. Sandwich undoubtedly has a most complete medieval plan, although there has been much rebuilding and re-fronting. It is also on the road to nowhere

so is less crowded than Rye, for instance, and consequently more pleasant. Strand Street has the most timber-framed and jettied buildings while Market Street is a fine space, although St Peter's church is a shadow of its former self, having lost both aisles and central tower in 1661. I lunched on the Quay and then walked round the town where every street is packed with high-quality building. Much of this was preserved despite economic decline for which the architectural historian can only be grateful.

Eventually, I walked out north along Strand Street past Manwood Court, in pale 1580 brick of nine bays with five crow-step gabled dormers and flanked by massive gable stacks. Beyond I turned right up Richborough Road, bearing right before the bypass bridge through a kissing-gate to follow the Stour north. I crossed the railway to Richborough Castle where there is an informative small museum as well as the remains of successive

Sandwich. Looking along Strand Street with its fine timber-framed houses jostling the pavement.

Roman fortresses, the Roman town, bath-houses and the foundations of the great symbolic entrance archway to Britannia province. I left via the west gate along Watling Street into the hamlet of Richborough (in fact, three farms), turning left opposite Richborough Farm on to the footpath through sheep-cropped water-

The Saxon Shore defences. Looking through the postern of Richborough's towering third-century Roman fortress walls towards the power station, the twentieth-century's contribution to these flatlands.

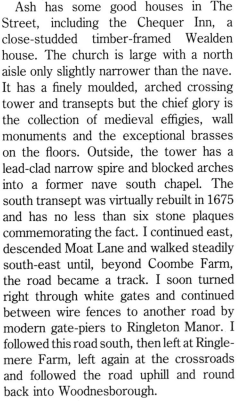

meadows to a road which I followed as far as a huge greenhouse complex. Here I turned right, crossed a stream and followed it south to a farm road. This merged with a lane which I followed through Weddington, mostly early nineteenth-century yellow-brick houses, into Ash.

Ash has some good houses in The Street, including the Chequer Inn, a close-studded timber-framed Wealden house. The church is large with a north aisle only slightly narrower than the nave. It has a finely moulded, arched crossing tower and transepts but the chief glory is the collection of medieval effigies, wall monuments and the exceptional brasses on the floors. Outside, the tower has a lead-clad narrow spire and blocked arches into a former nave south chapel. The south transept was virtually rebuilt in 1675 and has no less than six stone plaques commemorating the fact. I continued east, descended Moat Lane and walked steadily south-east until, beyond Coombe Farm, the road became a track. I soon turned right through white gates and continued between wire fences to another road by modern gate-piers to Ringleton Manor. I followed this road south, then left at Ringlemere Farm, left again at the crossroads and followed the road uphill and round back into Woodnesborough.

Greensand Hills

SURREY AND SUSSEX

Come, on the long-drawn clouds that fling
Their shadows o'er the Surry-Hills.
The dark-brow'd wood, the headlong steep,
And valley-paths without a crowd!
                    Robert Bloomfield

Walk 24

CRISS-CROSSING THE ROTHER DOWN TO RUINED COWDRAY

Midhurst and the Rother Bridges, Sussex. 12½ Miles. August 1989.
OS Pathfinder Sheet SU82/92.

Walking in the western Weald in the Rother valley through very beautiful lowland scenery is an object lesson in varied land uses governed by geology. Most useful land is in the valley of the river with its alluvial deposits, but to the north and south the greensand belt produces thin sandy soils only suitable for the roughest of rough grazing. These areas are now mainly heath or woodland and, while ideal for dog walking and riding, are of little economic use. Parishes reflect this by being long and narrow, the villages centred on the River Rother with its series of superb old bridges and arable fields on each side and, beyond, sandy heathland for common grazing. Where the soil is better, further arable continues. There are coppiced woodlands and modern conifer plantations while the iron-rich sandstones were worked for iron ore in the sixteenth and seventeenth centuries.

I started the walk from the car-park south of the A272 on the Elsted road in

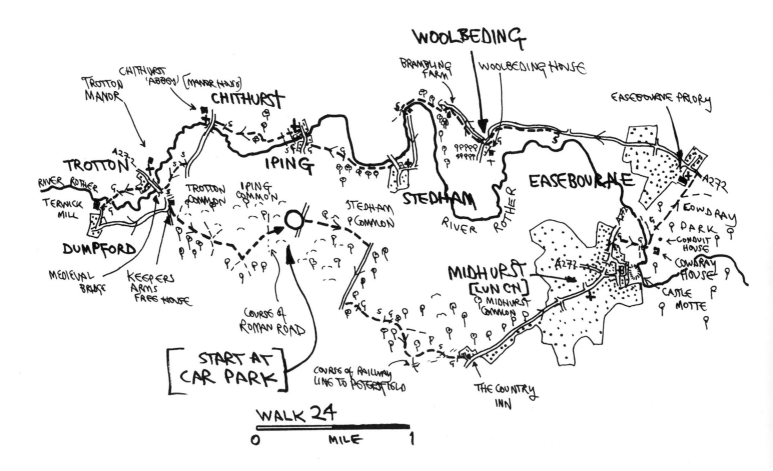

WALK 24

0   MILE   1

Iping Common, and walked east through heather, bracken, scrubby birch and pine along a sandy track, which becomes Stedham Common. At the road I turned right into Minsted Road, Stedham's access road to its commons and fields further south. Past a few toffee-coloured greensand houses and cottages dating from mid-nineteenth-century settlement in the common, I turned east before Minsted hamlet and crossed enclosures from the heath. Then across a stream which forms the parish boundary, returning to woodland, this time in Woolbeding parish. Continuing south-east and across the trackbed of the former Petersfield to Midhurst branch railway and into Bepton parish, I emerged at a hamlet formed by enclosure and settlement of Bepton's common heath. Turning left at the Country Inn, I walked into Midhurst down Bepton Road.

On the road into Midhurst the most striking building is Holy Mary's Catholic church (1957) by Guy Morgan in fine golden sandstone with a detached campanile. Midhurst is breathtakingly beautiful, particularly around the parish church on Church Hill, Edinburgh Square, West Street and South Street. Here spectacular timber-frames jostle with stuccoed fronts, header-bond brickwork, sandstone and old tiles to create a most intricate and heady mix. Of particular note is The Spread Eagle Hotel in South Street, a jettied timber-framed range and a gnarled painted south block. Part of the hotel is the old market house, originally open on the ground floor with a fine sixteenth-century timber-frame.

In Edinburgh Place two superb eighteenth-century houses, Bierton House and Gatehouse, have fashionable grey header brick with red-brick dressings to their sashed façades; the sides and rear are in less fashionable sandstone. The church was disappointingly rebuilt in the 1880s, except for the tower with its curiously dumpy shingled spire. Behind these, up St Anne's Hill (formerly Tan Hill) is the motte of the castle of the De Bohuns, fringed with towering sweet chestnuts.

Midhurst. Looking north up Wool Lane with tile-hanging over sixteenth-century jettied timber-framing.

There is plenty of choice for lunch in the town. North Street is spacious and generously laid out but poor on detailed examination. Exceptions include early nineteenth-century shop-fronts, the Angel Hotel, a splendid mid-nineteenth-century stuccoed front, and opposite on the corner of Lamberts Lane a large brick-fronted house with Venetian upper-floor windows and a provincial five-sided bay window clad in mathematical tiles. The school has a brick seventeenth-century bay with a shaped gable amid the stone ranges, some castellated, and the 'Schola Grammatica', a chaste Greek Revival building with panelled pilasters and a slated hipped roof.

From the car-park I walked along the causeway above the meadows towards the spectacular ruins of Cowdray on the other side of the Rother. The tall gatehouse gave access to this Tudor courtyard house with the hall range opposite, a striking element being the castle-like hexagonal kitchen. Built from 1492 to 1545 under three owners, the last being Sir Anthony Browne (later Viscount Montague), whose wealth came from acquiring monastic estates after the Dissolution, the house was occupied until a fire in 1793. Immediately north is the octagonal former conduit house, known curiously as the Round House, and beyond that the park and the famous polo ground.

I walked north with large lime trees on the left towards Easebourne Priory which presents stone cross-windows to the world and a discreet cloister garth away from it. It makes a superb composition and

The ruined Cowdray House, a slow-built and utterly Tudor courtyard mansion, seen from the west in jagged repose.

The unmistakeable yellow paintwork of the Cowdray Estate: a pair of greensand cottages in Easebourne.

attached is the parish church, brutalized by Blomfield, but distinguished by the Montague monument of 1592 moved here from Midhurst, with Montague kneeling above his two wives. From Easebourne I walked west, noting timber-framed houses with stone infilling, many with Cowdray Estate bright yellow paintwork, and down Hollist Lane to Woolbeding with its Frenchified Manor House. The church here is Anglo-Saxon with pilaster strips giving the clue in a yew-treed-lined churchyard. Continuing west, I dropped into the woods past Brambling Farm, emerging nettle-stung at Stedham Mill, a sandstone and brick-dressed group. Crossing the Rother I walked south to Stedham, its church with a south tower of 1670–77 and a very ancient yew held together by a hawser. Stedham Hall behind is a spectacular timber-framed house, mostly 1919 by John Malcolm. Stedham village has a delightful casual grouping of well-kempt brick, stone and rendered houses.

Along the south bank of the Rother I reached Iping, where the dignified perfection of Iping House with its tripartite sashes flanking a Doric pedimented doorcase and grey header brick façade contrast with the assertive and curiously out-of-proportion stuccoed Mill House in its garden containing a self-conscious chinoiserie-bridge. From the church (1840) in well-coursed sandstone, I continued west across fields and into woods flanking Hammer Stream, the parish boundary. Half a mile upstream is Hammer Pond, a relic of iron-working in the area. The new parish had its fields divided by 1859 enclosure gridiron hedging and the hamlet is a most beautiful grouping of a small unspoilt Norman two cell church and a fifteenth-century timber-framed manor house, now named Chithurst Abbey. The river flows by the Abbey, with its compound inserted stack, stone infilling to the ground floor and plastered infilling to the jettied upper-floor framing, set off by the sixteenth-century stone crosswing with its mullion and transome ground-floor window and brick lateral stacks with diamond flues. All is quintessentially English, down to the large topiaried yew hedge.

South along the road and into fields past White's Farm I saw the east elevation of Trotton Place peering from the other side of the river, a dignified house of about 1600 refronted in the early eighteenth century with a steep slated hipped roof with dormers and five bays of architraved sashes. Trotton church is outstandingly interesting for its memorial brasses, one of about 1310 to Lady Margaret Camoys the oldest surviving full-length female figure brass in England. Others are to Thomas Camoys, a Garter Knight who fought at Agincourt, and Elizabeth Mortimer, which is exquisitely done (if somewhat tricky to see under a perspex sheet). The roof is of high quality and was paid for by Thomas Camoys. The river bridge carrying the A272 traffic is one of the best in the Rother series, built in the late sixteenth century, five ribs supporting each arch.

Opposite, I walked through the hamlet and across fields to Terwick Mill, built in dark brown greensand and with its machinery intact. Down Terwick Lane to the Keeper's Arms for refreshment if open, before a final burst through Trotton Common where there is some sweet chestnut coppicing amid the heather, birch and oak scrub to Iping Common, noting on the right ancient tumuli covered in bracken. The Roman road marked on the OS map is covered in bracken and indecipherable; the car-park is reached accompanied (on this occasion) by swarms of persistent flies.

Walk 25

THE GREEN HILLS OF SURREY

Godalming and Puttenham, Surrey. 13½ Miles. August 1990.
OS Pathfinder Sheet SU84/94.

The country south-west of Guildford below the Hog's Back chalk ridge is mostly wealden clay deeply cut into by the River Wey, while north of Godalming golden-buff Bargate-stone forms a lower greensand sandstone outcrop. Charterhouse School is built from it and it is widely used in the villages on this walk, often combined with 'galleting': chips of dark-coloured upper greensand stone pushed into the mortar joints. The upper greensand runs along the foot of the Hog's Back, so called because the chalk here narrows to a mere ridge. Along the well-drained greensand foothills is the Pilgrims Way to Canterbury Cathedral and the Shrine of St Thomas à Becket (which is, in fact, a much older trackway).

This is prosperous countryside dotted with good sixteenth- and seventeenth-century timber-framed farmhouses and small villages. Within a fabric of neat fields are country houses in parkland, including Peper Harow and Loseley. The nineteenth century brought commuters and gentry whose wealth did not rely on land in Surrey, to Frith Hill for example, north of Godalming. Oddest of all are the shrines to the Victorian artist G. F. Watts, erected by his besotted widow Mary, at Compton: an art gallery, a short-lived Potters Art Guild and, most extraordinary of all, the Watts Chapel (1896–1901) in a cemetery above Compton. The chapel is an idiosyncratic hybrid Byzantine art nouveau style and every detail is heavily symbolic.

Puttenham church has a dominating fifteenth-century west tower but the rest owes more to Woodyer in 1861 than the Middle Ages. Puttenham Priory is an elegant stuccoed Palladian five-bay house of 1762, well-restored after careless hospital use. I turned left into Suffield Lane and climbed a stile on to a footpath above a pretty dry valley. At the road I turned right to walk into Shackleford beside a stream that rises north of Lydling Farm, a Bargate-stone house of about 1700 with hipped-roof wings and coved eaves. Shackleford has some Victorian estate cottages and a model dairy by Lutyens at Cross Farm. Down the Street, behind Dolphin House on the left, is a crinkle-crankle wall, commoner in Suffolk than Surrey. I took the right fork, opposite the tilehung Post Office stores whose north bay of 1690 in Bargate stone has a gable elevation with ornamental brickwork in somewhat rustic style, and headed south.

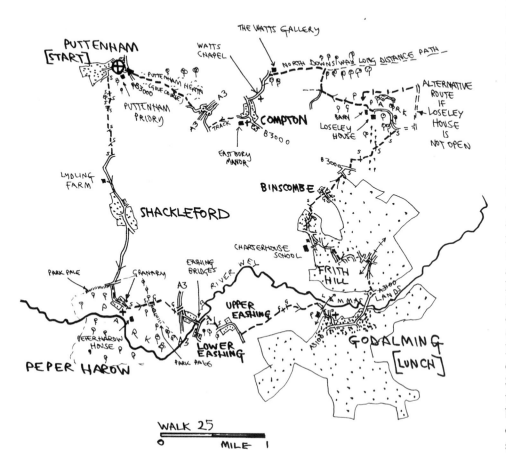

WALK 25

0   MILE   1

Agricultural plenty. The great granary at Peper Harow graphically demonstrates the Golden Age of corn production in late Georgian England.

At the junction I turned right, then left on to the drive to Peper Harow, passing through the pale of its medieval deer-park, landscaped by Capability Brown in the 1760s but retaining many older cedars and pollard oaks. In the estate village there are walled kitchen gardens, and to the left, superb farmyards and the seventeenth-century home farmhouse, tilehung above a Bargate-stone ground floor. Best of all is the granary whose tilehung upper two storeys are supported on five rows of five timber posts. The church was largely rebuilt by Pugin in 1844 in a style mimicking the evolution of a parish church: spiky late-Norman chancel arch, Decorated chancel and Early English north aisle of cathedral elaboration. Beyond, Sir William Chambers' stable court has Bargate cut to the size of bricks for some elevations. The yellow-brick mansion beyond of 1765–68, also by Chambers, is marred by 1913 additions, including the third storey and Cockerell's 1843 porch.

Over a stile I headed east past a modern farm-building and a decayed eighteenth-century dovecote, and continued over the hill to descend to a stile in conifers on the line of the old park pale. Beyond, the path crossed the A3 on a modern bridleway bridge to Eashing where, in less safety-conscious days, the petrol station was thatched. Through Lower Eashing and across the old bridges over the Wey, supposedly built in the thirteenth century by the monks of Waverley Abbey, I followed the road round past the dull former water-mill to the timber-framed Stag pub for a drink. Back at the bridges I followed the path by the river up to the road into Upper Eashing, whose best building is Jordans: a timber-framed wing with decorative circular panels to the gable, and five bays of early eighteenth-century brick-dressed Bargate stone. I followed the road round beyond Eashing Farm, also timber-framed, and then left on to a bridleway lane. This became a path past Far Cottage, then a lane descending into Godalming past Meath Home, formerly Westbrook Place of 1770 cloaked in mid-nineteenth Italianate stucco.

Godalming church with its lead-spired Norman tower is situated above the meadows along the Wey known as Lammas Lands where, after haymaking, the townsmen had rights to graze their stock. It is a much-added-to typical town church, sprouting aisles and chapels, in a churchyard full of good gravestones and chest tombs. North is a fine brick memorial cloister to the chief wireless telegraphist drowned in the Titanic in 1912.

Church Street winds to the stuccoed Market Hall (1814) which has a polygonal slate roof and sashed upper floor over an open arcaded ground floor: a very fitting building by a local architect, John Perry, although the town received its market charter long before in 1300. I noted the excellent timber-framed buildings at the end of Church Street and in High Street, including numbers 99–103 with three jettied storeys. The most peculiar buildings are number 80, W. H. Smith Travel, and numbers 74–6, dated 1663, both mainly brick with some stone and a profusion of ill-digested frenetic patternings and overdone cornices: late examples of artisan mannerism gone to chaotic seed. Past the stately chequer-brick Kings Arms and Royal Hotel of 1753 I turned left down Bridge Street to cross the river on Gwilt's 1783 bridge.

Across the river past the school (1872) with its bizarre Gothic turret I went straight on at the roundabout on to a path at the left of the Wey Inn. Over the railway foot-bridge on to Upper Manor Road, I worked my way through Frith Hill with its many Victorian houses. From Twycross Road I descended Sellars Hill past Charterhouse School, which moved here from London in 1872. It was designed by Philip Hardwick in Gothic style and is dominated by a spired tower. The chapel is by Giles Gilbert Scott who designed such disparate buildings as Liverpool Cathedral, Battersea Power Station and telephone kiosks! Past the school I turned right into Mark Way, then right into modern housing at Woodman Court and left of number 11 on to a footpath. I then turned left again in woodland to descend steeply to Binscombe with a Quaker burial ground characteristically without gravestones. Beside it, I followed a footpath to Green Lane, turning left then right. Right at the B3000, I turned left on to the footpath to Loseley.

Reaching the east drive I turned left to Loseley House, built for Sir William More in the 1560s, apparently using stone salvaged from Cistercian Waverley Abbey near Farnham. Originally, it had a west wing, demolished in 1835, but the great hall and principal rooms have survived (Open in the afternoons for guided tours from June to September; closed Sunday to Tuesday). The exterior is stately gabled with disciplined stone mullion and transom windows. West past the car park and out along a lane, I turned right at a bridleway sign to climb a sunken lane on to the greensand where I turned left on to the North Downs Way.

I followed this to the Watts Gallery behind the Potters Art Guild building of 1903. Further downhill towards Compton is the Watts Chapel itself, which is usually

Charterhouse School: Hardwick's striking 1872 roofscape in silhouette.

(Right): Red brick and terracotta symbolism on the exterior of the bizarre Watts Chapel.

open. From here I walked to Compton church with its famous two-storey Norman chancel, formed by inserting a vaulted gallery across the east bay. Remarkably, its late twelfth-century wooden balustrade survives. Beyond is Ewan Christian's Jacobean-style Eastbury manor of 1874, a solid Victorian mass in hard red brick and stone dressings. The Old Post Office antique shop has had its windows replaced by appalling UPVC ones (which makes one wonder whether the owner would put plastic legs on a Chippendale chair). I turned left into Eastbury Lane, then on to a track climbing into woodland. At the top I looked north to Voysey's Greyfriars of 1896 on the Hog's Back, a superb roughcast arts-and-crafts country house. At the road I turned right, then crossed the A3 on to the Puttenham Heath Road, and right on to a footpath leading to the Heath, now a golf-course, and back to Puttenham.

Sunlight illumines the extraordinary late nineteenth-century Watts Chapel near Compton: aestheticism colliding with Byzantine Greece and the art nouveau.

Rus in Urbe

GREATER LONDON

My eye descending from the Hill, surveys
Where Thames amongst the wanton vallies strays.
Thames, the most lov'd of all the Oceans sons.
Sir John Denham

Walk 26

THE MATCHLESS VALE OF THAMES FAIR-WINDING

Richmond and the River Thames, Greater London. 15 Miles.
November 1989. OS Pathfinder Sheets TQ06/16, TQ07/17.

In common with many in the book there are several ways to approach this walk. The buildings can be treated as exteriors and their interiors left for another time. Clearly, no one could complete this walk and a full tour of Hampton Court Palace, Ham House and Marble Hill in a single day, but you could split it into sections (thanks to public transport), or into two separate circular walks, utilizing the Teddington Lock foot-bridge over the River Thames when reaching the middle of the route.

Much of the route follows the River Thames as it winds through the London borough of Richmond, briefly entering Kingston Upon Thames. The amount of open space along the route is striking, including the great Royal parks of Richmond, the Old Deer Park and, most memorable, Hampton Court and Bushy Parks with their lime and chestnut avenues. Along the river there is also open country, Ham House Grounds and, on the west bank, Marble Hill Park. The benefit of all this greenery is that by separating the villages and towns from one another their distinct characters and historic cores can be the better appreciated, despite tails of development which absorb them into the Great Wen, London.

The scale and quality of what survives is no accident, for kings, nobles and other great men settled along the Thames west of London, the river being a better highway than contemporary roads. Sheen

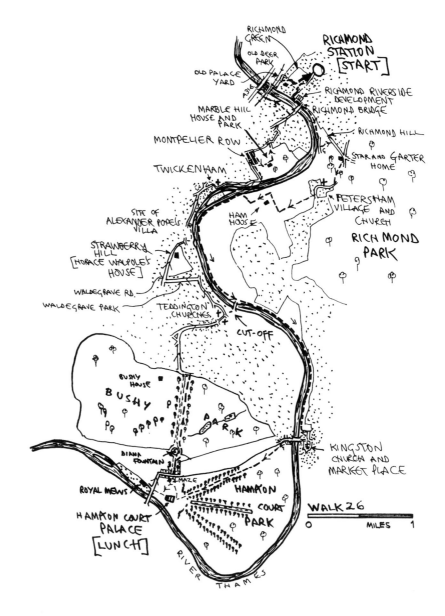

Palace, renamed Richmond Palace by Henry VII, and Hampton Court Palace, started by Cardinal Wolsey and taken over and completed by Henry VIII, attracted others like moths to a flame to build homes and villas along the river. These include Ham House (1610) for Sir Thomas Vavasour; Asgill House (1757), a summer villa for a merchant banker by Robert Taylor; Marble Hill built by George II for his mistress; Strawberry Hill, a medieval-type Gothick-fantasy castle by Horace Walpole (1749–66); and excellent Queen Anne and Georgian houses in Petersham, itself astonishingly rural. The list is endless but there are other particularly noteworthy buildings *en route*, including Montpelier Row, town houses near Marble Hill of 1720, and the comic opera Market House (1838–40) in Kingston Market Place. And through it all winds the River Thames, constantly alive with pleasure boats, strolling families and joggers on the banks.

I started the walk on Richmond Green, a large felicitous space where even Frank Matcham's exuberant terracotta Theatre of 1899 can be forgiven. The palace area is saved until later as I walked along the south-east side, with its mostly dignified Queen Anne and early Georgian town houses, all box sashes and cornice doorhoods on carved brackets. I left the Green into River Court, then right on to King Street and, past the post office, turned into Water Lane which descends to the river. Turning left on to the embankment I walked past Quinlan Terry's Richmond riverside development, a collection of classical office blocks recently completed. Much sneered at by Modernists as stage scenery and nit-picked by classical purists, I consider it a highly successful interpretation and, more importantly, so do the general public and the Prince of Wales! It is a composition of squares and individual buildings above a zigzag of ramped terraces and, in its careful craftsmanship and quality of materials, is a telling contrast to much tasteless classical pastiche. It merges well with the restored Tower House next to Richmond Bridge with its elegant five arches of 1774.

I continued along the river, merging with Petersham Road which I crossed to climb the footpath up to Richmond Hill. From here about 100ft above the river the view west along it is probably one of the best in London. Elegant houses lead south to the gates into Richmond Park, enclosed by Charles I, and opposite is the colossal Neo-Georgian Star and Garter Home (1921–24) by Sir Edwin Cooper, with Giant-order paired columns. Beyond this I dropped down through woods towards Petersham, a delightful village with a rich collection of late seventeenth- and eighteenth-century houses and a church of considerable character, partly medieval but mostly seventeenth- and eighteenth-century brick. Beyond this and opposite Dutch-gabled cottages, I turned right by a Jacobean-style lodge to walk to Ham House, with its sombre, remarkably complete interiors of 1672–74 and restored formal gardens (National Trust).

I then walked along the river bank to Kingston and its historic core, partly pedestrianized, with a large somewhat over-restored church and the market square. Across Kingston Bridge I turned into Hampton Court Park opposite the carbuncular Kingston Bridge House. Beyond the cattle grid I turned right, passed Hampton Wick Pond, and headed for the north-east double lime avenue focusing on the east front of Hampton Court Palace, the domestic masterpiece of Sir Christopher Wren. This is one of George London and Henry Wise's three great avenues radiating from the façade and associated with William and Mary's partial rebuilding of the Tudor palace. Every time I visit Hampton Court it seems better than I remember with Wren's great oak-sash windows, the real tennis court, the maze, the stupendously scaled kitchens and the texture of the Tudor brickwork, all seen above the heads of myriad visitors. The approach up the avenue is most impressive and reveals what the designers were after: a Palace-of-Versailles grandeur.

Out of the gates at the west I looked at Wren's house and the Royal Mews, also Tudor, before skirting the park walls and turning left into Bushy Park, also laid out by London and Wise with its six-deep avenues and the splendid Diana Fountain in a large circular pool. Herds of deer graze among the trees and to the west is the red-brick Bushy House of the 1660s built for the park ranger. Out of the park I turned left to follow the road round to Park Road, then right into Teddington High Street, relatively undistinguished but with a few nuggets, for example Georgian Elmfield House and Lloyds Bank of 1929 by Randall Wells. At the end is a curious juxtaposition of the small parish church, part sixteenth century, part Georgian, and on the south side the derelict but massive St Albans by W. Niven (1889) in towering Frenchified Gothic style, is incomplete and has smashed windows.

Turning left I walked up Twickenham Road, left down Waldegrave park and then right into Waldegrave Road to pass Strawberry Hill, Walpole's 'little plaything house' that he enlarged into a medieval battlemented house in early and influential Gothick, style, set 'in enamelled meadows, with filigree hedges'. Today it is a college. There are also some impressive later buildings, such as Sir Albert Richardson's grand brick chapel of 1962 modelled on Albi Cathedral in France.

Reaching the river, St Catherine's Convent is on the site of Alexander Pope's riverside villa. What a loss, for Kendall's lumpy Neo-Tudor replacement is no match judging by old prints. Continuing along Cross Deep I turned right into King Street, then into Church Street in the heart of Twickenham. Much is rewarding here, including the excellent church by John James (1714), but with a medieval west tower. Fine villas front the river and, beyond, the Orleans House Gallery, also by John James, is an elaborate octagonal garden room (1720), the only remains of a large mansion. Beyond is Marble Hill Park with its lovely stuccoed villa and on the west side behind its stable block is Montpelier Row. Marble Hill House has been beautifully restored and a visit is most worthwhile.

Leaving the park on to Richmond Road I

soon turned left to walk along Willoughby Road and Ducks Walk, then across Twickenham Bridge (1928–33), a grand three-archer by Dryland and Ayrton. Down on the other bank and back under the railway bridge I turned left up Old Palace Lane, admiring Asgill House at the corner, an exquisite villa with a canted centre bay and half-pedimented side bays restored in 1970. Turning right, I walked through Old Palace Yard with remnants of the Royal palace, and out through the Tudor archway back to Richmond Green. Turning right, I walked past Maids of Honour Row (1724), a terrace of three-storeyed five-bay brick houses with box sashes, to finish a walk with almost unmatchable historic interest.

Richmond Hill's monumental Neo-Georgian Star and Garter Home 'doth bestride the narrow world like a Colossus'.

Wren's masterly east front at Hampton Court: the columns frame Queen Anne's Drawing Room windows which look down three great radiating tree-lined avenues and the Long Water.

The Diana Fountain in Bushy Park. This 17th century composition in truth is surmounted by a figure of Arethusa, but the name persists.

A house fit for a mistress: George II's architecturally chaste Palladian villa at Marble Hill for Henrietta Howard, who became Countess of Suffolk for services rendered.

Walk 27

A STEEPLE ISSUING FROM A LEAFY RISE

Hampstead and Highgate, Greater London. 11 Miles. March 1990.
OS Pathfinder Sheet TQ28/38.

The remarkable survival of Hampstead and Highgate as villages owes much to the public spiritedness of the nineteenth-century Corporation of the City of London and others who purchased large tracts of heath, woods and open country, including Highgate Wood, Parliament Hill and Hampstead Heath. This from the 1860s aimed to safeguard what was valued, as the 'Great Wen' swept northwards. Other factors contributed as a tide of building swept past, including steep hills and fortuitous bypasses: Highgate by the Archway Road of 1813 and Hampstead by the easier gradients of Finchley Road to the west. This village quality is marked and the heaths and fields add to the *rus in urbe* character of the walk which also gives some fine views over London.

From East Finchley tube station of the 1930s with its statue of a kneeling archer aiming his bow towards London I crossed the High Road to walk through Cherry Tree Wood, actually mostly oak, hazel and beech. At the east end I left the park and headed along Fordington Road, crossed Woodside Avenue into Lanchester Road and beyond number 69 turned on to a tarmac path, crossing the bridge over the course of the long-abandoned branch railway to Alexandra Palace. I entered the delightful Highgate Wood, mostly oak and hornbeam and belonging to the Corporation of London. At a drinking fountain inscribed 'Drink Pilgrim, here! here!' I turned right and headed south and southeast to leave via Gypsy Gate, then crossed Archway Road to walk up Southwood Lane, originally a toll-free route past the Bishop of London's Hornsey deer-park, created in 1227, of which Highgate Wood is a remnant.

Opposite Jacksons Lane I turned right into Park Walk, a path emerging on North Road opposite two blocks of flats in International Modern style. These are Highpoint 1 and 2 by Lubetkin and Tecton of 1936–38, the right-hand one a marvellously pure-white rendered block full of Classical grace, while the left-hand one with caryatid pillars and brick and tile infilling is more suited for the English climate. I walked south into Highgate and, opposite Highgate School whose former pupils include Betjeman and Gerard Manley Hopkins, turned into West Hill with splendid Georgian houses on the north side and the 1854 reservoir alive with daffodils. Beyond the Grove on the edge of the hill stands Witanhurst, an enormous mansion of 1913 built for the millionaire Sir Arthur

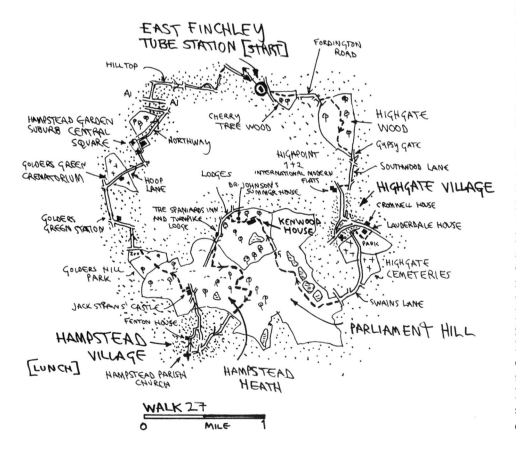

High Victorian Gothic almshouses of Holly Village, built in 1865.

Crosfield, famed for his invention of Sunlight soap. Returning eastwards, I visited the church by Vulliamy with its fine landmark spire, built in 1832 as the school chapel before Highgate became a separate parish. Further east, facing Pond Square, the Highgate Literary and Scientific Institution founded in 1839 indicates the cultural life of a village of writers and poets.

I turned right into the High Street, a most attractive street predominantly of eighteenth- and nineteenth-century yellow London-stock brick. Further downhill is an outstanding group: numbers 128 and 130 (early eighteenth century) and Cromwell House (1637–40), now beautifully restored as offices. Cromwell House has

much moulded brickwork, later box sashes replacing cross casements and a lantern cupola: a fine example of the Artisan Mannerist style. Opposite, Lauderdale House, colour-washed Georgian with pediments, conceals sixteenth- and seventeenth-century work (note the heavy moulded Tudor south doorway). I walked through its park, Waterlow Park, with fine views over London, to come out on Swains Lane and descend the hill past Highgate Cemetery. This famous cemetery is in two parts: the west is a nature reserve and contains the best architectural mausolea and monuments, mostly in a state of Romantic decay. It was opened in 1839 and at weekends there are guided

tours. The east cemetery (1854) is open daily and is famed for its Karl Marx memorial, still a magnet for deluded pilgrimage. Other influential persons buried there include George Eliot and Michael Faraday.

On the right are the tall mock-Tudor apartment blocks of Holly Lodge Estate and then, on the left at the Junction of Chester Road, the exuberantly High Victorian Gothic almshouses of Holly Village (now private houses) by H. A. Darbishire of 1865 for baroness Burdett-Coutts, a noted philanthropist. At the foot of Swains Lane I crossed into Parliament Hill and bore right to skirt Highgate Ponds, then walked uphill to enter the grounds of Kenwood House, owned by English Herit-

(Far left): Lubetkin and Tecton's Highpoint 2: A block of flats of 1938 in crisp International Modern style, complete with Surrealist caryatid figures.

(Left): In Highgate Cemetary Karl Marx glowers for ever at the cross, symbol of the 'opium of the people'.

In Hampstead Garden Suburb Sir Edwin Lutyens's vigorous Neo-Georgian Institute and School of 1908–10 dominate the east side of the Central Square.

The oddly named almshouses of Holly Village, founded by Baroness Burdett-Coutts in 1865: virtually all Victorian almshouses favoured the Gothic or Tudor style, here a spiky exuberant Gothic.

age. This fine stuccoed house was given its present appearance by Robert Adam in 1767–68; the great north portico was built in 1769 and the wings by Henry Holland. The service buildings have been adapted for refreshment and the view south from Lord Mansfield's house across the turf and woods to London is very fine. I continued west along a path to pass Dr Johnson's Summerhouse, a thatched rustic hut re-erected here from Thrale Place in 1967. Out by the Lodges, an elegant neoclassical screen of 1795, I turned left, passing the old turnpike lodge opposite the Spaniards Inn on the site of another of the Bishop of London's park gates. I walked along Spaniards Lane, then turned left to drop down on to Hampstead Heath and, at a clearing beside a gate into Kenwood, turned right, eventually crossing a five-arch bridge, turning right at a crossways and walked down an avenue of post-1987-storm-planted limes across East Heath.

I left the Heath for Well Walk, initially big Victorian Domestic Revival houses, then Georgian, including number 46, with a pretty Gothick oriel and door-case, and number 40, where Constable lived. Hampstead itself is a maze of small intimate streets and lanes, linked by alleys which, because of the hilly site, have delightful changes in level. Much of its expansion was associated with the chaly-beate wells discovered around 1700, which led to prodigious amounts of building peaking after 1800 when the Pump Room opened. My route crossed the High Street into Oriel Place, and then into Church Row, where excellent brick houses of about 1720 with richly carved modillion bracket hoods lead to the beautifully restored parish church. John Constable and Hugh Gaitskell, amongst others, are buried in the peaceful churchyard. The Church of St John by Sanderson, perhaps advised by Henry Flitcroft, dates from the 1740s and is in classical style with big Ionic columns and vaults. Inside are pedimented bench ends, galleries and a rich reredos.

Out of the church I went north up Holly Walk, passing the stuccoed Catholic church of 1816 in the middle of a Regency terrace. I continued onto Mount Vernon, then Windmill Hill and Hollybush Hill as far as Fenton House, a five-bay Georgian pedimented brick house owned by the National Trust. I lunched before heading north up Heath Street past the pond and, beyond Jack Straw's Castle, a weather-boarded and battlemented pub, I turned left to descend into the West Heath and walked along the valley floor. This led to Golders Hill Park which has a small zoo, and then Golders Green via West Heath Avenue. At Golders Green station I turned right up Finchley Road and then into Hoop Lane to pass Golders Green Crematorium of 1905 and 1938.

I was then in Hampstead Garden Suburb, founded largely by Dame Henrietta Barnett in 1906 and planned by Parker and Unwin from 1906 onwards, a deliberate contrast to the sooty Georgian and Victorian terraces further into London. There are two main architectural styles: Georgian concentrated around the Central Square area by Lutyens, and cottage vernacular in roughcast or brick, all with tiled roofs. Plentiful tree plantings and trim privet hedges complete a very delightful picture. I walked up Meadway, turned left into Heathgate and reached Central Square of 1908–10 with Lutyens's two outstandingly interesting churches, a most delightful mix of sweeping eaves and Baroque formality. The Anglican church has a spire, the Free Church a dome, and to the east the Institute is towering Neo-Georgian. I continued down Northway, walked left into Oakwood Road, then right across the Mutton Brook and Falloden Way into the northern part of Hampstead Garden Suburb with its mainly terrace cottages. Then I walked right on to Hilltop, crossed Ossulton Way into Brim Hill, now standard Suburbia, and eventually returned to East Finchley station.

Along the Chalk Hills

OXFORDSHIRE, BERKSHIRE AND HERTFORDSHIRE

. . . I found my lane,
And followed where it ran,
And gaps in hedges opened wide
As windows in the countryside,
With sudden landscapes breaking in
Upon the byway's privacy.
Arthur Stanley Wilson

Walk 28

THE RIDGEWAY AND THE WHITE HORSE VALE

Uffington, Oxfordshire, née Berkshire. 12 Miles. November 1989.
OS Pathfinder Sheet SU28/38.

On these walks perhaps a striking feature is the use of local materials for most buildings up until the mid-nineteenth century. After that transport improvements scattered materials all over the place, so in remote Oxfordshire/Berkshire hamlets Lancashire brick and Welsh roof slates are to be found. Until then building was on the whole truly vernacular, literally local. If there is building stone it is used; if not, timber, brick fired from local clay, or cob are used. Almost all the buildings along the route use local materials: chalk block quarried from the downs, flints found within the chalk and greensand from the foot of the downs, together with some sarsen stones. There is also timber-framing, particularly in Woolstone, brick and some cob.

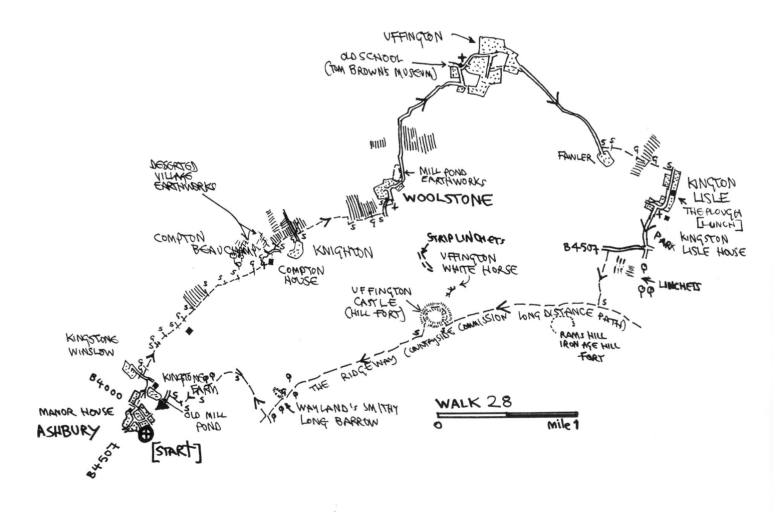

This walk falls naturally into two, the first part along the springline settlements north of the downs, the other along the ancient Ridgeway track which later became a drove road for flocks and traders avoiding town tolls. The parish boundaries are particularly interesting here, apparently following Iron Age estate boundaries and focused around farmsteads or hamlets along the springline with land stretching up on to the downs and north across the flat valley bottom to produce long narrow estates with a good balance of land. Many of these estates and hamlets never became parishes and the walk passes through several of them from west to east: Ashbury (a large village), Kingstone Winslow (a hamlet), Odstone (reduced to a single farm), Compton Beauchamp, Knighton, Hardwell, Woolstone, Uffington (the largest village), Fawler and Kingston Lisle. All had land up on the Ridgeway. Note Knighton Down, Kingstone Barn and Odstone Barn, for example. Long continuous north to south hedges descend the downs and cross the clay vale – many of these represent estate boundaries probably first defined two thousand years ago. Originally, these villages were connected by lanes, today mostly footpaths, the road now following the Icknield Way to the south, another ancient track running along the foot of the chalk downs.

The walk starts in Ashbury, a village of mainly chalk-stone houses, some with brick dressings, whose two former open fields were enclosed in 1772. The chalk-stone church is a spacious one inside but has a somewhat squat west tower. In the village College Farmhouse is a fine eighteenth-century chalk- and brick-dressed house, but the best by far is the fifteenth-century Manor Farm which is a hall house with traceried hall windows and a porch raised in brick in 1697. I crossed the B4009 and walked along the path to Kingstone Winslow which has a former water-mill, a pretty header pond and Kingstone Farmhouse of 1730. The farmhouse has three hipped-roofed late eighteenth-century rear wings which obscure the main block facing south. Next I passed

Odstone Farm, a double pile house with a steep stone-slated hipped-roof and all that remains of a hamlet, the only part of Ashbury parish not owned by Glastonbury Abbey. Beyond this and much mud, is a ridge and furrow field.

I continued east to Compton Beauchamp whose chalk-stone church has a stone-slated roof and pyramidal-roofed tower. Beyond is Compton House behind its walls and gardens. The church is mostly thirteenth century and the stone-bench sedile and pillar piscina in the chancel are noteworthy, as is the medieval stained glass which contrasts with the modern by Martin Travers (1937). The chancel walls are painted with foliage by Lydia Lawrence (1900) and the woodwork, including the rood and font cover, are by Travers, the whole effect somewhat precious and self-conscious. The house has a sixteenth-century courtyard plan in a moat with stone and brick elevations, but the distinctly French north front of about 1710 is perfectly situated at the end of a short lime avenue. In ashlar, it has a three-bay, three-storey centre with an order of Giant Doric pilasters above a rusticated ground storey and lower two-bay side wings.

Compton Beauchamp is a shrunken settlement and there are village earthworks west of the church and north-east of the house, then ridge and furrow of Knighton's former open fields on the left and its hamlet on the right with more chalk and brick and timber-framed and thatched cottages. I passed well south of moated Hardwell Farm, another deserted hamlet and one whose manorial boundary remains exactly as described in a tenth-century charter. The east boundary, now the parish boundary with Woolstone, is a spectacular double-banked affair running north to south. Beyond I walked through ridge and furrow to Woolstone which has a lovely chalk-stone church with a green-sand plinth. It is a two-cell building of the late twelfth century with a west bellcote and dragonhead stops to the chevronned north doorway. Inside, the fourteenth-century lead font is unusual and the church has a good crown-post roof. The lane

Polychrome brickwork: an alien intruder of 1877 in Woolstone village.

winds through a village of great quality with many timber-framed thatched houses as well as chalk-stone ones. It is intimate and has many trees, unlike the other villages on the walk. One odd house of 1877 has polychrome brickwork and north of the village are earthworks of a mill-pond.

I walked along lanes into Uffington with its spectacular church which has an octagonal crossing tower and a complete set of consecration cross roundels on the exterior, although the metal crosses themselves are long gone. The remarkable triangular-headed transept chapels and east porch are most unusual and look more Lethaby arts and crafts than medieval. Perhaps they are seventeenth-century rebuilds, but the main part of this large church is Early English (about 1250). Inside, there are finely moulded crossing and transept chapel arches and capitals,

Superb and astonishingly regular strip lynchets on the slopes below Uffington castle.

while the Saunders Monument (1603) in the south transept has one of those awkward effigies up on one elbow.

South-west of the church is the little chalk-stone school of 1617 with mullioned windows, now Tom Brown's Museum. The village is disappointing but there are several good houses and cottages. Out of the village I walked along Fawler Road and just before Fawler Manor, a big crosswing house, I turned left into fields across the settlement earthworks of Fawler to climb up to Kingston Lisle and lunch at The Plough. The village has many good houses including Thornhill House, a Queen Anne house of brick with cross-windows and timber-dentil cornice. The church is Norman with eighteenth-century graffiti on the north door, and in the chancel there are fourteenth-century wall paintings. The woodwork includes possibly Flemish bench ends carved with initials and instruments of the Passion, a handsome Jacobean chancel screen and a seventeenth-century pulpit. West of the church Little Farmhouse has an exposed cruck truss to its east gable wall, but Kingston Lisle

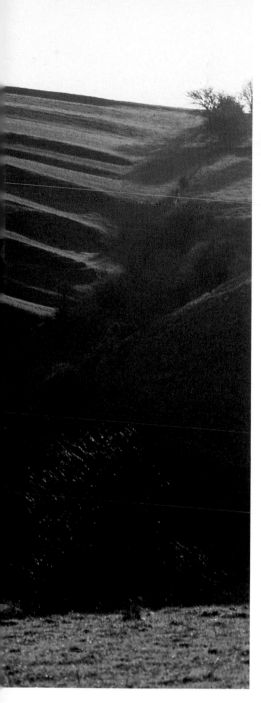

Looking north-west over the Vale of the White Horse from Uffington Castle hill-fort.

the White Horse and southwards over the Lambourn Downs, its ranks of arable hills stretching into the distance with occasional beech copses. Uffington Castle, an Iron Age hill-fort, is spectacular and beyond it the famous White Horse cut into the turf is genuinely of the Iron Age, its shape also seen on contemporary Belgic coinage. From up here the landscape is laid out below – hedges and areas of ridge and furrow clear.

I walked on to Wayland's Smithy, a chamber tomb of some complexity in a close surrounded by beech trees. It was so named in a charter of AD 955, so it is a genuine Anglo-Saxon coining. Wayland was an invisible legendary blacksmith who reshod overnight the horses of travellers. Beyond this I turned right off the Ridgeway and descended the track as far as a copse, then turned left into a steep valley to walk along the northern slopes of Odstone and Kingstone Coombes back to the road into Ashbury.

House is concealed within its well tree-lined park.

Climbing the path west of Blowingstone Hill and its coombe with strip lynchets I looked back to see Kingston Lisle House, its park and lake. The house has a three-bay south front with tripartite sashes and three hipped roofs behind parapets. On the Ridgeway itself I walked west, sometimes between widely spaced hedges and with fine views north over the Vale of

Like lonely sentinels these vertical stones guard Wayland's Smithy long barrow.

Walk 29

A CHAUCER IN THE CHILTERN HILLS

Ewelme and Watlington, Oxfordshire. 15 Miles. January 1990.
OS Pathfinder Sheet SU69/79.

This landscape of large straight-hedged fields contrasting with gently winding lanes to the north of the Chiltern escarpment is not merely the product of field consolidation but results from late enclosure. For example, the open fields of Ewelme and Benson survived until about 1860 and those of Brightwell Baldwin were enclosed after an Act of 1802. Interestingly, unlike other parts of the country, the lane network remained virtually untouched by the Enclosure Commissioners. Scenically, the walk is dominated by the well-wooded Chiltern Hills and passes mainly over gault clay, greensand and chalk. There is much timber-framing and brick but also extensive use of limestone, some from the Portland beds to the immediate north. Flint is of course common but the most notable material is the grey bricks produced from iron-free lime-rich clays at the foot of the Chiltern chalk. These were expensive and used for show fronts in the eighteenth and early nineteenth centuries, usually in extravagant header bond.

I started in Benson, a small town on the old Henley to Oxford road that largely ignores the nearby River Thames. The church has a fine ashlar west tower

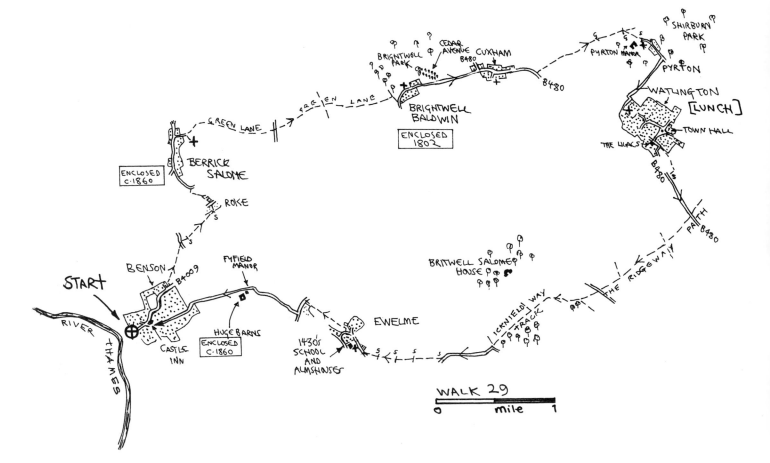

The former Castle Inn in Benson has a semicircular Georgian brick bay closing the vista up Church Road.

(1765–81) but is otherwise very heavily restored medieval with a Victorian chancel. Walking east along Church Road the view is terminated by the three-storey semi-circular bow of the former Castle Inn of grey header bricks with red dressings and three sashes per storey. To the left the stuccoed eight-bayed White Hart is currently boarded up awaiting conversion to offices. Heading north-east along Watlington Road past the Sun Inn dated 1763, I turned left beyond Sands Way on to a tarmacked footpath to Roke Marsh. Behind the Horse and Harrow inn a group of three modern houses look like remarkably well-converted weather-boarded and tile-roofed barns.

Straight across I continued on a footpath to the hamlet of Roke, also in Benson parish, then by footpath to Lower Berrick which has a cluster of fine stone houses and also a timber-framed house. North past several good houses and cottages into Berrick Salome proper, I turned right beyond the Chequers, passing more grey headers and red dressings, to the church with, to the north of the junction, the Innocents, a splendid colour-washed rubblestone three-bay thatched house (about 1600). Berrick Salome church is quite bizarre with an 1890 gingerbread squat west tower, porch and dormers concealing an interesting medieval church with excellent provincial woodwork includ-

ing a west gallery of 1676 and nave roof of 1615. Back on the track I followed Hollandtide Bottom, the old road between Berrick and Brightwell Baldwin, now a pleasant green lane.

Brightwell Park remains behind flint and brick walls, but the mansion has long gone. The church is delightfully situated in what appears to be an inlet into the park. Inside, this mainly fourteenth-century building has a good collection of medieval glass, a Jacobean pulpit with tester and in the Stone Chapel an extraordinary monument to that family consisting of four flaming urns in arched niches of about 1670, overpowering in scale and topped off by painted black flames licking over the

Britwell Salome House. The Palladian mansion and column seen from the Icknield Way along the foot of the Chilterns.

chapel ceiling. Opposite, the Lord Nelson has an attractive timber loggia and, just beyond, the Old Rectory of 1802 has a slated mansard roof and stuccoed elevations. On the left a decayed and gale-damaged cedar avenue in Brightwell Park converges on the road and an ashlar-fronted lodge. I continued into Cuxham, another attractive village with an elegant stone-built Old Rectory of about 1800 with sashes and Doric porch. The church has a Norman west tower and medieval pews with buttress ends.

Beyond Chestnut Farm cottages I turned left on to a footpath alongside a pollarded willow fringed stream, then across a field into Pyrton, a winding hamlet, whose church was rebuilt by Buckler in 1856. He reused the Norman south door with its hood-mould of grapes, leaves and fruit and the high chancel arch. Opposite is a charming stuccoed and bay-windowed former vicarage. Out of the village I turned right to walk into Watlington along a road which gives an excellent view of the south front of Pyrton Manor, an E-plan early seventeenth-century brick house with eighteenth-century sash windows. Ahead, Watlington church tower peers over modern estates. Almost at the main road, I turned sharp left to look at the church whose fifteenth-century tower escaped a virtual rebuild in 1877. The church was locked, its yard near-derelict, the whole distinctly unloved.

I walked south from the lych-gate, then left to emerge at the end of Church Street. Watlington is a remarkably coherent historic town fortuitously preserved by a refusal to accept railways in the nineteenth century. There are many fine brick fronts and timber-framed buildings, including the jettied Old Barley Mow in the High Street. Several grand eighteenth-century houses such as Well House and High Street House, both with box sashes, testify to Georgian prosperity. At the end of High Street is the brick Town Hall (1665) with toothed arches. I walked down Couching Street, which stops at the Lilacs, a big timber-framed house with a three-flued central stack, then left into Brook Street, continuing straight on to a path. Rejoining the B480 I soon turned right on to the Ridgeway Path, an official long-distance path, that for this stretch is off the Chiltern ridge and following the Icknield Way, an ancient trade route part prehistoric and part Roman. I followed this west, leaving the Ridgeway Path at North Farm to continue west along the Icknield Way green lane. To the north I saw Britwell Salome House of the 1720s with a pedimented centre block linked to lower pavilion blocks, all with slated hipped roofs and in brick with stone dressings. At the left is a cupola-ed stable range and in its park a tall memorial column of 1764.

Reaching the road, I followed it until a bend where, on a footpath, I crossed a ploughed hill, then passed through pig bungalows and crossed another ploughed field into Ewelme. This is a village set apart by its breathtaking sumptuous church and attached almshouses and school, all of the 1430s, founded by the Earl and Countess of Suffolk. The alabaster effigy of the Countess, a granddaughter of the poet Geoffrey Chaucer, is quite outstanding and pristine, while below is a macabre stone cadaver. The south-east chapel with restored 'IHS' lettering covering its walls, the screens with original iron mullions and the towering pinnacled font cover crowned by a figure of St Michael, make this a rare church. The brick almshouses are private but the porch is impressive. And the brick school, founded in 1437 appears to be still in use as a primary school!

Opposite, Forde Farm is early nineteenth century in coursed rubble with brick dressings and sashes and has a large weather-boarded and tile-roofed barn with two wagon porches. I walked through the village and turned right at the cress bed, then left on to a path past well converted barns, one flint, the other weather-boarded. Left at the road and then right, I walked west along the north perimeter of RAF Benson. Fyfield Manor has a good stuccoed front of nine bays, originally two storeys in 1790 but with a third added in 1840 when the front was given a Belgravia Italianate look. Older work is concealed within. This is the site of a deserted medieval village, while behind it is one of the most enormous barns I have ever seen: L-plan with at least five wagon porches and an awesome sweep of tiled roofs.

Rich corn country. In the eighteenth century a barn of colossal size was needed for the Fyfield estate's crops, and this is only half of a L-plan giant.

The road leads into Benson which has many good houses. However, some buildings like the shopping parade, for example, do the town no favours. Particularly fine are Barclays Bank and Kemp House, nine-bayed Georgian buildings with segment-headed sashes, Kingsford House with grey headers and red dressings, and seven-bayed Castle House of brick dressed stone, coved cornice and box sashes, gabled dormers and the three-storey brick bow already mentioned as a hinge in the streetscape. Here I turned into Church Street and back to the car.

Ewelme School, founded in 1437 by the Earl and Countess of Suffolk, the Countess being the granddaughter of the poet, Geoffrey Chaucer. An early use of brick in this area.

Walk 30

A DISTANT NOISE OF BATTLE

Newbury, Berkshire. 13 Miles. May 1990.
OS Pathfinder Sheet SU46/56.

The Kennet and Lambourn rivers converge on Newbury from the chalk downs along lush flat valleys while Newbury itself lies on the Reading Beds, a mixture of clays, light-coloured sands and pebbly flints. Other Eocene deposits include clays for fine red 'cutter' or rubbing bricks, as well as for other bricks. Flints are widely used but the predominant character of the villages and farms in these gentle rolling hills is red brick with a fair amount of timber-framing. To the south of Newbury most farming is pastoral with thorn-hedges and oak standards. It is gentle walking country with extensive woodland on the sandy soils of the Reading Beds, much of it formerly coppiced hazel.

I parked near Hamstead Marshall church, beside the remnants of the great mansion, Hamstead Lodge, built for the Earl of Craven in the 1660s. The house disappeared after a fire in 1718, leaving extensive walled gardens and no less than eight sets of gigantic gate-piers. Several pairs are associated with the walled gardens south-south-west of the church, while others surround the weed-choked site of the mansion. This was a solid block eleven bays square, of three storeys with lantern cupolas and dormers to a steeply pitched hipped roof. It was once claimed to be based on Heidelberg Castle and designed by Sir Balthasar Gerbier, a Dutch architect rival of Inigo Jones, but this must be an earlier house of about 1620. The 1660s house was probably by Captain William Wynde. The parkland survives with great ancient oaks, limes, sweet chestnuts and cedars and is most picturesque.

The church has good Jacobean woodwork while two pairs of gate-piers loom over the churchyard south wall with shell niches on each side and urn finials, both in brick with stone dressings. I walked west along the road, turning the corner to the west side of the walled garden which has a pair of stone gate-piers with pine-cone finials. These walls surround the large but inferior 1985 Neo-Georgian Craven House. I retraced my steps to Craven Hill, a lane of dwellings formed from estate barns and service buildings, and headed along it to successive pairs of gate-piers. Southwards the east wall of the walled garden has two further sets of gate-piers, one pair in a semicircular recess, as well as the site of the house.

I continued through the gate-piers by the churchyard to follow the track downhill and then right into the drive through the Park. Beyond the lake on the left is a very good Norman motte-and-bailey castle. The drive skirts the lake and heads uphill to Hamstead Lodge, now a nursing home,

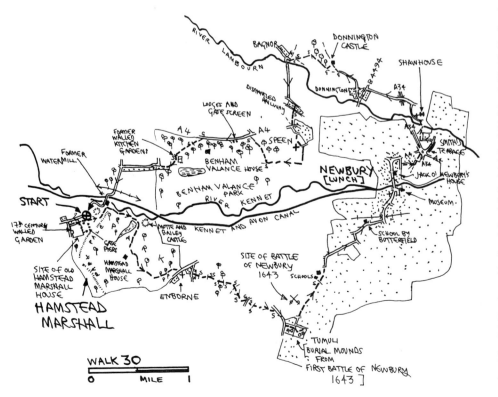

through a conifer wood. At its edge was a tumulus; a further two were in the park beyond. One of these has a plaque indicating that the tumuli are mass graves for those who were killed in September 1643 at the first Battle of Newbury during the Civil War. Although these mounds have not been excavated properly, this is indeed possible as the Royalist guns were positioned here during the battle.

From the north-west corner of the park I walked down Battle Road, across Essex Road on to a footpath with fields on the left and gardens on the right, and then skirted a school. Reaching Oaken Road I followed it round into Fifth Road through the suburbs of Newbury. At the end I turned left into Buckingham Road, then right into Enborne Road to walk into Newbury, passing St Nicholas School by William Butterfield of 1859, a somewhat quirky Victorian Gothic building with steep gables and a pyramidal spire. At the junction I turned left into Newbury which, in spite of

The Nag's Head on the road into Newbury. A Victorian three-dimensional pub sign.

Dwarfed by gate-piers at Hamstead Marshall, almost all that remains of the Earl of Craven's 1660s palace, and a hint of its scale and quality.

built in the middle of the park in 1720 but much altered and extended. The path skirts the stuccoed two-storey house to rejoin the drive which I followed out of the park, passing between widely spaced seventeenth-century cedars.

Out of Hamstead Park I crossed to Enborne church, a delightful stone-dressed flint building mostly Norman with heavy-handed late Victorian additions. I walked east past the rear of the Georgian rectory and turned right into Church Lane. Just before Old Lane Cottage I turned left on to a footpath, marked as a recreational path, and followed this across lush pastures and a gentle valley to Wash Common. At the road I turned right and, opposite Wash Common Farm, left into a football field and

Newbury's Northbrook Street with the shop-fronts mercifully obscured to give some idea of the quality of the townscape: seventeenth-, eighteenth-and nineteenth-century frontages march into the distance.

a fair number of good buildings, does not have much consistency as a town. This is partly because of truly horrific shop-fronts and partly some less than successful modern infilling, for example Pearl Assurance House, a 1960s slab block rising above Georgian town houses. Nearby, the multi-storey car-park has some success in domesticating an incongruous building type, but its tawdry towers have all the faults of illiterate 'referencing' to the past.

That said, in Newbury there are many fine individual buildings, including the museum, a jettied building of 1626–27 in Wharf Road off the Market Place with fine carved brackets and ovolo-mullioned windows. The Gothick archways (1770) into the churchyard are most elegant with their ogeed gables while the church is Tudor and paid for by 'Jack of Newbury',

Shaw House, finished in 1561 and now a school, seen beyond the shadow of its fine eighteenth-century wrought-iron gates.

that is John Winchcombe, a cloth merchant who had over a hundred looms. His house survives though refronted in Northbrook Street beyond the balustered bridge over the Kennet. Its north elevation with close-studding and original oriel window is visible in the alley-way. Above part of the appalling shop-front of Camp Hopson is a façade of 1669 with superimposed pilasters flanking each bay, all in brick. At the end of the street by the 1926 clock tower I turned right on to London Road and, opposite the charming battlemented Gothick St Mary's House, turned down Park Way, then left into a park. At the terracotta statue of Queen Victoria I turned left and soon went under the A34/A4 roundabout via a subway to walk along Shaw Road with Smith's Terrace (1823) on the right, a very long brick terrace with a central pedimented carriageway.

I turned left down Hutton Close and right, almost back at the A34, to walk to Shaw where a fine E-plan mansion of 1581 is now a school. In brick with stone dressings, including cornices and mullion and transom windows, it was built for Thomas Dolman, a successful clothier, who had carved the repellent Latin tag on his porch: 'the toothless envies the eater's teeth and the mole despises the eye of the goat'. Next to it is Hansom's Neo-Norman church (1840) with a Butterfield chancel of 1878 in uncompromising Gothic. Beyond, I turned left to cross the A34 on a bridge and walked to Donnington, a village with good brick almshouses of 1602 built round a courtyard. I followed signs to Donnington Castle whose gatehouse of 1386 survives together with the foundations of the oblong castle, which sits amid the star-shaped earthworks of Civil War gun platforms from the twenty-month siege of 1643–44.

I descended south-west to the path and followed it, initially through woods, to Bagnor, a strung-out hamlet along the River Lambourn. I turned left down a straight road and, at the junction, left, then right on to a path between houses, across a field and then the A4 at Speen. Past the war memorial cross, I soon

Donnington Castle: a walker approaches.

turned right to the Victorian church of 1860 and 1878. The church has a fine collection of monuments, including Lady Elizabeth Castillion (who died in 1603) in Spanish widow's hood and farthingale and an 1806 Canova wall tablet to the Margrave of Ansbach.

From Speen church I walked towards the old school and then south on to a footpath and west above the water-meadows. The path then turned right up a green lane to the A4, which I walked along westwards, passing the superb stone lodges and gate-piers with their Tuscan pedimented archways to Benham Valence Park. I followed the park wall west to a pedestrian gate on to the footpath, descending though woods and then across its parkland to a walled garden and estate cottages, only glimpsing Capability Brown's stone mansion. Out of the park I walked west and, beyond the Red House pub, turned left to walk back to Hamstead Marshall church, crossing the Kennet and Avon canal of 1811 with its stuccoed wharf buildings, now a house.

Walk 31

THE WAY THROUGH THE CHILTERNS

The Tring Salient, Hertfordshire. 16 Miles. April 1990.
OS Pathfinder Sheet SP81/91.

The Tring Gap has long provided a route through the Chiltern Hills with the earliest being the Roman road, known as Akeman Street, now the A41. The Grand Junction Canal, later the Grand Union, wound through from London to Northamptonshire during the 1790s, and this walk follows part of its route as well as two spurs, the Aylesbury Arm (opened in 1815), and the Wendover Arm (opened somewhat earlier). Both spurs are very narrow with locks only 7ft wide. The walk follows the dry, scrub-filled centre section

of the Wendover Arm (which did not hold water financially or literally) and skirts one of the large feeder lakes excavated to store water for the locks of the Tring Summit: Wilstone Reservoir. The canals were supplanted by the London and Birmingham Railway, now part of the London Midland Region, which also sweeps through the Tring Gap. Along the foot of the Chilterns the Upper and Lower Icknield Ways represent much older trade routes. Hertfordshire controls the Gap and juts out into the Vale of Aylesbury

beyond, and, as the vicar of Wigginton described it to me, 'sticks into Buckinghamshire like a sore thumb'.

I started in Ivinghoe in Buckinghamshire, a most attractive village with mainly brick and timber-framed houses. The cruciform church with its central tower and needle spire or 'Hertfordshire Spike' has a marvellous interior, with local (Tottenhoe) chalk-stone capitals with vigorous stiffleaf foliage. It also has bench ends (1500) with poppy-head finials of which some are treated as faces, fifteenth-century roofs enriched with carved angels, and a fine ornate Jacobean pulpit with tester. In the carriageway of the King's Head Restaurant are crucks either side and the Youth Hostel near the church in Old Brewery House is a tall Georgian house of three bays with tripartite sashes to the outer bays and a Doric arched door-case, obviously a prosperous brewery. Attached to the churchyard wall is a long thatch hook which was used to pull burning straw off roofs.

I walked west and, opposite the Bell, turned on to a footpath beside a stream and skirted housing, heading generally west to the Cheddington Road where I turned right and then on to a footpath before the railway signposted 'Cheddington 1 mile'. This led to a pedestrian swing bridge over the Grand Union canal where I turned left to walk along the canal which winds along the contours and past Pitstone Wharf, which is alive with colourfully painted narrow boats. I passed a pair of locks whose gates were dated from 1862 to 1885, a white painted lock-keeper's

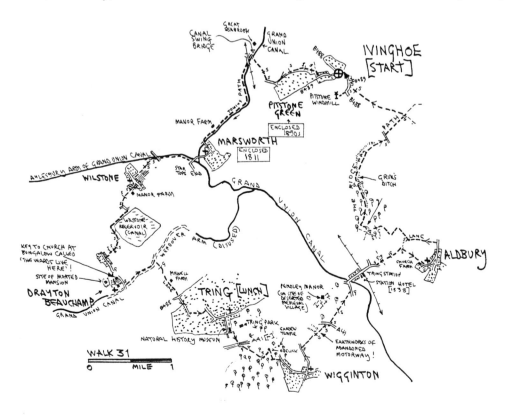

WALK 31

Canal boats on the Grand Union Canal near Marsworth.

cottage (1909) and a yellow stock brick engine house with a slated hipped roof. Passing Manor Farm I saw earthworks of the shrunken village and the interesting timber-framed house, partly clad in yellow stock brick carried up from the London brickfields by canal.

Past the timber-framed and thatched Ship's Stores and under bridge number 130 I climbed up to the road through Marsworth, a small village with a number of timber-framed cottages. The church in chequered stone and flint was dramatically over-restored in the 1890s by the amateur architect Vicar F. W. Ragg, who was assisted by his wife. It is extraordinary with fruity out-of-scale capitals and corbels and a wealth of foliage panels and inlay in the chancel. The south chapel altar is a tomb chest with macabre skull-laden panels.

I continued west down the lane and, beyond Marsworth Junction, turned right on to the tow-path of the Aylesbury Arm of the canal which drops via a series of locks from the main canal level. Most lock-gate mechanisms have dates ranging from 1851 to 1893. Under a road I soon turned left into fields at a footpath sign to walk to Wilstone, a curious village with mostly late-nineteenth-century terraces, a few older buildings, including a jettied timber-framed one and a flint church of which only the nave was built before the benefactor went bankrupt in 1860, the east and west walls hastily and cheaply completed in brick. Continuing south, I turned right into Chapel End Lane, and then into the fields through a group of converted barns to reach the road. Briefly along the road to the car-park I climbed to the Wilstone Reservoir and skirted it, initially along the dam crest and then along a path through willows before crossing fields to Drayton Beauchamp.

This remote village straggles towards the church, and I crossed a field with medieval fish-ponds on two sides and a large moated site with a modern house replacing the manor house demolished in 1760. I got the church key from the bungalow at the south-east corner of the field called 'The Wards Live Here' and passed the Old Rectory to the church, a chequered stone and flint nave and a banded ironstone and limestone chancel, all battlemented. Inside, the splendid Newhaven Monument of 1728 has his lordship reclining on a sarcophagus and, added in 1732, her ladyship on a kind of shelf in front.

I walked south past the former National School (1844) and then left on to the old tow-path of the Wendover Arm with the canal a scrub-choked ditch. In half a mile I turned right to climb out of the valley and continued across the main road into Miswell Lane, then left along a path through a playing field, skirted a school and turned right to walk up to the road. This led into Tring, a somewhat disappointing town. The church has another spectacular baroque monument with Lord and Lady Gore reclining on the plinth of a huge urn. The High Street has one or two good buildings, including the Bell Inn where I lunched. I headed south down Akeman Street which has a Baptist Chapel which was rebuilt in 1832, and is, as the plaque informed me, 51 sq ft. At the end of the street by the Zoological Museum based on the collections of Lionel, Second Baron Rothschild, I turned left past 1880s Rothschild cottages: timber-framed, tilehung and rendered. Then I turned right on to a path that leads into Tring Park. Across the

The Aylesbury Arm of the Grand Union Canal, opened in 1815, descends via a series of locks into the flat Vale of Aylesbury.

motorway bypass I climbed through the severed park to the woods, looking back at the mansion, a somewhat undistinguished building of the 1860s apparently encasing a seventeenth-century house. In the woods I climbed a yew avenue to an

Pitstone windmill. A post-mill built in 1627 but much repaired.

Tring Park. A garden temple in decay seen from the obelisk in the woods where the Ridgeway Path climbs towards Wigginton.

obelisk where another avenue gives a view of a temple-fronted building.

Climbing out of the wood, I briefly met the Ridgeway Path, the Countryside Commission Long-Distance Footpath, before turning right to walk through Wigginton which has a charming flint church with a belfry. I walked north along the lane called The Twist and rejoined the Ridgeway Path to follow this, passing at a distance Pendley Manor, a Victorian rebuild and the site of a village destroyed in 1440 by Sir Robert Whittingham for a deer-park. At Tring Station, the Royal Hotel (1838), a large stuccoed building, and the railway workers' cottages nearby, date from the building of the London and Birmingham Railway whose station has now been replaced by a modern box.

Beyond Westland Farm I left the Ridgeway Path and continued straight on over fields and then right to Aldbury. Immediately north-west of the church are what appear to be the earthworks of the long-demolished manor house. The church has a south-east chapel enclosed by a stone screen with high-quality monuments, and the village is like a picture postcard with a green that has a pond and stocks. There are many fine houses here and a curious village bakehouse with a tall octagonal flue. North of the village I turned left on to a green lane which then weaved around fields back to the woods, where I rejoined the Ridgeway Path. This followed the Grim's Ditch northwards, a great Saxon linear earthwork probably intended as a boundary between tribal groups or clans. After a mile or so the path emerged on to sheep-cropped downland with wide views off the chalk ridge. Just before Incombe Hole, a fine deep coomb, I left the Ridgeway Path, turning left to walk down towards Ivinghoe. Reaching the road, I diverted south to Pitstone Windmill, a post-mill of 1627 but much repaired, standing in the arable, before walking into Ivinghoe.

Walk 32

WITHIN A SINGLE PARISH BOUND

Great Gaddesden Parish, Hertfordshire. 12 Miles. May 1990.
OS Pathfinder Sheet TL01/11.

This walk is restricted to a single parish in the Chilterns which caught my eye and that of Mike Kilburn, the landscape and theatre historian: Great Gaddesden. Looking at the 1:25,000 map there is a strikingly regular pattern of long narrow fields in the east of the parish which may indicate an ancient form of land division. Medieval parishes in the Chilterns were often characterized by large numbers of relatively small common fields in contrast to Midland parishes where two to four great fields formed the basis of their communal agriculture. Great Gaddesden had about thirty, but its pattern of rectangular closes with characteristic reverse-S-curved hedges fossilizing the cumbersome turn of the ox-plough overlays a much older field pattern, dating from when the plateau above the Gad valley was first systematic-ally cleared for cultivation. This may have been in the Iron Age or Roman period and later adapted to common-field agriculture. An examination of the 1838 Tithe Map suggests that the whole plateau was divided into a grid of rectangular fields. A similar pattern seems discernible in the neighbouring parish of Flamstead and Bedmond further to the south. Perhaps this area formed part of a huge Roman estate, related to the creation of the nearby great Roman *oppidum* or town of Verulamium, modern St Albans.

The actual cropping of these smaller and more numerous Chiltern common fields was less regimented than in the Midlands, different crops being grown side by side in the same field. They also tended to have more hedges long before they went out of comon farming. In the seventeenth century the copyhold tenants secured through a lawsuit considerable independence from the lord of the manor, consolidating a process that had started by the sixteenth century whereby strips in the open fields were exchanged to amalgamate and rationalize holdings. By 1600 much of the open arable had been enclosed by hedges, but this slow consolidation preserved much of the old pattern even today when arable lands threaten so many ancient field patterns in the Chilterns.

This is mainly timber-framing and brick country with some flint walling. Chiltern chalk underlies the area, and there are several old chalk pits within the parish, while the plateau is capped with loamy clay with flints and pebbles and the valley side by chalky clay, also with flints.

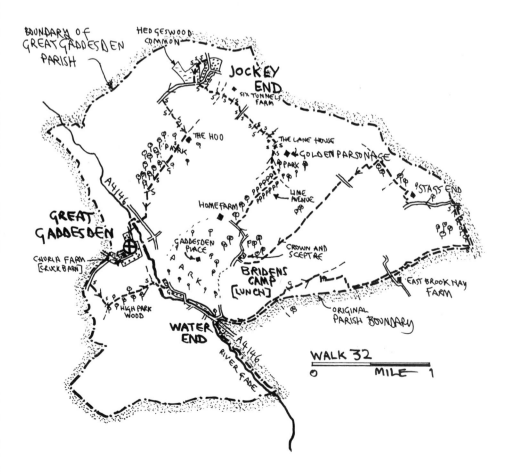

The route passes through the most interesting parts of the parish and could be divided into two loops, starting and finishing at Great Gaddesden church. The church is mainly rendered with the tower in exposed flint rubble, while the chancel has quoins and buttresses in reused Roman brick, possibly from a local, as yet unearthed, villa similar to that excavated in the 1960s at Gadebridge Park. Inside, the 1730 Halsey chapel contains a splendid series of Halsey family memorials, the best of which consist of busts within draped baldacchinos framed by fluted pilasters supporting open segmental pediments, all four from the earlier eighteenth century. The nave arcade has local Tottenhoe chalk-stone stiffleaf capitals and a good fifteenth-century roof. The church lies behind cottages, a pub and school, above the flat valley through which the river Gade winds with cress beds and ponds.

We left the churchyard at the south-west corner, noting the barn conversions to the south which include a large late-medieval cruck barn, at present unconverted and only repaired. In the field are earthworks which indicate that Great Gaddesden originally extended further west, and fringing this field are a number of fine timber-framed houses, including Glebe House with a Tudor brick porch.

We followed the lane uphill, bearing left at the junction on to a deep lane along the parish boundary, flanked by an eight-species hedge that could go back to at least the twelfth century. At the 1:12 gradient sign we turned left over a stile, signposted Potten End, and went through a massive 25ft thick hedge. Walking alongside a hedge, we turned left into Highpark Wood, which showed little sign of being much over two hundred years old but is shown within the same boundaries on the 1838 Tithe Map. From the wood we descended to the river in its beautiful valley.

Ahead on the brow is Gaddesden Place, the home of the Halseys whose memorials so enrich the church, set in sheep-grazed parkland. The house by James Wyatt (1775) has a big four-columned Ionic portico with pediment, but was rebuilt after a fire in 1905 and replaced Golden Parsonage as the family seat, seen later on the walk. We crossed the meadow diagonally to a foot-bridge and reached the main A4146 road at Water End. Turning right we passed a number of good seventeenth-century timber-framed and brick houses with mellow old tiled roofs. Across the somewhat perilous eighteenth-century three-arch brick bridge the river becomes a water feature in the park.

At the junction opposite the Red Lion,

The view of Gaddesden Place of 1775 in its parkland as you descend towards the Gade valley from High Park Wood.

we turned left by an ash and sycamore copse and, at the bend, right onto the public bridleway signposted to Stags End. This was the original parish boundary. Many hedges on this walk have been cut down but, thankfully, there is vigorous regeneration by maple, hazel and hawthorn. The hedge on the left includes ancient laid oak, hornbeam and ash. Just beyond an ancient pollarded oak the path goes right and skirts a copse of dead elms.

Twisted three-hundred-year-old sweet chestnuts remain from the park of Golden Parsonage, whose 1705 wing is seen beyond.

The field on the left is part of the open-field network probably enclosed in the early seventeenth century. The path follows its south hedge, then turns right to skirt another larger field. We continued east; crossing a lane, the path becomes a trackway. At the end we turned left to follow the parish boundary north through woodland. At a road we bore left, passing

Stags End Park, a stuccoed two-storey early-nineteenth-century villa with a shallow slated hipped roof and Doric pedimented portico, called Tags End in 1838. Beyond it we turned right on to a footpath and left beyond a wood to head for the road.

At the road we turned right, then left on to a track signposted Bridens Camp.

The track ran between two of Great Gaddesden's open fields, now arable, skirted the Big Wood and reached Bridens Camp, a hamlet of estate cottages, to lunch at the Crown and Sceptre, a beer-shop in 1838. We continued north-east and, beyond the sports field, turned left on to the concrete road to Home Farm, signposted Great Gaddesden. At the

The ancient lime avenue, at least three hundred years old, which leads to the Halseys' former mansion, Golden Parsonage.

wood we turned right with another of the open fields on our right. Beyond the wood the path entered a lime avenue where a ring count on a fallen tree gave a minimum age of 300 years. This avenue is very impressive and must relate to Golden Parsonage ahead. At the end, we turned left on to a footpath to skirt Golden Parsonage, a five-by-five-bay brick house of 1705 with large brick angle pilasters and a moulded cornice. In fact, this is the surviving wing added to a seventeenth-century house demolished when the Halseys moved to Gaddesden Place. In the pasture to its west are sweet chestnuts, at least one of which must be seventeenth century and obviously part of its park, Golden being a corruption of 'Gaddesden'.

We walked through pastures following a footpath across the grain of the rectangular former open fields to Jockey End, passing two seventeenth-century farmhouses, Lane House and Six Tunnels Farm, the latter with six octagonal flues to its stack. Jockey End has a few timber-framed houses but mostly comprises nineteenth-century cottages with an Ebenezer Chapel (1845). We walked west down Bradden Lane, having crossed Hedgeswood Common which continues as a wide grazing verge. Opposite Widmore Farm (about 1830), we turned left on to a footpath parallel to an overgrown green lane. This led to The Hoo, a three-bay Georgian house with a Doric columned and entablatured door-case and Neo-Georgian rear wings. The remnants of its Park are clear with a number of sweet chestnuts and old trees isolated in the arable to the west. We headed south-west past The Hoo's façade, eventually entering the mainly coniferous Hoo Wood to descend into the valley, emerging from the woods with a spectacular view to the church. At the road we crossed, bore right into the water-meadows, crossed a foot-bridge and headed back to Great Gaddesden church.

East Anglian Angles

NORFOLK, SUFFOLK AND ESSEX

*It is a reverend thing to see an ancient
castle or building not in decay.*
Francis Bacon

Walk 33

CHURCHES OF THE SALT-MARSH EDGE

Blakeney and Cley-next-the-Sea, Norfolk. 12 Miles. June 1990.
OS Pathfinder Sheet TG04/14.

This walk, entirely on the chalk, is very different scenically from the Chilterns, although a continuation of the chalk spine of southern England. In Norfolk the chalk, undulating rather than hilly, is mainly overlain by glacial deposits, including boulder clays and sands, the latter producing heathland amid the arable. For example, Salthouse Heath and the Downs, a narrow ridge of glacial moraine containing vast quantities of flint pebbles running from Blakeney to Glandford, although sections have been quarried level.

These pebbles and beach pebbles, extensively used for building, give the area its architectural character. I should think three-quarters of the buildings on this walk and most of the boundary walls are built in smooth white flint pebbles with brick dressings, although there is also a fair amount of colour-washed render to be seen. The River Glaven divides the route, winding north through lush watermeadows towards the sea, while chalkland descends fairly abruptly to the coast road. Beyond are the salt-marshes, now mostly nature reserve or pasture protected from the sea by a high shingle bank.

I parked on the B1156 side of the River Glaven in Glandford, an early twentieth-century Norfolk Vernacular-style estate village, with gabled flint and pebble cottages, including a purpose-built shell museum. Shell-collecting was one of the hobbies of Sir Alfred Jodrell of nearby Bayfield Hall who built the museum and the village. He found the small church a ruin and lavishly rebuilt it, cramming it with high-quality woodwork, including an elaborately cusped hammer-beam roof, pews and chancel screen, all dating from 1899 to 1906. He used the skills of woodcarvers Frank McGinnity and Walter Thompson whose portraits are on the dado frieze either side of the door. They also carved on the bench end of Jodrell's pew Landseer's 'The Shepherd's Chief Mourner', with the carver's dog substituted. The only discordant note is the marble angel by Bazzanti in the north chapel, a syrupy tribute to Jodrell's mother.

I crossed the Glaven in its watermeadows by the foot-bridge next to the ford. Once up the hill the fields are mostly arable with occasional woodland. I passed a sand and gravel pit and, where the road turns right, I carried straight on into a green lane called Hurdle Lane, emerging opposite an attractive group of pebble- and brick-dressed farm-buildings with pantile roofs. The former farmhouse, Swan Lodge (1840), is in more expensive brick.

I carried straight on and the road soon passed through Taylor's Wood, a fine ancient woodland with neglected sweet-chestnut coppicing. It also has oak and ash

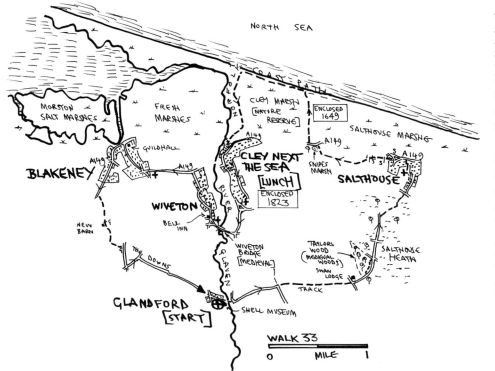

WALK 33

0   MILE   1

Salthouse church and the sea looking north: few places in England have a north facing coastline.

coppices, although these are now somewhat invaded by sycamores and coarse purple rhododendrons. The wood occupies a classic ancient wood location with its east boundary on the parish boundary bank. I walked within the wood parallel to the road and beyond, at crossroads, continued straight on, signposted Salthouse. I passed through Salthouse Heath, sandy country much overgrown by hawthorn and gorse with open areas of bracken and small oaks and birches everywhere. After half a mile I bore right on a surfaced lane into the heath at Bard Hill with fine views over the sea, the salt-marshes and Salthouse. I descended steeply into Salthouse village with its pebble cottages, to turn left at Pear Tree Cottage on to the footpath to the church.

Salthouse church interior is flooded with light from its tall aisle windows and, apart from the earlier tower, is of about 1500. It is full of interest, including the 1513 former chancel-screen dado with painted figures of saints, reused in sections all over the place, and old quarry tiles on the floors. In the north-west corner of the

churchyard buried beneath ivy are the remains of a small square flint chapel. I left the churchyard through the north gate down a narrow lane to the coast road: Left to the triangular green flanked by rendered and pebble cottages, I went to the right of Bardhill Cottage over a fence stile into the fields. The path runs roughly parallel to the road with good views over the marshes. Once upon a time Salthouse was a port with a channel called Salthouse Mayne Channel but, in 1637, a Dutchman called Van Hasedunck began the embanking of the marshes and cut off the channel. Despite protests, in 1649 the whole of the Cley and Salthouse Marshes were reclaimed.

The path reached the road beside the reedy Snipe Marsh pond and crossed over to the east embankment of Cley Marsh, less civilized than Salthouse Marshes and a nature reserve noted for its bird life. At the sea I turned left on to the great shingle bank and then inland to walk along the west dike (1649) above the Glaven, briefly on the Norfolk Coast Path. Ahead, Cley-next-the-Sea and its windmill wraps round

Cley-next-the-Sea windmill rears above the houses: a landmark for miles around.

the end of the chalk ridge. The castle-like tower to the left is an addition by Guy Dawber to Cley Old Hall, a large seventeenth-century flint house with brick dressings and mullioned windows.

Cley, formerly a thriving port, has some fine houses, including one of about 1700 in brick behind a small railing-ed court and The Gables, seven stuccoed bays with sashes and neoclassical door-case. Most odd is Whalebone House with its cornice entirely of knucklebones, which also frame decorative flint panels. The bulk of the village is in render or pebble with brick dressings. I continued south to the church which faces Cley Green and is well away from the sea. This church is quite outstandingly interesting with the early fourteenth-century Decorated work attributed to John Ramsey, the master mason of Norwich Cathedral lady chapel, and his nephew William. The quality of the inventive foliage and tracery carving is superb, as are the ruined transepts, the great west doorway, the traceried parapets and the clerestory with its alternating arched windows and cinquefoiled circular windows. Inside there is medieval woodwork

incongruously tacked on to Victorian pitch-pin pews and six excellent misericords in the chancel.

Out of the church I crossed the green and headed south, turning right at the junction to cross the medieval single-arched Wiveton bridge into Wiveton, whose church has flushwork battlements, early Victorian box pews and fine views from the churchyard across the Glaven to Cley church. I turned right at the Bell Inn and wound through the reclusive pebble-built village to the coast road, then left and along the north pavement to Blakeney church, again well away from the sea end of town. It has a beacon tower at the chancel end that looks like the tall 1435-bell tower's little brother. Another good church, the chancel is Early English with a seven-lancet east window and rib vaults, a contrast in scale after the large airy nave with its soaring hammer-beam roof.

Beyond the church I took the second right to walk down the most attractive main street to the Quay. Many Blakeney cottages have Blakeney Neighbourhood Housing Society plaques, founded by Norah Clogstoun (1886–1963). Most of

the houses and cottages are in pebble or colour-washed render, apart from the brick warehouse buildings, now shops, by the quay. I turned right to the fourteenth-century vaulted brick undercroft which is called the Guildhall, but is more probably part of a merchant's house. I walked west along the Quay, noting the Red House

Whalebone House in Cley-next-the-Sea has a cornice entirely of knucklebones which also frame panels of cobbles.

Blakeney Quay looking west with the eighteenth-century Red House on the right.

which stands on the right, a long low two-storey Georgian façade with Greek Doric porch and central pediment, its name indicating the rarity of wholly brick elevations at this date.

I followed the road past the King's Arms to the crossroads with the A149 and continued straight across through the 'suburbs' of Blakeney. Just before the crest of the hill, I turned left at a footpath sign to follow the path south-east towards Glandford along a scrubby heathy moraine ridge bisecting rich arable country. Beyond New Barn I reached the road and turned right, then left, and right again, to walk back into Glandford, initially at the foot of The Downs, a brackeny continuation of the ridge.

Walk 34

ALONG MELFORD BY THE STOUR

Long Melford and Cavendish, Suffolk. 13½ Miles. July 1990.
OS Pathfinder Sheet TL84/94.

There is now little clue to the medieval wealth of the Stour Valley for the sheep have mostly been replaced by cornfields. Vast fortunes were built on wool and its processing into cloth. For example, Long Melford church was spectacularly financed by a number of wealthy fifteenth-century clothiers whose gifts are commemorated in Gothic-lettered inscriptions all over the exterior. The north aisle has stained-glass figures depicting friends and relatives of the Clopton family of Kentwell Hall, major benefactors to the church, completed by 1496. Long Melford is in every way the centrepiece, but there is much else of interest, including Cavendish and the delightful church at Pentlow.

The countryside, underlain by chalk, is expansive and gently rolling with large golden cornfields. Oaks are now the main hedgerow tree, but some of the woods are disappointing, for example medieval Stanstead Great Wood retains its boundary bank and ditch and a fringe of older trees, but has been replanted with conifers. However, more worthwhile is the mile-long lime avenue leading to Kentwell Hall planted in 1678.

I started from the church at the east end of Glemsford, a long curving village with pockets of older buildings amid modern housing of indifferent quality. The church, much rebuilt between 1447 and 1475, has a flushwork south side and looks north over the valley of the River Glem. I walked south and turned right into Bells Lane, past the former silk factories, once the basis of Glemsford's nineteenth-century expansion, but now housing. I followed the road round and turned right at Tye Green into Cavendish Lane, grateful after a mile for the shade from roadside poplars.

Beyond the large hall and crosswing Blacklands Hall I reached Cavendish. Turning right, I walked along the attractive main street with thatched cottages and hall houses, nearly all colour-washed and plastered. The large green, very picturesque and much photographed, has many good houses, including Manor Cottages, a high-status sixteenth-century house with three jettied gables and heavily moulded mullioned and transomed windows to the jettied outer bays. The church is behind a picturesque L-plan range of pink-washed thatched cottages, rebuilt after a 1971 fire. Visually, they are a perfect foil to the church with its splendid tall west tower whose stair turret is crowned by a skeletal timber bellcote. The clerestory is tall Perpendicular work, graceful, battlemented and surfaced in flushwork panelling.

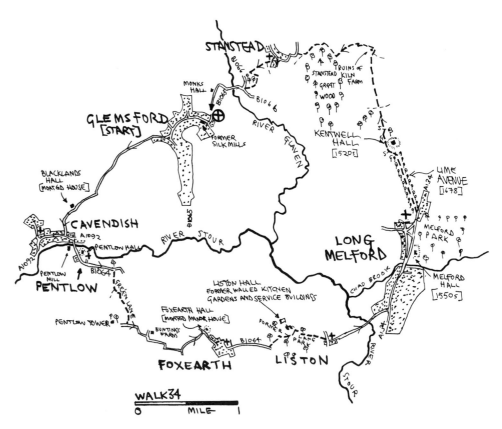

Retracing my steps east down the main street, I turned right opposite the Memorial Hall to cross the River Stour into Essex. On the right, Pentlow Mill has an eight-bayed house in eighteenth- and nineteenth-century brick, and mill buildings in range. I followed the road round to Pentlow church, flint and pebble rubble with an apsidal Norman chancel and a fourteenth-century round tower. The north chapel of about 1600 has crowstep gables and three excellent Jacobean effigies, all sharing one tomb chest. Pentlow Hall (1500), north-west of the church, is a large moated timber-framed hall and crosswing house, altered about 1580.

I continued along the road, turning right opposite a copse into a green lane. Glimpsing Rectory Tower, a polygonal brick tower built in 1858 as a filial memorial by Reverend Bull, I turned left at the road to walk east with pasture on both sides, turning right by Ropers Farm into a minor lane, then left to Foxearth. I turned right at Foxearth Hall, a delightful fifteenth-

century moated hall and crosswing house with compound brick stacks. Past the Foxearth Brewery buildings (1907), now being converted to houses, I turned left to the church which has a fine Perpendicular battlemented north aisle. The rest of the church is Victorian or heavily restored with a tower of 1862 in sombre-black knapped and squared flints with white stone dressings. Inside, the church is superbly fitted and decorated in Victorian medieval style.

From Foxearth church I walked south, noting the old brick seven-bayed vicarage of 1702 with a coved plaster cornice, and the timber-framed *cottage-orné* lodge at the gates. East along the road, I turned left at the footpath sign on to a metalled track. This leads past the service buildings of Liston Hall, a mansion now demolished and its park turned over to arable. The walled kitchen garden and other buildings survive. Out of the 'park' Liston church has an early sixteenth-century mellow brick west tower with crowstep battle-

ments, the rest being in flint and pebble rubble. Continuing east, I crossed the River Stour in its meadows, then the course of the old railway, into Suffolk and Long Melford.

Long Melford lives up to its name, expanding south from the Green along Hall Street for nearly two miles. By the thirteenth century it had a market charter and by 1400 was known as 'Long' Melford. Its wealth was based on cloth, which declined by 1700 only to recover as a local market and industrial centre. Hall Street has a bewilderingly expansive range of high-quality houses, the majority timber-framed, mostly concealed by colour-washed plaster or refronted to bring them up to date. The Bull Inn has reversed this trend and the brick façade has been removed to expose the timber-framing, while others have excellent Georgian fronts, such as Mansel Hall with its Venetian window and sashes, or later refrontings, including the Victorian front to the Gables. Several others have

Long Melford Green looking north with the church tower; to the right, the Holy Trinity Hospital almshouses, founded in 1573.

The Lodges to Melford Hall whose turrets and stacks crowd on the right.

exposed timber-framing, but there are also brick villas and cottages contrasting in scale with industrial buildings such as the nineteenth-century four-storey Old Maltings. The street is wide with occasional grassy areas and trees, all artlessly effective as the street curves gradually north.

I lunched and crossed the Chad Brook to the Green, a large triangular grassy arena bounded on the right by the walls to Melford park, and to the left the 1860 school and rows of good houses. In the distance the rebuilt 1573 Holy Trinity Hospital or almshouses screen the church. Beyond the walls, Melford Hall (National Trust) is based on the house built about 1520 for the Abbot of Bury St Edmunds within his much older deer-park. This park

was enlarged and landscaped between 1580 and 1613, incorporating many oaks from pre-existing hedgerows. The house was enlarged and remodelled for Sir William Cordell between 1554 and 1578 on a courtyard plan. The east range has gone, opening the courtyard to the east, and many windows became sashed in the eighteenth century. The staircase inserted by Thomas

Long Melford. Suffolk's supreme 'Wool Church': its windows seem to go on for ever, its walls sumptuously enriched by 'flushwork'.

Hopper in 1813 is remarkably monumental in scale, sweeping away from the sixteenth-century great hall.

The church, rebuilt between 1460 and 1496, is outstandingly interesting, and the Clopton Chantry is a remarkable survival with much original decoration, if somewhat faded. The church interior is cool and spacious with elegant quatrefoil piers below three tiers of Perpendicular wall panelling, the upper two glazed for clerestory windows. The eastern chapels and the off-centre Lady Chapel are by contrast intimate small-scale spaces. The latter, accessible only from outside the main church, has an ambulatory aisle all round. Outside, the church is nearly all flushwork with a very long nineteen-window clerestory. The 1727 Georgian brick tower is cased in 1903 flint and stone.

From this remarkable church I continued north up High Street and turned left into the lime avenue to Kentwell Hall (Open at various times), a very attractive moated brick mansion of about 1525, built on an E-plan by the Clopton family. Its two ogee-roofed turrets were copied at Melford Hall thirty years later. The footpath skirts west before heading north to Kiln Farm, now reduced to a couple of flint outbuildings. I turned left to follow the remnant of a hedge and skirt Stanstead Great Wood into Stanstead village, partly along the parish boundary. Stanstead Hall is mid-nineteenth century with paired Dutch gables and its barns well converted to houses, except for the lifeless fibre-cement slates. The church is mostly Perpendicular and inside are the Royal Arms of Queen Anne. South of Stanstead church I turned right at the converted barns and skirted Scotchford Wood. Descending to the road I turned right, then left across the River Glem to climb back to Glemsford church.

Walk 35

A LOFTY CASTLE GUARDS THE COLNE

Halstead and the Hedinghams, Essex. 14 Miles. May 1990.
OS Pathfinder Sheets TL63/73, TL83/93.

While not noted for building stone, the boulder clays of this part of Essex contain numerous pebbles, flints and stony formations, some of which can be used for rubble work. The nearby chalk also provided much flint, although better stone was imported for dressings and columns, Hedingham Castle using the renowned Barnack limestone from Northamptonshire. Timber-framing and brick are the normal secular materials, the former usually rendered and often with decorative pargetting in panels. The landscape is an ancient one of narrow winding lanes with scattered farmsteads, originally surrounded by small irregular fields and scattered oak and ash woods. This fertile landscape has suffered extensive hedge-grubbing to make bigger, more economic arable fields for growing fodder beans, oilseed rape, barley and wheat.

I parked in Chapel Street car-park in Halstead and walked uphill along the High Street towards the parish church, away from the River Colne. It is a fine wide street with the plots laid out in the thirteenth century when the market was established, the streets round the church being earlier and less regular. Premaberg House, number 24, is a towering Georgian house, and next to it Chantry House retains fragments of Bartholomew, Lord Bourchier's college of chantry priests, founded in 1412. Opposite, the White Hart, a fifteenth-century hall and cross-wing house, has ornate vinescroll-carved barge-boards. The church, built in flint and pebble rubble with limestone and some chalk-stone dressings, is well set in a churchyard with many chest tombs. Inside, the Bourchier monuments are of great interest. The Bourchiers were a very powerful medieval family, Lord Chancellor Robert fighting at Crécy and dying in the Black Death of 1349. His tomb chest is occupied by effigies of his parents, while to the west his son John, a Knight of the Garter and governor of Flanders, and his wife, lie under a tall canopy, their effigies dating from around 1400.

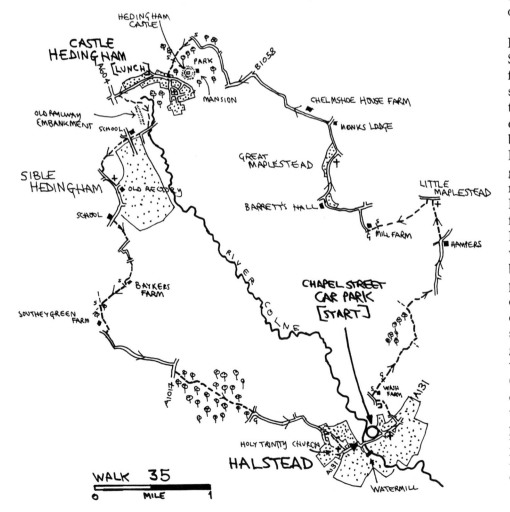

Halstead Mill. In this painted weather-boarded mill spanning the River Colne, the Courtaulds set up a silk works in 1826.

Leaving the churchyard, I walked up Head Street, with more fine houses, and turned left into Mill Chase. I bore right of the mill cottage on to a path behind Tudor-style almshouses and cottages of the 1920s built for the Courtaulds, descendants of sixteenth-century Huguenot refugees who brought weaving and cloth-making to Halstead. At the road I turned right, then right again past a converted barn and Wash Farm, a jettied house with grouped chimney shafts and much exposed timber-framing to the rear. I followed the footpath, partly along the winding remains of old lanes, skirting at one point Fitz John's Grove, an ancient wood shared by three parishes, to reach the road and turn left. At Hampers, a fifteenth-century hall

and jettied crosswing house, I crossed fields to Little Maplestead church.

Little Maplestead church is a rare example of a church with a round nave modelled on the Holy Sepulchre church in Jerusalem. The village and church had been given in 1185 to the Crusader military order of the Knights of St John of Jerusalem, founded in 1092 to protect pilgrims in the Holy Land. This church is difficult to interpret owing to an almost complete rebuild in the 1850s, but the walls could have been twelfth century, altered when the six piers of the nave were built about 1335. Out of the churchyard I turned left by a pond on to a footpath, following a hedge west down a shallow valley. Beyond Mill Farm, a

seventeenth-century lobby-entry T-plan house in pink-washed roughcast, I followed a lane uphill, then left on to a road. Across a stream I passed fifteenth-century Barrett's Hall Farm and, on the left, Barrett's Hall, a yellow-brick-fronted villa of about 1820. Right at the junction, I walked uphill to Great Maplestead, a village with several good pargetted houses and cottages, and even terraces of flint cottages with brick dressings called 'Stone Cottages'.

Opposite, the east apse and tower of Great Maplestead church are Norman, the latter half rebuilt in brick after lightning struck in 1612. The south transept was extended in the early seventeenth century to house the quite extraordinary Deane

A monument to less than healthy filial worship in Great Maplestead church: the Deane monument to Anne and her son Sir Dru, who erected it in 1634, presumably still alive then.

monuments: the one to Anne Deane has her standing in her shroud below a canopy with clouds and angels in relief, with her son Sir Dru lying on his side at her feet who 'here prostrate at her Feete Erects this Monument April ye 14th. 1634'. Opposite, her husband, Sir John, rests on his elbow below a canopy with their children's effigies on a shelf.

Out of the church I continued to the junction and turned left into Monk's Lodge Road, then left to pass Chelmshoe House Farm (about 1730) in red brick with a pedimented Gibbs-surround door-case and an eighteenth-century brick dovecote in its orchard. At the B1058 turned left and then right into Rosemary Lane to skirt the tree belt around Castle Park. I followed the road round and, opposite Yeomans, took a footpath that led to a green lane into Castle Hedingham. At Pye Corner, a good group of houses and cottages, I turned left up Bayleys Hill and entered the Castle grounds (Open Easter to October daily, 10.00 a.m.–17.00 p.m.).

The castle on its motte, built by the De Vere Earls of Oxford, is initially screened, and I saw first the early eighteenth-century service block and mansion. The shorter two-storey service block has a central pediment, while the taller mansion has seven by five bays with a timber modillion eaves cornice. Across the fine Tudor bridge over the moat, the towering keep built in about 1140 has a curiously crumbly top contrasting with the remarkable fine ashlar walls. Inside, the two-storey great hall with its huge diaphragm arch and gallery is a fine space.

The remarkably well-preserved Norman keep of about 1140 at Castle Hedingham from the south.

Castle Hedingham. Typical houses in Church Ponds Lane face the churchyard in the centre of this compact historic town.

From the Castle I walked down Castle Lane into the village, one of the most attractive in Essex with splendidly winding streets lined with good buildings, some timber-framed, some brick and many rendered. Notable are Falcon Square and St James's Street, but finest of all in the centre is the church with its sixteenth-century brick tower. Inside, the church is late Norman with alternating octagonal and cylindrical piers and a soaring early-sixteenth-century double hammer-beam roof. Beyond the richly traceried chancel screen of about 1400, the chancel contains stalls with misericords and the superb black marble-topped tomb chest of John, Earl of Oxford, 1539, and his wife.

I walked west out of Castle Hedingham to the hamlet of Nunnery Street, the long-vanished nunnery having been near Nunnery Farm, a sixteenth- and seventeenth-century pink-washed farmhouse.

Over the river I turned left along the river bank and then southward. Right at the road I soon turned into Christmas Field, skirted a school, crossed the A604 main road and followed the track immediately right of a lodge, ignoring the lane signposted 'Rookwoods Only'.

Reaching the road, I turned left to walk into Sible Hedingham which has a somewhat over-restored but attractively situated church. The Old Rectory behind extensive garden walls is a seven-bay brick house of about 1714 with box sashes and a later Bath-stone Ionic porch. I continued south over the stream, right into School Road and, opposite the school, left on a footpath leading to a lane which wound through Cobbs Fen. Across another road I followed the drive to Bakers Farm, a large sixteenth-century timber-framed hall and crosswing house with four north gables and two massive compound stacks. Beyond a pond I climbed a stile and headed west to the right of a narrow pasture along the valley slope. At a stile I climbed to modern farmbuildings and skirted these to reach the road at Southeygreen Farm, which has a crosswing and a large stack. Left at the road I walked past scattered farmsteads to the junction. Here I turned right, then soon left on to the track through Broak's Wood, keeping bearing steadily southeast.

Reaching the road, I followed it into Halstead, passing Holy Trinity (1843) by George Gilbert Scott and Moffatt in yellow brick with stone dressings: a most unusual and interesting Victorian church. At the river bridge are Dutch-gabled houses, The Causeway, which lead to the spectacular white-painted three-storey weather-boarded mill in which the Courtaulds set up a silk works in 1826.

Walk 36

NO OTHER PALACE IN THE KINGDOM WILL COMPARE

Saffron Walden and Audley End, Essex. 15½ Miles. September 1990. OS Pathfinder Sheet TL43/53.

This walk in the chalky north-west corner of Essex crosses gentle broad hills under immense skies. There are also parks with towering limes and oaks, ranging from the spectacular Audley Park to Debden Park, now ghost-like after its mansion was demolished in 1936. I lunched in Saffron Walden, a remarkably complete historic town with a splendidly amorphous ruined castle keep, an outstanding church, a townscape of superb quality and a seemingly endless number of fine timber-frames as well as many fine Georgian houses. Immediately west is Audley Park, landscaped by Capability Brown in 1762, utilizing and expanding a medieval deer-park and earlier formal gardens. These surround Audley End, a Jacobean mansion of prodigious size built for Thomas Howard, Earl of Suffolk and Lord Treasurer to James I. Much was pulled down in the early eighteenth-century to create a more manageable house, but it is still immense. Pargetted timber-frames, colour-washed render and mellow brick dominate the older buildings, while local flint and some clunch are also used.

I started in Newport, a long village cruelly bisected by the railway which cuts through what was formerly a green. It has a number of good timber-framed houses, including Monks Barn, an outstanding Wealden house with close-studding and an oriel coving carved with the Virgin and angels. The railway makes the green a peaceful backwater and it has the best house in the village: Crown House, its

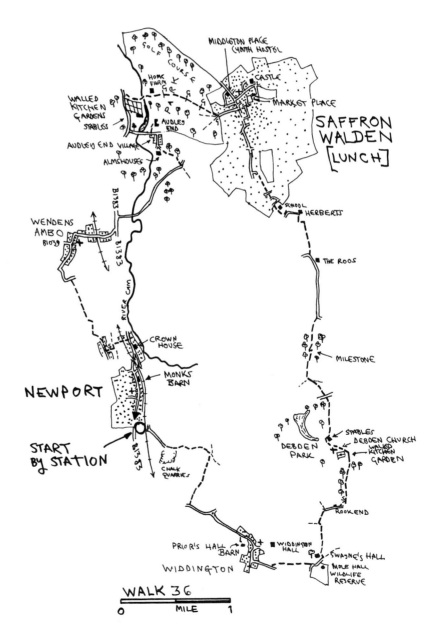

WALK 36

0   MILE   1

1692 front elaborately pargetted with panels of foliage, swags and even a crown projecting from the wall above a grand shell-hood door canopy. The large church, whitewashed inside but curiously lifeless, has a superb and rare late thirteenth-century oak chest with painted figures in the lid. The church is west of a jumble of lanes and a complete contrast to the more ordered main street.

At the station I crossed the railway on the foot-bridge, then walked right along the lane, before bearing left beside Needham Chalk's quarry into a green lane to climb out on to arable lands. As the hedges vanish, I turned right by an electricity pole on to a track to descend to the road by Shiptons Farm. Left towards Widdington, I turned right at the English Heritage sign to Priors Hall Barn, a magnificent medieval eight-bay aisled barn with a crown post roof (Open April to end of September, weekends 10.00 a.m.–6.00 p.m.). At a pretty triangular green I turned left to the heavily restored church beyond the Old Rectory with a Georgian brick front to a medieval house. Back at the Green, I turned left, passing a cottage with green soda bottles built into the flintwork, then left into Cornells Lane. At the second footpath sign on the left, I turned into arable to head diagonally right to an isolated oak tree, then the gap to the right of the woods.

At the road I turned left with the wildlife park on the right. At the end I turned left to skirt the grounds of Swaynes Hall, a large yellow-ochre-washed pargetted house with a massive stack of six-square flues. Behind the house at a footpath post I turned right to follow the hedge north. Past Rook End I bore left across a small field to a stile, then left to follow the track north to Debden and the walled former kitchen gardens, to demolished Debden Park. The church has an octagonal yellow-brick east end (1793) in Gothick style with pretty pinnacles and Coade-stone plaques. The thirteenth-century nave arcades lead to steps in the Gothick east end, which has a ribbed plaster vault and elaborate pendant bosses. This end is quite refined,

delicate and utterly Georgian: not remotely medieval.

West from the churchyard, I turned right at Debden Hall's eighteenth-century stable block and followed a metalled track through remains of parkland. It descended to the road with a glimpse on the left of the park's vast lake. Straight over the road through hedgeless arable, I entered the corner of Howe Wood. In the middle of the wood is an eighteenth-century turnpike milestone which gives the distances to Cambridge, New Market and Debden Hall. The track left the wood and soon reached the road. Beyond The Roos, a seventeenth-century house with barns and a duck pond, I continued north along a track which led to the outskirts of Saffron Walden. I skirted a fenced school playing-field and worked my way through housing estates, eventually emerging on Debden Road.

Turning right into Debden Road, I walked downhill into Saffron Walden, so called from the saffron grown here for use in dyeing and medicines. The market was moved here in 1141 from Newport by Geoffrey de Mandeville who probably also built the castle keep. To explore the town, I turned right off High Street into Gold Street which, besides jettied timber-

framed cottages, has a Georgian house with a high archway to former maltings at the rear. From here I turned right into George Street, then left to weave through the alleys to Market Place. Out of the north-east corner with The Common on the right, I turned left by the rugged flintwork of the Norman castle to walk down Church Street, then right down Museum Street to Castle Street.

I retraced my steps to the very large and stately parish church and entered under the west tower with its elegant crocketted spire. Inside, it is light and airy with large Perpendicular windows and slender piers. It was largely rebuilt between about 1450 and 1525, partly by the Royal master masons Simon Clerk and John Wastell. From here I returned to Church Street and the Sun Inn with its virtuoso display of pargetting and lime-washed timbers, as they would have been originally. Right at High Street, I continued into Bridge Street passing Myddleton Place's Youth Hostel, a superb close-studded and jettied timber-frame with a carved dragon post at the corner. Back uphill, I turned right into Freshwell Street and walked via Park Lane to reach High Street opposite the Cross Keys Hotel, richly framed and jettied. Right into

Gold Street in Saffron Walden: early seventeenth-century timber-framing.

Audley End. The Lion Gate is surmounted by a Coade stone lion with the posture of a pointer, all alert and straight-tailed.

High Street, I turned right on to Abbey Lane past the Almshouses, founded in 1400 but rebuilt in 1834.

At the end of Abbey Lane I went through the gates into Audley Park, turning right and right again on to a path across a field, not down the lime avenue. This path follows the bank of The Slade with views to the left of the Temple of Concord in the main park, then of Audley End itself, and to the right is the north part of the park now a golf-course. At the road past the huge walled gardens that serviced the mansion with fruit, vegetables and flowers, I turned left, soon passing the west front of Audley End seen beyond a cricket match (perhaps) and the lake with the Jacobean brick stables on the left. At the junction I turned left, then into the grounds through Lion Gate. Audley End has recently been very well restored by English Heritage and is well worth going inside. Emerging into daylight it is sobering to realize this is only a fragment of an enormous Jacobean courtyard house.

Back through the arch I turned left, then right past the old post office where I had a cup of tea. I continued between eighteenth-century terraces of one-and-a-half-storey rendered cottages with gabled dormers, then had glimpses of the diamond stacks and Elizabethan brickwork of the College of St Mark, almshouses with two quadrangles and a higher chapel. Past Abbey Farm and right at the road, I followed it to the main road to Newport. Here I turned left, then right into Wendens Ambo. The church with some Roman and Tudor brick has a Norman tower with a thin spire, a 'Hertfordshire Spike', and a short nave and chancel. Inside, a medieval chancel screen, a fifteenth-century pulpit, and rare but faded wall paintings in the chancel are to be seen. I walked past attractive rendered cottages, then left and left again by a K6 telephone kiosk towards Duck Street. I followed the lane round passing several good houses, including Blythburgh House, timber-framed to the rear and pargetted and pink-washed to the front. Left, signposted 'To Rookery Lane', then opposite Norton House, I turned right on to the bridleway south back to Newport.

Audley End's eighteenth-century estate village has rows of pretty rendered one-and-a-half storeyed cottages facing each other across the street.

In Middle England

BUCKINGHAMSHIRE, BEDFORDSHIRE AND CAMBRIDGESHIRE

As one who long in populous city pent,
Where houses thick and sewers annoy the air,
Forth issuing on a summer's morn to breathe
Among the pleasant villages and farms
Adjoined, from each thing met conceives delight.
John Milton

Walk 37

HOW DELIGHTFUL ARE THY TEMPLES

Stowe and Buckingham, Buckinghamshire. 13 Miles. April 1990.
OS Pathfinder Sheet SP63/73.

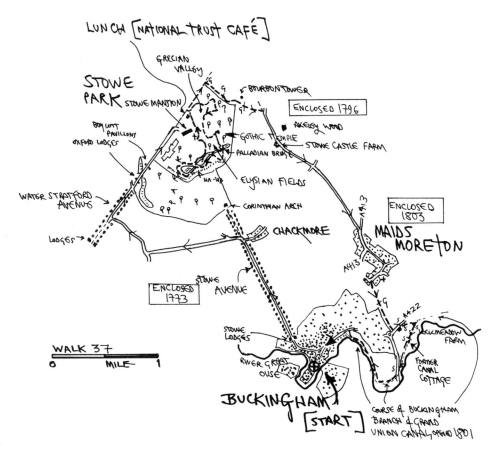

Stowe Landscape Gardens are a remarkable survival of that peculiarly English genre, the picturesque naturalistic landscape park, a form that was widely imitated all over eighteenth-century Europe and indeed North America. Stowe is of European importance and all the more fascinating for the evidence of its evolution from a formal layout to the romantic naturalism we see today through adaptation, remodelling and blurring of woodland edges. The gardens to the south and west of the mansion are more open with large irregular-shaped lakes, while the east and south-east parts have secluded valleys as their focus, the Elysian Fields and the Grecian Valley. These Greek names reflect the cultural milieu of the early eighteenth century when the classics were highly revered and the Augustan and Georgian periods were seen as revivals of Ancient Greek and Roman culture. The landscape park is focused on a miraculously large surviving number of garden buildings, almost all in classical style and many of temple form. With a deep blue sky and the conifers framing some of the temples the visitor almost feels himself transported to a Roman glade.

The Temples arrived at Stowe in the sixteenth century as sheep farmers but soon diversified into wool (and also marriage to heiresses). Government posts, then an avenue to enrichment, followed and, in 1676, Sir Richard Temple built a red-brick house that remains the core of the present Stowe mansion. The development of the landscape park and the house relate to periods when his son – also

Richard, made Viscount Cobham in 1718, and a prominent Whig politician – was out of power and favour. Much of the remainder of this task was undertaken by Richard, Earl Temple, Cobham's nephew who inherited the estate. Further work was done by the Marquis and then Duke of Buckingham. The gardens were landscaped by Charles Bridgeman, William Kent, and also 'Capability Brown' to whom

their present appearance owe much. The best architects of the day were used for the garden buildings, including Vanbrugh, Gibbs and Kent, while the mansion with its tremendously long south front took its present form under Earl Temple in the 1770s. Bankruptcy in the 1840s led to the great sale of the household contents and the position never really improved until Stowe School was founded in 1923. The

School struggled with an overwhelming legacy of historic buildings until, in 1989, the National Trust received the landscape gardens. I timed the walk to coincide with the school holidays when the grounds are open, and followed the route in the National Trust guide.

I started the walk in Buckingham, a compact town with many fine historic buildings of Georgian appearance. For years the town was in decay and has only revived relatively recently with the arrival of the private University of Buckingham and nearby Milton Keynes. The parish church on the old castle site has an eighteenth-century core, but now is very efficiently Gothic. I walked out of Buckingham down West Street past Castle House whose early eighteenth-century sashed façade conceals large Tudor and Jacobean wings. Beyond the former barracks of the Yeomanry militia I turned right onto Stowe Avenue. This is flanked by suburban houses up to a pair of pretty lodges. Beyond, the Grand Avenue runs arrow-straight towards Stowe, saved from housing by Clough Williams-Ellis who bought it. The elms have gone and the avenue has been replanted with beeches and horse chestnuts. The avenue undulates and from the first crest I saw the Corinthian Arch and, framed by it, the portico of the mansion itself a mile away. At the bend I turned briefly into Chackmore before heading west, leaving the main road. At a T-junction I turned right and soon passed Boycott Farm, an eighteenth-century stone house with hipped dormers and Victorian sashes on the site of a deserted medieval village.

At the next junction I turned right into Oxford Avenue where the limes and oaks survive well. This follows the course of a Roman road and heads straight for the park. Across the road I passed through the Oxford Lodges, in fact gate-piers by Kent relocated here with the addition of pavilions in 1760. Through these the drive crosses the Oxford Bridge (1761) and passes between the Boycott Pavilions (1728) by Gibbs, with their French domes (1758) by Giambattista Borra. The drive

Stowe Park: the approach to the mansion looking north-east from the 1761 bridge over the Oxford Water to the Boycott Pavilions.

then continues, flanked by beech and lime avenues, past the school campus, mercifully hidden mostly by trees. It then passes across the great north front of the mansion with its quadrant colonnades either side to the car-park where tickets can be bought or cards shown. The National Trust route takes in all the significant temples, columns, arches and other garden buildings in an admirably complete

Stowe Park: the Queen's Temple. This eighteenth-century garden temple is now a music room for Stowe School.

way: starting in the Grecian Valley, then heading down the east side of the Elysian Fields, across the Palladian Bridge to walk along the south side of the lakes. The route then continues along the north side of the lake to return up the west side of the Elysian Fields. Just beyond the round Temple of Ancient Virtue concealed in trees and bushes is the medieval parish church of the village cleared away by the Temples. Inside is a poignant tomb to Martha Penyston who died aged twenty-five in 1619: she lies on the tomb chest and at her feet is an infant daughter's effigy. The route finishes at the Temple of Concord and Victory which is in parlous condition, its plaster cornices and entablatures decayed and the side walls rebuilt in Fletton bricks. Behind the temple is the cafeteria where I had a snack lunch. It would be invidious to pick out any of the garden buildings, for the ensemble is absolutely stunning and I cannot agree with Horace Walpole who in the 1750s called them an 'Albano glut of Buildings . . . let them be ever so much Condemned'. A tour of these remarkable gardens is the most exciting architectural experience.

Back at the car-park, I continued north-east with a decayed gazebo and the Wolfe Obelisk (1759) sitting amid the sheep-cropped pastures. Beyond the end of the park I turned right to cross a field and, beyond an avenue of red oaks, skirted a copse to head south-east, initially aiming for a granite obelisk (1864). I passed the Bourbon Tower, originally a gamekeeper's cottage but given an earthwork surround and octagonal turret in 1845.

Reaching the road past some spectacular ridge and furrow I walked south with Akeley Wood and its lodge on the left, a half-timbered much gabled mansion by George Devey of the 1860s, extended by Sir Ernest George in 1911. On the right is the quite extraordinary Stowe Castle, a three-sided battlemented castle with turrets, open to the east with a lean-to farmhouse within, and built in the eighteenth century as an eyecatcher for Stowe. I continued along the road which dates

Stowe Park: the Gothic Temple of 1741 by James Gibbs in rust-brown ironstone. It has been restored and converted into a remarkable holiday home by the Landmark Trust.

Buckingham's Old Gaol, recently carefully restored, was built by Lord Cobham of Stowe in 1748 because the summer assizes had nowhere to hold miscreants!

from the 1801 enclosure into Maids Moreton, so called after the Peover sisters who built the church in the mid-fifteenth century. Past Upper Farm, with 1624 on the stone stack, I continued straight on down Main Street which has a number of thatched late-timber-framed cottages and a school dated 1854. At the end I turned right into Church Street and passed Maids Moreton Hall, a late nineteenth-century pile of little distinction. The Church, although aisleless, is a superb Perpendicular example with fan-vaulted porch, west doorway canopy and tower. Inside are the original chancel screen, high-quality sedilia, a dole cupboard and a near-complete set of painted and incised consecration crosses. Outside, the west tower has most unusual belfry openings and the church is one of the finest in the county. I walked west and then left to the A422 Stratford Road.

I turned left and, beyond Lockmeadow Farm, descended to the line of the Buckingham Branch of the Grand Union Canal which was opened in 1801. Now long abandoned, its course is marked by three or four trees and the public footpath along the site of the tow path. The path then skirts a surviving canal cottage and follows the canal ditch west to cross the bypass and head for Buckingham. I followed the riverside walk beside the Great Ouse until beyond the sports field where I returned to the road and walked into Buckingham, passing the market place and the Old Gaol, a Gothick 'castle' of the 1740s, and the imposing Town Hall of the 1770s surmounted by the swan of Buckinghamshire.

Walk 38

WALLS OF CLAY

The Witchert Country, Buckinghamshire. 17 Miles. October 1989.
OS Pathfinder Sheets SP60/70, SP61/71.

In a belt west of Aylesbury are a number of villages whose cottages have rendered walls. These are mostly built in 'witchert', Buckinghamshire's version of the cob or earth-wall construction more usually associated with Devon and Dorset. Still used until the 1920s, witchert is a corruption of 'white earth' which roughly describes the lime-rich sub-soil. Placed in heaps alongside a plinth wall of local fieldstone, it was thoroughly soaked, mixed with chopped straw and laid in 'raises' or 'berries' about 18in high. As each layer dried a further one was smacked on top until the required height was reached, doors, windows and floors being built in as needed. The surface was then dressed smooth by a sharpened spade. Provided the tops are protected from the weather a witchert wall will last for centuries, and there are many seventeenth-century houses in the witchert villages. Witchert was used for dwellings, farm-buildings, boundary walls and even chapels. Houses were usually rendered, but many outbuildings and walls were not, so these can be examined closely. The walls, often over 6ft high, curve and swoop to give a sense of enclosure and intimacy.

I started the walk in Stone, a parish whose open fields were enclosed in 1777 and whose church has a Norman font vigorously carved with men fighting animals. I walked east along the main road past the pantiled village hall by Clough Williams Ellis, and turned left on to a drive by a small witchert thatched cottage on its right, a survivor of three tiny houses. Further down is Woodspeen, a seventeenth-century witchert house. Beyond a modern estate and the hamlet of Upper

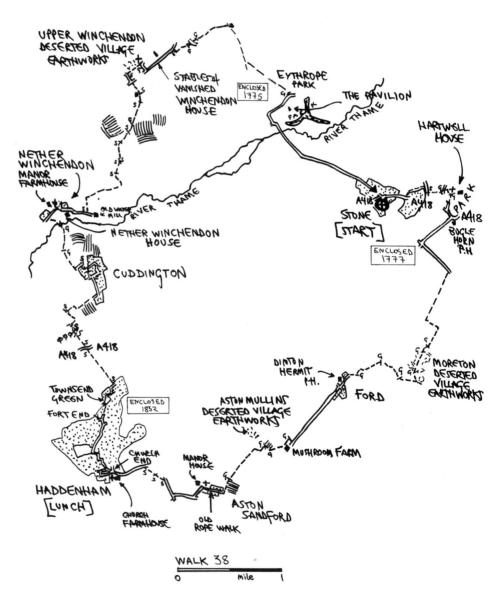

WALK 38

0   mile   1

Hartwell, I crossed a field to walk alongside a mid-nineteenth-century wall in large, somewhat friable-looking Portland limestone blocks. This surrounds part of the grounds of Hartwell House and the track skirts the Old Rectory, partly of 1582 but now Georgian in appearance. Opposite, I went through gates in the park wall to Henry Keene's octagonal Gothick church (1755), now roofless, with Hartwell House beyond, a superb Jacobean mansion, recast in the eighteenth century by Keene and now a country-house hotel, beautifully restored by local architect Eric Throssell. Back out of the gate past the fine stables, I continued alongside the park walls, inset with ammonites or 'bugle horns' and dated 1855, to turn right at the Bugle Horn Inn.

I walked along the Portway and then left at The Firs (about 1860) in polychrome brick, the wing of an intended school, while opposite limestone walls are dated 1862. Turning right at the Old School House I headed south, now on Swan's Way, a Buckinghamshire County Council waymarked bridlepath. Following this, I crossed the clear earthworks of the deserted medieval village of Moreton, now permanent pasture, walking up the holloway of the main street to the moated site beyond which some farm-buildings remain, although the 1767 barn has collapsed.

Leaving Swan's Way and heading northwest and west, I passed Moat Farm, a medieval hall house, into Ford. I had a refreshment at the Dinton Hermit Inn, named after John Bigg, a local hermit, once secretary to the regicide Simon Mayne of Dinton Hall who had signed Charles I's death warrant. Beyond the crossroads, I passed witchert cottages, the former Strict Baptist Chapel – part 1712 witchert part 1852 chequer brick – and, on the right, Manor Farm, a good early eighteenth-century house.

Where the lane becomes unfenced I was in the former manor of Aston Mullins whose village was cleared for sheep in the fifteenth century. Weaving round the mushroom farm sheds I crossed the Great

Ground, now subdivided but originally a field of 140 acres. Traces of ridge and furrow indicate the former village open fields, last ploughed 400 years ago. I continued alongside the hedge into Aston Sandford, again passing through ridge and furrow. On the left beyond a thatched barn is a long pantiled building which was a ropewalk. The church is notable for the thirteenth-century stained glass figure of Christ. The eighteenth-century medieval

Manor House has a large free Tudor-style south block by Gilbert Scott of 1867.

Haddenham is the witchert country's capital: all around are high boundary walls, outbuildings, cottages, houses and villas in the material. This long, straggling polyfocal village was a settlement of smaller freeholders who farmed the open fields in common until 1832. Along Aston Road is Grenville Manor, timber-framed but stone fronted of 1569; on the left is Church

Farmhouse, a fifteenth-century timber-framed wealden hall house. The church is marvellously situated on the south side of Church End green, a space surrounded by houses of interest and a witchert wall on the north side. The church has a dignified Early English tower. Inside, note the Norman font with two dragons chasing their tails, the fifteenth-century screens, the elegant nave arcades, the bench ends including the one with a plough carved on it, and the medieval glass in the north-east chapel.

There are several pubs serving meals. After lunch, I continued north up Gibson Lane, then the Croft, before turning left down a path flanked by witchert walls, and then right at the King's Head up High Street. More fine buildings: difficult to select, but note the witchert Methodist Church (1822); Oak Beam Cottage, number 22, with exposed medieval cruck trusses; and Dove House, number 4, timber-framed with massive stone stacks, diagonal brick flues and a circular dovecote in the garden. At Fort End I crossed into Fern Lane and, passing the Old Brewery

Capital of the witchert country: Haddenham's Church End.

Witchert walls wind along a footpath off Flint Street in Haddenham.

Seventeenth-century timber-framed cottages in Nether Winchendon.

(1846), walked along the path between witchert walls to emerge at Townsend Green. Along Rudd's Lane, left into Rosemary Lane, and left on to a footpath out of the village by Cobwebs with ornate Tudor-style chimney stacks grafted on to a seventeenth-century witchert cottage in 1921.

Across the A418 and into Cuddington I passed ridge and furrow in the landscaped grounds of the witchert villa Dadbrook House (about 1850). Cuddington has an attractive church and many witchert buildings; crucks like The Pitchings, Spurt Street; and stone houses, including Tyringham Hall, Lower Church Street (1609), with mullioned and transomed windows, the surviving wing of a major mansion. Heading down Tibby's Lane, I skirted converted witchert farm-buildings looking like overblown bungalows, right down the road. Then I crossed the River

Where Wesley first preached after his ordination: Upper Winchendon church looking westward to the deserted village earthworks and the Vale beyond.

Thame and into Lower Winchendon, a scattered village with mainly timber-framed houses. The church is outstanding, with box pews, a three-decker pulpit and squire's pew and a west gallery. I walked east past the gates to Nether Winchendon House, an open courtyard house. The south range incorporates a medieval hall and tudor solar wing, all much altered around 1800 in Gothic style by the owner Scrope Bernard, an amateur architect. Philip Tilden added more this century, including ornate Tudor-style chimneys.

Just before Winchendon Mill I turned left into a ploughed field, following the 'CW' waymarks of a County Council Cir-

cular Walk. Heading across Winchendon Hill, I descended into a valley flanked by medieval strip lynchets and with superb ridge and furrow, on the valley floor. In Upper Winchendon I walked up the limes avenue to the church. On the left are the earthworks of another village deserted by 1700 and, most spectacularly, the remains of fish-ponds. The mainly twelfth-century church with everything diligently labelled has an unspoilt whitewashed interior retaining much of its medieval woodwork, including a chancel screen, pews and best of all the fourteenth-century pulpit, three-sided and carved from a single piece of timber.

South of Upper Winchendon church is

the former barn and walled kitchen gardens of the vanished eighteenth-century mansion of the Whartons, whose stables only survive. Turning through Eythrope Park Farm to a footpath which rejoins the Swan's Way by a Lodge, I descended into Eythrope Park, now mostly ploughed. I was now in Rothschild country, for the route goes close to Eythrope's service buildings: the Homestead, now dwellings, has buff timber-framing and roughcast, brick and conical-roofed turrets, while the Pavilion (1883) itself is largely unseen. Bridge Lodge by George Devey is a fine composition, a cross between a Swiss chalet and an Elizabethan cottage. Up the road and I was back in Stone.

Walk 39

THE RIVER GREAT OUSE, SLOW-WINDING THROUGH A LEVEL PLAIN

Around Olney, Buckinghamshire. 12 Miles. October 1989.
OS Pathfinder Sheet SP85/95.

The River Great Ouse meanders lazily through the gentle rolling north Buckinghamshire countryside, cutting low cliffs at the edges of its flood plain. It is rich agricultural country with much arable but, mercifully, also areas of pasture. Because of this, ridge and furrow is relatively scarce. The field patterns are mostly late eighteenth and early nineteenth century, Olney parish being enclosed in 1767, Cold Brayfield in 1801 and Newton Blossomville in 1810. In this former elm country there are few hedgerow trees except for occasional ashes, a deeply regrettable result of the ravages of Dutch elm disease. Yet in Cold Brayfield parish, the contrast is marked, for here the 1801 enclosure favoured oaks which mostly survive.

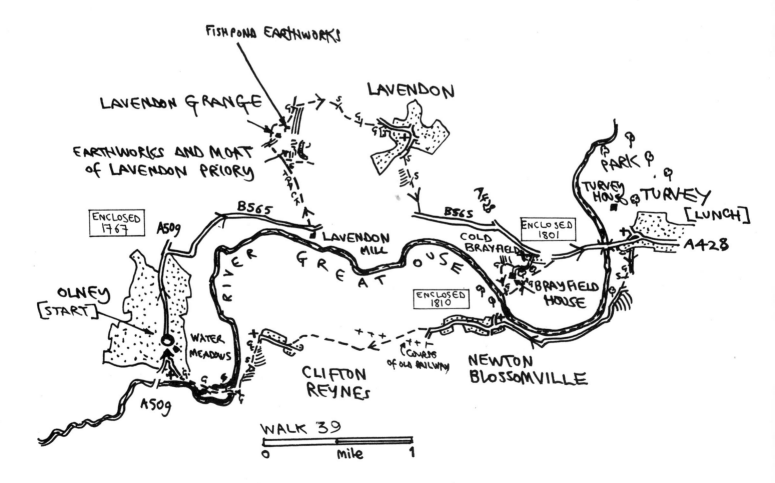

I set off from the market place in Olney, at the heart of this most attractive small stone-built town. Olney has an architectural homogeneity accidentally caused by a disastrous fire in 1786; most of its best buildings belong to after this and before 1850, although a few pre-date the fire, including on the south side of Market Place the proud early-eighteenth-century red-brick house in which the depressive poet William Cowper lived from 1767 until 1786. Now the Cowper and Newton Museum, this building is refreshingly unmodernized and exactly how a country museum should be. John Newton was curate of Olney from 1764 to 1780, a prodigious preacher and author, with Cowper, of hundreds of hymns called The Olney Hymns. His pulpit survives (as an exhibit) in the parish church – Newton's chequered career as a slave-trader gave him a breadth of experience and appeal that packed his church. The gardens of the Vicarage (1767) and Cowper's house interconnected, and the poet's summerhouse survives.

The town plan is interesting with the earlier part between the river and the market-place more irregular in plan, while the planned borough runs north as a single wide street flanked by long narrow burgage plots and parallel back lanes: Olney is recorded as a borough by 1237. The church, brutally over-restored inside, is notable for its magnificent fourteenth-century spire with four tiers of lucarnes which dominates both the town in a disembodied way and the surrounding countryside.

Walking north up High Street, the stone houses, mostly continuous, present a dignified classical harmony. Note particularly number 6 with a recessed centre and Ionic pilasters; Olney House, number 15 with rusticated ground storey and Venetian windows; number 23 with eighteenth-century tripartite sashes; number 56, a 1920s façade inscribed 'Bucks Lace Industry', a reminder of an important former industry; and Orchard House, number 69, given art nouveau features by A. E. Anderson in 1904. At the north end of town is a small artisan suburb of about

Provincial grandeur: Venetian windows and rustication on one of the best houses along High Street (north) in Olney.

1900 built to service a large boot and shoe factory of about 1895, now Bumpus Haldane and Maxwell, a many-gabled sub-Queen Anne building and an outlier of Northamptonshire's huge nineteenth-century boot and shoe industry.

Beyond the old railway embankment, I walked to Lavendon Grange where there are good, if unclear, monastic earthworks: a moat and fish-ponds of a Premonstratensian house founded in the twelfth century; a small stone country house of about 1620;

a seventeenth-century farmhouse; and a complex of barns and coach-house converted to a house. The paths into Lavendon village follow the line of the former route from Warrington. A plaque on Lavendon churchyard wall commemorates the Jarrow Hunger marchers who passed through the village *en route* for London in 1936. The church itself has an Anglo-Saxon tower and nave and a good south porch in local Middle Jurassic limestone with orange-brown Northamptonshire ironstone dressings. The village is mostly limestone but disappointing. On the footpath off Olney Road I saw ridge and furrow and stone-pits to the right.

Cold Brayfield has a long stone terrace of early nineteenth-century estate cottages with double-fronted sash windows, other estate cottages and a small parish church. Within a well-wooded park,

Brayfield House is a most attractive Regency villa-style two-storey country house with a nine-bay south front having a verandah with step-through sashes and a central bay with a pedimented third storey. Back up from the river I walked into Turvey in Bedfordshire. On the left Turvey House peered out from its parkland, a Nash-like palace with Giant Corinthian columns and pilasters flanking end pavilions and centre bay, a truly massive entablature and an attic storey. It is said to date from 1794 but looks more 1830.

Across the river bridge, partly medieval but mostly about 1800, into Turvey, I lunched at the Three Fishes which has flood-marker plaques of 1797, 1823 and 1947, all well above the pavement. The pub has a superb Jacobean porch dated 1624. Turvey has many fine buildings and a general air of Victorian estate housing: old

houses have nineteenth-century decorative barge-boards and bracket eaves. Holmwood House is particularly striking with a sententious tag in the barge-boards, 'Except The Lord Build The House Their Labour Is But Lost That Build It' and, architecturally, a High Victorian confection. Turvey Abbey to the east is a refreshing jumble of simpler verities a range of gables, later box sashes and imported balustrades from Easton Maudit in Northamptonshire.

To the west, the church is on the north side of a pleasant triangular green with nineteenth-century estate cottages curving away south-east and the gate lodge to Turvey House on the west. The heavily restored church is richly rewarding with a quite outstanding collection of Mordaunt family monuments ranging from 1506 to 1601. Most striking is that to the second

Regency repose: Cold Brayfield House whose park runs down to the River Great Ouse.

A moral writ large: the Higgins family mausoleum in Turvey churchyard built in Jacobean style with pinnacles and lettered balustrade.

Lord Mordaunt, raised above his two wives on a straw mat intermittently supported on three short columns: possible in stone, of course, but curiously surreal. In the churchyard the Higgins mausoleum of about 1847 is a square brick structure with pinnacles and a Castle Ashby balustrade.

Out of Turvey I followed the south bank of the river where the road is above a tree-lined 20ft cliff for some distance into Newton Blossomville, mainly a limestone village with a pleasant small stone school of 1822 paid for, the plaque says, by Rev. Joseph Goode, the curate. The church,

near the river, is very attractive with some good curvilinear Decorated tracery, a Tottenhoe stone font and a narrow thirteenth-century nave with a surviving lancet window in the porch. Across fields to the very small village of Clifton Reynes, with a very fine church renowned for its oak effigies of about 1300, a rare survival, but also interesting old glass, an excellent font and good nave arcades. The Old Rectory to the south is a Georgian enlargement of a seventeenth-century building with marvellous views from the ridge over towards Olney.

The path through the pastures has ridge

and furrow which stops at the cliff edge. I then dropped down amid the hawthorn scrub to cross the river, and walked west across flat pastures in the valley bottom. At Olney the Mill House is of two periods, an early nineteenth-century tripartite sashed rear block and a west front block of much greater elaboration: late eighteenth century of five bays and three storeys, architraved sashes and a nice door-case with a Doric broken pediment. I visited the church and walked back to the Market Square, noting more fine Georgian and early-nineteenth-century stone houses.

Walk 40

A GRAND AVENUE TO A GRAND MANSION

Wimpole, Cambridgeshire. 12½ Miles. May 1990.
OS Pathfinder Sheets TL24/34, TL25/35.

Around the villages in this undulating chalk land overlaid by rich boulder clay laps a tide of almost hedgeless arable: a carpet of fodder beans, rape, barley and wheat; pasture only remaining as small closes immediately around the villages. This is not flat Cambridgeshire, for an east-west ridge of chalk rises over 40m above the villages on the walk. Along this ridge runs the Mare Way, an ancient track much utilized as a parish boundary, but the focus of this walk is undoubtedly Wimpole Hall in its great park and a barrier to the relentless march of the plough.

Before recent Dutch elm disease attack, Wimpole imposed itself on the surrounding countryside by running a spectacular double elm avenue southward from the Hall across country for 2½ miles in about 1720. It was never a drive, solely a vista and a remarkable one at that. The National Trust are slowly replanting it as a double lime avenue, but it will be years before it makes much sense in the landscape. The Chicheley family's Hall (about 1640) survives as the core of the centre block. Wings were added by 1711, and the Hall was much altered by Edward, Lord Harley around 1720. Harley used James Gibbs, the architect of St Martins-in-the-Fields in London and he was responsible for the splendid chapel with its outstanding *trompe-l'oeil* paintings by James Thornhill. In 1741 Harley sold Wimpole to Philip Yorke, Lord Chancellor Hardwicke, and the house rapidly assumed much of its present appearance under the architect Henry Flitcroft. His son employed the great Sir John Soane to remodel the Library, install the plunge bath and remodel part of the house for the *tour de force* Yellow Drawing Room, (1791–94). In 1840–42 Kendall was employed to remodel parts of the house and build the 1851 stables in a restrained Baroque style.

The mansion sits in parkland which descends broadly from north-west to south-east with the highest and most hilly parts west of the house. The parkland turf, grazed by sheep and cattle, lies like a carpet over village earthworks and ridge and furrow. The parkland expanded from a small area around the house to its present

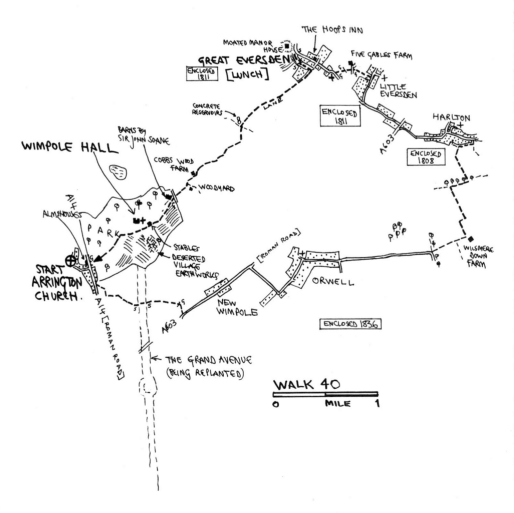

a period of expansion were demolished and the arcades bricked up around 1600 when the population declined. The village migrated to Ermine Street where the best buildings are found, including the Hardwicke Arms Hotel of two eighteenth-century builds. I walked south, past this, and turned left on to a footpath through arable, signposted to New Wimpole, which crossed the currently vestigial Wimpole Avenue, giving views of the Hall south front. Past Cambridge Road Farm the path followed its access track, reaching the Cambridge Road, like Ermine Street on the course of a Roman road. I turned left and walked through New Wimpole, in fact mostly paired gault-brick estate cottages built in the 1840s in a free Tudor style. Gault brick shades from grey to yellow and was locally produced in the nineteenth century, supplanting red brick for most uses. The villages along the route combine colour-washed render with red brick for pre-1800 houses and yellow gault-brick for post-1800 houses, all roofed in either thatch, plain clay tiles or, in the nineteenth century, slates. New Wimpole was built for estate workers and was placed well outside the Park, a belated replacement for the original village cleared in the seventeenth century.

Out of New Wimpole I followed the main road and then turned right to walk into Orwell down the splendidly named Hurdleditch Road. This led into Town Green Road. The green shown on the 1837 enclosure map has been built over and the ugly grocery shop occupies part of it, the timber-framed house with a jettied crosswing and the whitewashed thatched cottage behind being its former east edge. Lordship Close, modern houses grouped round and echoing the gault-brick former school of 1883, occupies the site of a former motte or castle. The church is at the junction and has a chancel which was rebuilt in 1398 by the then rector, with a fine wagon roof with ornate bosses and shields at the intersections and misericords to the choir stalls. The interior is whitewashed with quatrefoil-plan piers.

I walked east down High Street, a mix

Pedimented excellence: Wimpole's parish church of 1749 by Henry Flitcroft is very much subordinate to the great house and full of fine family monuments.

600 acres, absorbing the villages and cultivated open fields of the parish of Wimpole and probably a settlement called Ratford. It was originally a formal layout around the house, but this was extended and a series of axial avenues were laid out by Charles Bridgeman in the 1720s. In the 1760s the ubiquitous Capability Brown was employed and he naturalized the park considerably, with more being done by Humphry Repton in the early 1800s.

I parked near Arrington church which is a good example of village history reflected in stone: the aisles added around 1300 in

of plastered cottages with thatched roofs and slated gault-brick houses and cottages. Number 30 is sixteenth century with a crosswing, and is thatched and colour-washed with a thatched cob garden wall. Out of the village I continued east along Orwell Road between arable lands for a mile. At the end I carried straight on through a shelter belt on to a metalled farm road. At Wilsmere Down Farm, a house and model farmyard of about 1800, built soon after Barrington parish was enclosed in 1796, I turned left to follow the path uphill, eventually turning right to walk parallel to a tree belt along Mare Way. Then I turned left at a footpath sign to descend into Harlton, an attractive village with the church tucked away behind the main street. I turned right into Coach Drive to visit the church, noting the Old Rectory of 1843 in Regency style with an Ionic porch and sash windows. The church interior is whitewashed with elegant nave arcades of the later fourteenth century, no clerestory and tall aisle windows. The plain leaded windows combine to echo the cool interiors of a Sanraedam painting. The chancel screen in clunch is rare and the elaborate reredos has its thirteen niches filled by modern figures. Against the nave south wall and currently undergoing restoration is the enormous Fryer monument (about 1631), coloured and in alabaster, of a high coffered arch carried by a male and a mourning female caryatid and four figures: Sir Henry and his parents kneel, while his wife Mary reclines below on her elbow.

I walked west, passing a painted clunch

Wimpole Hall's brick and stone beyond the forecourt piers and railings.

ashlar house with a slate roof on the right, crossed the Cambridge Road and walked into Little Eversden, turning right into High Street and right again into Church Lane to the church, which has a good timber-framed north porch. Back along High Street I turned right beyond Rectory Farm on to a footpath which crossed a lane by Five Gables Farm, a fifteenth-century hall house with a superior crosswing of the seventeenth century having close-studded framing and three oriel windows. I continued on footpaths to Great Eversden church in its stone-walled churchyard surrounded by horse chestnuts. The aisleless

Kendall's Stables at Wimpole of 1851 in an elegant and restrained Baroque style are in a fiery red brick, only partially restrained by the stone dressings.

church is all of a piece, having been completely rebuilt after it had been struck by lightning in 1466, while the crumbling porch is dated 1636. Opposite the church the Homestead is sixteenth century with a jettied upper floor and, to the north-west of the church, Church Farm has a big fifteenth-century weather-boarded aisled barn.

I lunched at the Hoops pub and continued along the main street to Manor Farm, a hall and crosswing house set in a moat and given an eighteenth-century front with fluted pilastered door-case, sashes and a modillion eaved cornice. I returned parallel to the road across a ridge and furrowed pasture and a trackway to Wimpole Road, where I turned right. The village straggles south-west along the lane

before the track climbs the chalk ridge. At the crest it meets Mare Way by two circular concrete reservoir tanks, crosses it and descends to Wimpole to reach the road at Park Farm. This has a Tudor style-estate farmhouse (1860) and behind it thatched barns apparently designed by Sir John Soane. South of this, I entered the Park via a kissing-gate and walked across ridge and furrow towards Kendall's stable block. I visited Wimpole Hall and the Home Farm, had tea, and continued west through the Park on the Harcamlow Way, which leads to the fine west gates. Opposite the gates are Almshouses by Kendall built in 1846, with shaped gables to the wings and porch in late Elizabethan style. Out of the gates I turned left, then right, back to Arrington church.

Walk 41

STEEPLES ALONG THE GREAT OUSE

St Ives, Cambridgeshire, née Huntingdonshire. 7 Miles. May 1990.
OS Pathfinder Sheet TL27/37.

St Ives is a classic planned medieval town. Around 1110 the owners of the manor of Slepe, the abbots of Ramsey, obtained a charter granting a fair for Easter week on the ground between their church at Slepe and their new bridge over the Great Ouse, and here they laid out their town. The present All Saints parish church is on the site of this church and the memorable bridge with its chapel, a replacement (about 1415) for the original bridge. The town obtained its name from the bones of St Ivo which had been obtained in the eleventh century, and the fair was a runaway success, rapidly becoming one of the four most important in England. Goods travelled up the Ouse from all over England and Europe as the fair sprawled over surrounding fields; the Abbots had made a sound investment. The walk route is never far from the River Great Ouse with church-yards remarkably close to the river. There are also superb river meadows rich in varieties of grasses and dusted with buttercups when I walked them.

Parking in Houghton at the Green, in fact grassless with a Gothick village pump and a thatched shelter, I looked north to the now anonymous fifteenth-century former George and Dragon Inn, its left-hand crosswing with exposed timber-framing and the hall range with a big lateral stack added in the sixteenth century. I walked

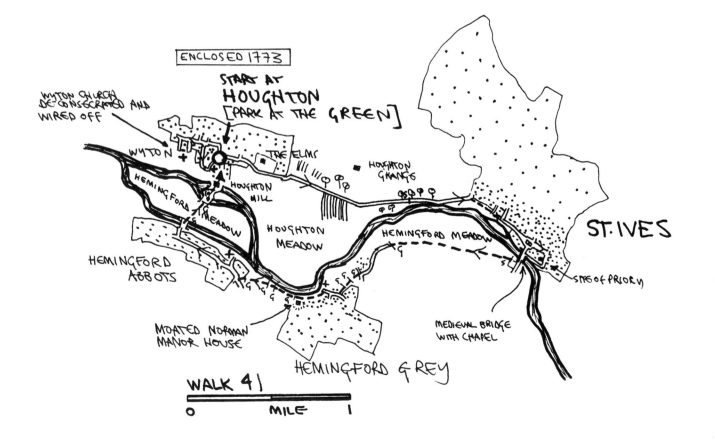

west down Huntingdon Road past Fern-leigh with its mansard roof and 'tumbled-in' gable brickwork, then past thatched and colour-washed cottages. Many later houses are in local yellow gault brick. Beyond the jettied Three Jolly Butchers Inn, dated 1622 on its central chimney, I was in Wyton. Here are more yeoman houses, including jettied and thatched Magdalene House and Stuart House (1648), with a jettied and gabled room projecting over the entrance. Inter-spersed are humbler one- and two-bay thatched cottages, many with 'Norfolk' casements sliding sideways, a particular feature of East Anglia and Yorkshire where unsurprisingly they are called 'Yorkshire sashes'.

Beyond Stuart House I turned left down Rectory Lane, hoping to visit Wyton church, but this has been closed and sold into private hands, securely cut off with barbed wire within its unkempt former churchyard and its fittings dispersed. I returned to Huntingdon Road via Church Walk and retraced my steps as far as Green Lane where I turned right. This passes the school and becomes a footpath curving east to join Chapel Lane. I visited the parish church which has a fine tower, square with an octagonal bellchamber below a fine spire with two tiers of lucarnes. Inside, the north nave arcade is somewhat let down by the mean brick aisle of 1871. Opposite, the former United Reformed Chapel (1840) with modillioned eaves, pediment gables and porch is now a residential centre. Back at the green I walked east down Thicket Road, and out past the gault-brick Elms, a mansion of 1868, set in virtually intact Victorian land-scaped grounds.

I continued along the road which jinks across a stream and follows the Ouse Valley Way, a waymarked recreational path. On the left the land climbs about 20m above the valley, but on the right are pastures which were part of the open fields of Houghton before the Enclosure of 1773. A narrow close curving away from the road contains three ridges or 'selions' of ridge and furrow. This narrow close must indicate an earlier enclosure out of the common fields, presumably by agree-ment. The next field has five selions, the next, eleven and both are now a nature reserve and SSSI (Site of Special Scientific Interest) as old hay meadows, although originally plough-land.

The lane continues, sometimes close to the river, into St Ives, emerging by the parish church, mostly fifteenth century and rubble with Barnack limestone dress-ings. The tower is surmounted by a tall elegantly proportioned spire and the churchyard backs directly on to the river. Church Street has several excellent houses, notably Barnes House with full-height bay windows flanking a fluted Doric pilastered door-case. I walked down a path called Church Place, then right, then left into the Waits which appears to have been a riverside wharf. This continues into Broadway, which widens out to be-come the market-place somewhat over-built towards the bridge, reappearing as Market Hill to the east. There is much of quality here from small gault-brick terrace cottages upward, including stuccoed Bur-leigh House, set back from the road be-hind a high wall, and number 37, early eighteenth-century red brick with a modillioned timber cornice. I lunched at the Bubble 'n Squeak café in Coach Mews; excellent value.

Further up Broadway are several pros-perous houses, while Crown Street, fac-ing the market infilling, has a fine early eighteenth-century house in red brick with rubbed brick band courses and cornice as well as stately segmental-headed box sashes. Beyond, Market Hill has a statue of Oliver Cromwell, irreverently adorned with a yellow sun-hat, a resident in the 1630s. After more interesting houses, a spiky Free Church by John Tarring (1862–63) with a tall spire, and the low-key Corn Exchange and Town Hall, I turned right down Priory Road. Just before The Rid-ings a stretch of buttressed wall is part of a medieval barn belonging to long-vanished St Ives Priory. At the end I turned right down an alley to a lane by the Oliver Cromwell Inn whose ornate

An illustrious resident: Oliver Cromwell lived near St Ives in the 1630s and his statue has a place of honour in the market-place.

wrought-iron sign came from an inn on the Quay. More fine houses on the Quay and along Bridge Street include the Manor House with its four jettied gables, now much altered. The superb medieval bridge is faced in Barnack limestone-ashlar with one of four surviving bridge chapels in England. Preserved by being converted into a house, it unbelievably had two storeys added in brick, only removed this century. Over the bridge on the left are two good Georgian houses and on the right the bland modern Dolphin Hotel re-grettably replaces another.

Crossing the car-park south of the hotel, I climbed a stile into the flat expanse of Hemingford Meadow to head west through its lush grasses, leaving through a kissing gate into a lane, and then right

St Ives: the medieval bridge with its chapel seen from the Quay is a memorable sight.

on to a footpath into Hemingford Grey. I turned right at the road, passing a former maltings with terraced workers' cottages. The church is marvellously situated by the river beyond the grounds of red-brick Hemingford Grey House (1697), now a conference centre. The church lost its spire in a hurricane in 1741 and now has ball finials to the spire stump and tower angle finials: a most striking solution. From the church I continued along a footpath and, beyond a good end-of-lane group of houses, walked along the river bank. This passes the moated Hemingford Grey Manor House which is a rare Norman first-floor hall house with an eighteenth-century brick gable elevation facing the river, but the rendered west elevation retains Norman arched windows. This

Hemingford Grey church has its feet virtually in the River Great Ouse, its stumpy spire the result of a hurricane in 1741.

Houghton Mill rears above the water.

was the home of the author of the *Green Knowe* books, Lucy Boston, and a few years ago she had shown me and walking friends her house. She died, aged 97, two days before I did this walk.

I continued west through meadows to Hemingford Abbots, and right down a lane by the Axe and Compasses Inn to visit its church which has a graceful ashlar recessed spire. Inside, the plaster has been stripped off the nave walls revealing the changes that it has undergone, including remains of earlier windows. The sixteenth-century nave roof is very fine with remains of original paint on the east bay. The screen in the tower arch has glass engraved by David Peace in 1974 to celebrate the church millenary. Back at the through road I turned right and soon on Common Lane passed late seventeenth-century brick houses with Dutch gables, and other good houses, before turning right into Meadow Lane on to the river meadows, then across the Great Ouse to Houghton Mill. This is a former water-mill owned by the National Trust (Open on many afternoons from 2.00–5.30 p.m.). From here I followed the lane back to the Square in Houghton via Mill Street.

Walk 42

A PILGRIM TO BUNYAN'S HOUSE BEAUTIFUL

Ampthill and Silsoe, Bedfordshire. 16 Miles. April 1990.
OS Pathfinder Sheet TL03/13.

The greensand sandstone ridge running across central Bedfordshire provides the scenic focus for this walk. To the north the scarp drops relatively steeply to the flat lands through which the River Great Ouse winds – these are the Oxford Clays. From Houghton House I saw clusters of brickworks chimneys dotting the plain below. Southwards the land is undulating, eventually giving way to the gault-clay vale. The main building material of churches is rich brown greensand while the brick earths produce red brick and the gault its characteristic smooth yellow to grey brick.

The walk passes through parts of the great Duchy of Bedford and De Grey of Wrest Park estates. From the 1840s on, both undertook an extensive programme of building attractive brick cottages in Tudor style for their estate workers, partly to offset the effects of enclosure which had produced a large landless labouring class. In the old common fields

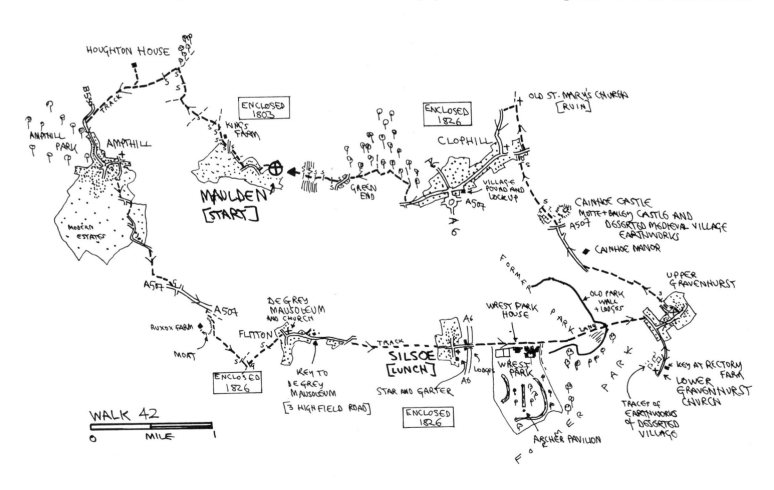

almost every villager owned some land, but the Duke of Bedford in the 1790s and the de Greys in the 1820s secured enclosure by Acts of Parliament and small landholders disappeared. On this walk the common fields in Maulden parish were enclosed in 1803 for the Duke, while the de Greys' steward, Thomas Brown, secured the enclosure of Flitton, Silsoe and Clophill in 1826. The other notable feature of the landscape are the great parks, mainly on the greensand, including Ampthill and Wrest Parks, both medieval in origin.

Maulden church, uphill away from the village, is mainly a rebuild by Benjamin Ferrey of 1859, although the chief interest is the octagonal mausoleum north of the church, also of 1859. Here several of the seventeenth-century Bruces of Houghton House are buried. I left the churchyard to follow the Greensand Ridge Walk, a Bedfordshire County Council waymarked path, through Maulden village which has a scattering of older cottages, mainly typical Bedfordshire steep-roofed single-storey buildings with rooms in their roofs. Also in the village are a number of Bedford Estate cottages with hood-moulds to the lattice casements and gabled upper-floor windows. These are recognizable by the Ducal coronet above a letter B and are often dated. The Greensand Ridge Walk continues north past King's Farm, a Bedford Estate farmhouse dated 1852, into rolling pastoral landscape, eventually reaching the top of the ridge with fine views north over the Bedfordshire Plain.

Leaving the waymarked path I walked down a young avenue to Houghton House, the hillside mansion of the Bruces looking north over the flat lands and said to be the model for Bunyan's 'House Beautiful'. Although a ruin one can gain an impression of what it was like and English Heritage information boards include reconstructions of the mansion before its partial demolition in 1794 by the Duke of Bedford. This E-plan house has remains of advanced architectural features of about 1630 refined enough to be attributed to Inigo Jones, regrettably without a shred of evidence. I wandered through the roofless rooms and returned to the Ridge Walk, leaving it where it goes into Ampthill Park, a Royal hunting park favoured by Henry VIII.

The road descends into Ampthill which is focused around the market-place. On the west side is the Bedford Estate Moot Hall of 1852, a rebuild in the normal estate style but with the cupola from the earlier building reused and curiously out of scale.

Houghton House: these pinnacles and roofless walls, and clustering chimneys mark the spot where stood . . . the mansion of the 'fair, and wise and good'.

Ampthill market-place has a striking combined water-pump and obelisk dated 1785. Beyond is the Bedford Estate's Moot Hall of 1852 with a reused and out-of-proportion cupola from its predecessor.

Opposite is a water pump incorporated in a stone obelisk on a pedestal (1785) erected by the Earl of Upper Ossory who demolished buildings that had infilled the market place. Obviously prosperous in the eighteenth century, Ampthill has many fine Georgian houses and refronting of timber-framed earlier buildings and, by 1800, the town was 'reckoned the genteelest in the county'. In passageways and on gable elevations the earlier timber-framing can be seen, for example on the Ampthill Tandoori in Dunstable Street.

There are some good Georgian shopfronts, but the chief interest is the superb large Georgian town houses nearer the church. The church is curiously village-like in feeling after such high-quality urbane sash-windowed architecture and is situated at the north end of a small square with the cliff-like Dynevor House 1725 on the rainwater heads, on the west side. The church is in toffee-coloured greensand and has an excellent medieval roof with angels while in the chancel an Ionic column topped by an urn is the memorial to the Second Earl of Upper Ossory of 1818.

Out of the church I walked down Church Avenue to a footpath behind suburban gardens, through housing to the road which I crossed to skirt a football pitch and then across fields to a crossroads with the A507. I walked along the roadside east and then right across a stream towards Ruxox Farm in a large dry moat. The path skirts this and then heads south-east alongside lime trees. I followed the path over streams and through former meadows into Flitton. I turned left into High Street, then up Wardhedges Road, and into Highfield Road to number 3, where I got the key to the church from the Stimpsons. I retraced my steps downhill to the church, which is relatively routine. However, attached to it is the De Grey Mausoleum, started in 1614 and completed in 1705, a cruciform building crammed with very high-quality monuments for the Wrest Park family ranging from the seventeenth century onwards. Well worth retracing my steps.

Wrest House: the 1834 mansion of the de Greys by Cléphane, unusually, in French style, and its parkland an agricultural college.

Having returned the key, I continued east to Silsoe which has a good north-south main street, now relatively quiet since the A6 bypass opened. There are a number of fine timber-framed houses, including the terrace numbers 17 to 29 and several de Grey estate cottages. I lunched at the Star and Garter and then visited the church of 1829–31, a competent green-sand Gothic church. I walked east past mansard-roofed lodges, across the A6 in its cutting, and along the arrow-straight chestnut avenue that leads to Wrest House in its vast park, now mostly farmed as part of the Agricultural College. The House and its walled garden and service buildings occupy a very large area and are in French Louis XV style with tall case-ment windows and mansard roofs designed by Cléphane in 1834. The formal gardens to the south include the wonderful Baroque Pavilion by Thomas Archer of

about 1710 (Open at weekends from April to September). In the distance to the north the Brabury Lodges and long stretches of somewhat dilapidated park walls can be seen. I continued east out of the park past Gravenhurst Lodge and on to the Gravenhursts. I turned right at the road to walk south to Lower Gravenhurst church, getting the key from Rectory Farmhouse opposite. This unspoilt church in the care of the Redundant Churches Fund is on the site of a deserted medieval village, now ploughed.

Back uphill, I visited Upper Graven-hurst church and headed across fields to Cainhoe Manor, then crossed the A507 to Cainhoe Castle, the large Norman motte and bailey castle of the powerful d'Albini barons. The earthworks to its west are those of the village deserted soon after 1350 and apparently a result of the great fourteenth-century bubonic-plague epide-

mics that swept Europe in 1349 known as the Black Death. I continued north across fields to Clophill, where the medieval church is a roofless ruin, up the hill; the present church in the village is of 1849. I walked through the long straggling village which has many older houses and cottages and, at The Green, a nineteenth-century lock-up and pound for stray animals. Beyond the A6 at Hall End I turned right past Long Thatch and before Hall End farm, a timber-framed house with cross-wings, up to the edge of Maulden Wood to follow its edge west to Green End. Through this on a tarmac lane, I turned right by Medbourne House, a roughcast lobby-entry-plan seventeenth-century house, on to footpaths to the west. In the first field holloways and house platforms indicated a deserted settlement and beyond this was ridge and furrow, and then Maulden church.

GLOSSARY

artisan mannerism A builder's style of 1620 to 1660 usually in brick with exaggerated gables, cut brick pilasters and window surrounds, and elaborate doorhoods.

art nouveau A style of 1890 to 1905 with sinuous curves and stylized wave-like foliage.

arts and crafts style A late Victorian revival of traditional craftsmanship and styles.

ashlar Smoothly cut blocks of stone with fine joints.

baroque Late seventeenth- and early eighteenth-century style using exaggeratedly large classical elements including columns, a dramatic use of space and mass.

campanile Detached (usually) bell tower.

capital A carved block at the top of a column or pier.

clerestory The upper windows above the aisles in a church.

Coade stone Artificial stone developed by Mrs Coade of Lambeth in 1769.

cob Walls made from earth or clay mixed with straw.

coppice Trees cut to ground level and cropped for poles, palings, furniture, and so on, on a five-, ten- or fifteen-year cycle. hazel and chestnut are common coppice trees.

cornice A moulded projection at the top of a wall, classical in style.

cottage orné Early nineteenth-century style imitating rustic cottages.

croft Small-hedged or fenced fields within villages.

crown-post A post rising from a tie-beam to the collar-beam in a roof truss.

cruck Pairs of large timbers rising from the ground to the apex of a roof.

cupola Small-domed turret on a roof, often open-sided or with a clock face.

Decorated Gothic Medieval style (1280 to 1370) with elaborate window tracery.

double-pile A house two rooms' deep in plan.

dressed stone/dressings Worked and finished stone used round window and doorways or for string courses, quoins (corners) or decorative bands.

Early English Gothic This medieval style (1190 to 1280) is characterized by the lancet or tall narrow window and later by plated or unmoulded tracery.

enclosure Literally putting a hedge or fence round an area. Used to describe fifteenth- and sixteenth-century enclosing of common fields for sheep or stock fields, or from 1650–1870 for private farms, often by an Act of Parliament.

entablature The lintel area with cornice and fascia above classical columns.

estate (style) Tudor or other historical styles used by large estates, particularly in the nineteenth century, for workers' cottages and farm-buildings.

flushwork Flint panels in dressed stone used in medieval East Anglia often as tracery or inscriptions.

furlong A group of strips in open-field farming.

galletting Small chips of dark stone pressed into mortar joints, common in the greensand areas of Kent, Surrey, Sussex and Hampshire.

gazebo A garden room, often square and set up high to give views both over gardens and countryside.

Georgian Architecture from about 1710 to 1830, characterized by the sash window.

Giant (order or pilasters) In classical or Georgian architecture columns or pilasters two storeys high.

Gothic Medieval pointed-arch-style architecture, 1180 to 1540.

Gothick Georgian revival of medieval Gothic, inaccurate but highly decorative. Often used stuccoed and ogeed arches.

hall house Medieval house based on a hall or large room open to the roof.

holloway In deserted villages or other earthworks the course of a lane or street below the surrounding ground level, often between house platforms.

International Modern 1920s and 1930s flat-roofed concrete walled style.

Iron Age The name given to the iron tool- and weapon-based cultures in England from about 400 BC to about AD 100.

Jacobean Early seventeenth-century architecture characterized by strapwork decoration and Renaissance forms and detail from France and the Low Countries.

jetty In timber-framed construction projecting or oversailing upper floors.

lancet Tall narrow pointed arched windows in Early English Gothic building.

lynchet, linchet Terrace ploughing of steep slopes, usually medieval and often on marginal land.

lucarne Unglazed gabled window in a medieval spire.

mathematical tiles Hanging tiles with brick-shaped lower parts which combine to look like solid brickwork. Found in Surrey, Sussex, Kent, Wiltshire and occasionally elsewhere.

motte A castle mound.

mullion A vertical division in a window.

Norman English Romanesque from 1050 to 1180. Initially wholly Norman in influence but after about 1080 increasingly English in inspiration.,

ogee Arch or roof with a double curve, the upper part concave, the lower convex.

open fields Form of medieval agriculture where arable land of village is farmed in common by strip-farming methods.

oriel A bay window that does not reach the ground.

Palladian Sixteenth century Venetian Renaissance style of Andrea Palladio introduced to England by Inigo Jones and revived in the early Georgian period. Characterized by elegant Classical proportions, stucco, columns and pediments.

pargetting Ornamental plastering of outside walls, in panels or relief, and a notable characteristic of East Anglia and Essex.

parterre Sixteenth- and seventeenth-century formal garden beds, often on terraces.

pediment A low-pitched triangular gable of classical design, usually at the top of columns.

Perpendicular Late medieval Gothic style (1330–1540) characterized by rectangular panels of tracery and strong vertical emphases.

pilaster A shallow projecting square column with base and capitals in classically derived architecture.

pollard Technique in which a tree is lopped above cattle-browsing height.

portico Classical porch, usually with at least three columns supporting a roof or pediment gable.

ridge and furrow Medieval ploughing technique in which the fixed ploughshare heaps soil into ridges with furrows in between. It helped drainage (they almost always cross contours) and in common farming identified individual holdings.

rustication V-shaped joints which emphasize the blocks, usually in stonework.

selion An individual ridge in ridge and furrow country.

stiffleaf Early English Gothic-carved foliage style.

strip A parcel or group of selions or ridges in ridge and furrow. A group of strips makes a furlong.

stucco Render with ground-stone content, or more commonly any white render.

sunken way A lane worn down below the level of surrounding land, only possible before the age of tarmac roads!

transom A horizontal division in a window, often combined with mullions.

tripartite sash A window of three lights in which (properly) the outer two are half the width of the middle sash.

Venetian window A tripartite sash with a higher arched central light.

vermiculation Cutting away the surface of ashlar stone to look worm-eaten.

vernacular Literally local style. Any building that is not 'polite', usually cottages, farmhouses and barns, and not country or gentry houses.

wealden In hall and crosswing timber-framed houses a type where there is a single roof carried past the recessed central hall bays on brackets.

witchert Buckinghamshire cob or earth walling, based on limestone sub-soils.

FURTHER READING

Buildings

Clifton-Taylor, Alec, *English Parish Churches as Works of Art*, (Batsford, 1974).

Dixon, R. and Stefan Muthesius, *Victorian Architecture*, (Thames and Hudson, 1978).

Pevsner, Nikolaus (Founding Editor), *The Buildings of England* (Penguin). Every English county is covered in one or, occasionally, two volumes, published at various dates.

Service, Alistair (General Editor), *The Buildings of Britain*, (Barrie and Jenkins, 1982). Four volumes are published: Anglo-Saxon and Norman; Tudor and Jacobean; Stuart and Baroque; Regency.

Landscape History

Archaeology in the Field Series, (J. M. Dent, 1975–78). Various authors cover aspects of landscape history, such as Fields, Villages, Towns and Woodland.

Hoskins, W. G., *The Making of the English Landscape*, (Hodder and Stoughton).

Hoskins, W. G. and Roy Millward (Editors), *The Making of the English Landscape,* (Hodder and Stoughton). An ongoing selection of volumes for each county.

Rackham, Oliver, *The History of the Countryside*, (J. M. Dent, 1986).

Taylor, Christopher, *Roads and Tracks of Britain*, (J. M. Dent, 1979).

Index